THE MOST IMPORTANT TWENTY YEARS OF YOUR LIFE WILL BE THOSE YEARS BETWEEN FORTY AND SIXTY.

How well you live those twenty years will definitely determine the elevated quality of your life, RIGHT UP TO AND THROUGH YOUR HOPEFUL HUNDRED YEARS.

Think of this book as the quintessential motivational manual for the 40 to 60-year-old American man! It is truly a first, designed specifically for every man going through The Great Transition - that critical time period where ever man will lay the foundation for the second half of his life.

Sir, I do hope at the end of this 400-page journey of positive power, you will arrive at a higher level of self-satisfaction, and increased purpose for the balance of your life.

Copyright

Publisher: Abundant Press

Author: Ken Dab-Row

Title: Age My Ass

Subtitle: Your Great Transition into the Greater Half of Your Life

ISBN: 978-1-948287-21-0

For More Information, please visit:

AgeMyAss.com

Dedications

I dedicate this book and its creation and content, to my very close and cherished protege and friend, Rob Friedman.

Rob – as successful in business as you and Jeff Frieden (love you too, Jeff!) have been, and the very sizable wealth you have acquired, it pales in comparison to your human values. Every positive word contained in this text are qualities you possess in abundance. This book would never have been written without your constant encouragement over the last twenty years. Rob, you are one of the fairest and finest human beings I have ever had the privilege to have entered my life. Your humanity and caring exceeds explanation.

And to Adam Smith, my very dear and closest confidant and friend, whose loyalty has been as close to unconditional, as is humanly possible. This book would have never been completed without your patience and understanding, and total commitment to the "Age, My Ass!" project. Adam – I would not, and could not have done it without you.

Also to my son, who I consider closer than a son, Terry Bahr, for his highly intelligent and always in control stability under all and any existing conditions. A quiet, but ever present giant of caring and concern. A magnificent human being. And to Terry's precious and priceless wife of forty-five years, Emy, whose strength of character and caring nature are beyond calculation.

Tribute to some special people who have made my life exceptional.

To my two precious granddaughters, Gina and Amanda, thank you for your caring and devotion for a lifetime.

To Donald "Frosty" Fosnot, who rose above every negative that confronted him (and they were numerous) to achieve great success as one of the top executives of one of America's largest privately owned businesses – Conair. And like Rob Friedman, is a person of the very highest character and integrity. And to his wife Kathy – a very thoughtful, sensitive lady. And to his sister Darlene, one of the most caring, responsible women I've ever met, and to her sister, Patty, a glamorous and caring lady.

To Annie Pena, whose unconditional caring for the welfare of my Millie and me, has been and still is so totally complete. So exceptional, it can never be measured in words alone. And to her husband Eduardo, and my beloved adopted grandchildren Hadassah and Josued – I love you!

To Vic Gruber - tough as nails, smart as a whip, and a profound sense of honesty.

To Tim Pohlman – a very special guy in my life, and his wife Susan.

Thank you Darrell and Judy Willis for your prayers.

To George and Tuesday Coates. Two of the finest humans you'll ever meet.

A special thanks to Dennis and Wendy Carey. You are two of God's finest.

And also special thanks to Mike and Brenda Cagliostro.

To Gary Barbera, a most brilliant man who has matured in so many positive and productive ways.

To Pat Hickey - one of the best at his business.

To Clay James - a mogul in the car business.

To Charlie Chalom – a life force and realist who takes no prisoners.

To Harry Rausch. I'm as big a fan of you as you are of me. Your name should be Mr. Tenacity!

To John Bailey - a great and respected legal mind, and even more respected as a decent, civil human being.

To Tal Harel – such a mench! The epitome of maturity.

To Heather Stern – my chosen and only goddaughter, and her gorgeous mother, Maureen.

To Joe Nobriga, who has wisdom and self-respect beyond his years.

To Paul Briley, who I love dearly, and his wife, Nid.

To Shaun and Shannon Briley.

Thank you Martie Robson for your constant caring and encouragement.

To my gal-pal, Super Mom KC Campbell.

To Paul Raymond – out of sight but never out of mind.

To Pat Newton – one hell of a great guy and any man's equal.

To Mohamed – I love ya! Fight the good fight, it's never too late.

To Ted Borgous - a life force that never quits.

To Jerry Taitleman – a great fighter in the ring, but even a greater friend outside it, and his beautiful wife, Marge.

To Gary Bahr, whose bravery and will is unimaginable.

To Lee and Cathey Ledford and Robert and Bernadette Hogan.

To Jack and Ellen Gaar, my very efficient and conservative financial advisors.

To Judy Stephans – God bless you, honey.

And to my very special adopted sons, Mike Glass – a body building promoter of iconic proportions; Charles Bradshaw, and his son Phillip.

To Walter Friedman - a finer, more well-tuned mind would be hard to find. And to Lance Friedman, I appreciate you as much as you appreciated me.

To Chuck Polizzi – we accomplished the unimaginable. I'll always love ya!

To Ralph Cohen – an exceptional man who allowed me to make exceptional things happen.

Finally, to my Las Vegas family of close and very cherished friends: Anna Bailey - a most elegant, dignified, beautiful woman. Diane and Willard Booth – a true, friendly, giant of a man with a great love for life. And to Diana and Paul Balfour – a man of exceptional and superior musical and comedic talents. Thank you all. Yours truly, and my magnificent Millie, have a much clearer and far reaching perspective and beautiful view of life, having your shoulders to stand on.

And in memorium of my seven closest friends, America Nobriga, Jim Spero, Dr. William "Bob" Bailey, Dr. Loren Stern, Dr. John "Jack" Briley, Danny Zimmerman, and Dan Casabian. Fellas, if you can hear me through another dimension, thanks for a lifetime of friendship.

Table of Contents

Introduction & Biography

By Adam Smith

It has been my pleasure to have known Ken as a friend, mentor, and bombastic father figure for over thirty years. Just like many other people in Ken's life, I was drawn to that huge persona and positive attitude. For the past twenty or so years we have worked together with me serving as his producer and de facto manager, so when the idea came along to try and bottle this genie of positive power, it was only natural that we should work together on the "Age, My Ass!" project, and all that goes along with it, including this book.

Ken in his mid-50s (about the time we first met)

"Age, My Ass!" was designed for men over forty to help them with what Ken calls "The Great Transition"; that time between forty and sixty when men start setting the foundation for the next forty or more years of their life. Ken remembers well that time in his life, and more importantly, the decisions and choices he made that he credits with helping to make him the ninety-year-old powerhouse he is.

"Age, My Ass" is the culmination of the years, phases, and stages of the life of Ken Dab-Row. Ken belonged to a unique generation that was based on values that some people would call old-fashioned. His attitudes and priorities were lived with power and purpose, and of course influenced by his heart and soul. One of Ken's top priorities was his love and respect for the written and spoken word. In Ken's case, words spoken with power, with finesse, some with anger, but most with love and compassion.

But before we start, I'd like to give you an example of how Ken practices what he preaches. It's taken several years to develop and write this book, and about half-way through that process, Ken suffered a mini-stroke, the effects of which caused a definite change to his lifestyle, including driving (which is something Ken truly loves – being behind the wheel). Without the wheels under him, he could have stopped there. And why not? Lots of guys in their late eighties would take a stroke of any kind as a message to start easing down. So Ken could have stopped. Stopped coming into the studio to do commercials, stopped traveling, even stopped going to the gym. But he didn't. In fact, true to his form, he figured out how to beat it! He did everything he could to not let the physical effects of a stroke slow him down, and within a few short months was back on track. He truly is an amazing man who refuses to be beaten, and whose spirit and determination are infectious.

Of course, no one is born in their late eighties, but instead truly are a product of their life experiences. So to that end, we offer a brief biography where you'll learn about the events that helped Ken discover who he was and ultimately shaped who he would become. In preparation of this short biography, I thought about that age-old question: What would you consider your greatest accomplishment? Knowing Ken as I do, and

Ken in his early 60s

having spent more than the last thirty years in his presence, I pretty much already had the answer without even asking the question. For Ken, certainly his broadcasting career is high on the list, but he would tell you that simply living a great life and loving each day of it is his greatest accomplishment. For Ken, there have been challenges and struggles, love and loss, failure and success, but he has accomplished a long, fulfilling and rewarding life.

Even at ninety, people thirty to fifty years his junior are still drawn to him and still asking the same questions they did when he was in his fifties. Wanting to know how he accomplished his level of fitness and maintains his exuberance at this late stage of life. For Ken, it's not a mystery but rather a simple formula whose key is the loving of life and living it to the n-th degree. But most important, the loving of yourself in it.

It's safe to say Ken is not and never has been shy, inhibited, or meek, and that he has always been free spirited and boisterously bigger than life, especially when he belts out a song or uses the spoken word. He frequently acknowledges how fortunate he is that he was blessed with those "pipes", and that they've stayed intact all these years. That was a true gift of God and nature, but the rest was not. From his early days in Philly, to his life as a teen set out on the world, to his career as one of the most recognizable voices ever heard on American radio, to his incredible physical and mental condition, these

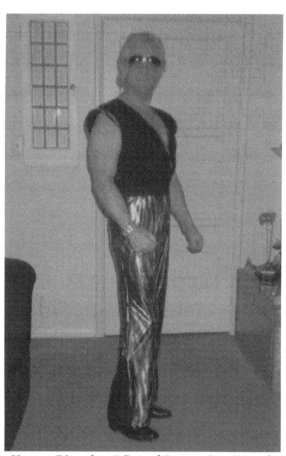

Ken at 70 in his "Grand Pappa Rap" outfit

were the result of a man who is committed to the things he values, and has stayed committed to them his entire life. But it has been a labor of love and joy built on a rock-solid foundation of those five words that connect his crest's five-pointed star: Honesty, Loyalty, Trust, Courage, and Commitment.

There is one last point that should be made on the subject of accomplishments. It is in man's nature to want to leave his mark, something that says "I was here." Being an announcer or a physical phenomenon might do, but there are many who will tell you that Ken's monument is the people whose lives he has literally changed, or even saved. Real people that Ken opened his heart to over his ninety years. People in need, or who were lost or hurting, or were simply missing something, who connected with his unique, upbeat style. It might have been one simple meeting that lasted less than an hour, or taken place over a thirty-year friendship, but the one thing you could count on Ken for, no matter who you were, whether he agreed or disagreed, you could count on his compassion, his caring, and his human concern. But just as important, he is more than capable of sometimes giving you a motivating stiff kick in the ass! Many of his close friends and supporters have often joked about how things will be when he goes to his final reward. Many can see Ken fearlessly sitting down one-on-one with God, sincerely debating how best to better humankind's destiny. But in the end, when they really get to know each other, they'll probably be arm in arm, just a couple of old timers, sharing some pie-in-the-sky ideas and hitting heaven's gym. Joking aside, he has straightened out and smoothed life's path for many people down here on earth, (and I include myself on that list) and those people will continue to meet and beat fear and compete in life as they carry and continue to spread the winning message during life's long positive journey of "the mind, the money and the muscle". That, my friend, is the true lasting accomplishment that has been for ninety years - and still is - Ken Dab-Row.

Part one – Growing up

It all started in May of 1931, when Ken opened his mouth for the very first time. Ken will even tell you he remembers that first breath. After that first slap on the back by the doctor, he said "Hey doc, take it easy … I was only put together with one screw!"

He was raised in a working-class Philadelphia neighborhood at the start of the great depression. These were tough times, but his parents, Faye and Sidney, provided a good home with solid family values. And believe it or not, this man whose powerful, confident voice has been heard millions of times on the radio across America throughout his 50-year career, actually stuttered as a child. So at twelve years of age, Ken took speech therapy. He would visually line up the words of his thoughts in his mind's eye and see them and speak them. He would write down his opinions on any aspect of life that spiked his interest, then read it as many times as it took to deliver it with perfect pace, interpretation, passion and clarity. This process lasted for almost a year, after which the stutter was completely eliminated. Then to further develop his speaking skills, he would repetitiously repeat progressively difficult tongue twisters at a rapid pace. And by fifteen he had mastered his oratory skills. This was during an era, the 1940s, when live conversation was the most important means of communication. So by the time he reached sixteen, Ken had highly developed his speaking skills to go along with his naturally powerful voice.

Where Ken grew up during his youthful days of the late '30s and early '40s, families were first or second generation from Europe and Russia with strong accents. So his very American speaking skills opened up the world to him, at a time when whatever ethnicity you were, that was the neighborhood you lived in. In fact, you almost never left the neighborhood – it became your life. But Ken had a problem with that, because the world he wanted to live in and was curious about was much bigger, more exciting and interesting than just the neighborhood. So out of that curiosity, around fourteen or fifteen years old, he left the protection of the neighborhood to explore what were then the mean streets of Philly. And although he would fearlessly take on all comers, being a skinny kid with a hair-trigger temper, the outcome wasn't always positive. No doubt it was that mouth and fearless attitude that led to a lot of fist fights and Ken getting in plenty of trouble as a youth. As a result, he knew he needed more muscle, so at fourteen he developed an interest in body building and boxing. Over the following months he put on the muscle and became a skilled boxer, and after a couple of years and a couple of hundred street fights, he finally got the message and smartened up: Ken figured no matter how many fights you win, if you stay angry in life, you ultimately lose. So he got his anger in check and started to look for positive outlets for his energies, which led to, of all things, poetry. He discovered that weaving words was far less dangerous than weaving in and out of punches.

No doubt the manipulation of the English language through poetry helped him understand how to tell a story and how to engage the listener. So began his education as a wordsmith, and between the ages of fourteen and seventeen he found his niche using that powerful speaking voice as a barker and a pitchman on the boardwalk of Atlantic City and on the midways of traveling carnivals. Ken even became a backstage singer at burlesque houses for the bumping and grinding burlesque queens.

Part two – The acting bug

By eighteen he had settled into what would become the most lucrative venture of his young life, and also a great learning experience. In 1949, along with twelve other men nationwide (all past thirty, while Ken was only eighteen) he had become a fixture at Sears and Roebuck stores demonstrating the then-new wonder appliance called the pressure cooker. Traveling from store to store, from Maine to Virginia, completely on his own, making very good money and having total freedom, he lived his life to the limit.

And by the way, talk about making big money at a young age. A hundred and fifty to two hundred bucks a week in 1949 was a lot of money. Think about it: a loaf of bread was ten cents, a gallon of gas fifteen cents, a new car nine hundred to fifteen hundred dollars, and a house in a middle-class neighborhood was six to twelve thousand dollars. In other words, what a dollar would buy in 1949 would take twenty-five to thirty dollars today. So imagine being eighteen today and making two hundred fifty to three hundred thousand dollars a year. And making that kind of money for over two years. In that two-year period, Ken made and spent today's equivalent of over a half a million dollars.

By 1951, World War Two had come and gone, but there was still a need for men and women in the military to staff bases in Europe and to create a presence for the brewing conflict in Korea. Ken was about to be drafted in the Army for two years, but instead he enlisted in the United States Air Force for four years. By the way, leaving the private sector for the Air Force also represented a pay cut, from about seven to eight hundred dollars a month, down to seventy-two dollars a month. But in the end, it was worth it because of where it led Ken to next. Now where do you put a pitch man in the Air Force? In the control tower directing traffic, of course! This lasted about a year when another opportunity presented itself where his vocal skills and convincing powers would also be of great service. He joined the Air Force Special and Information Services, a group designed to educate troops through theater on how to conduct themselves as foreigners in England.

At the time, 1953, just seven years after World War Two, the Air Force still had over forty air bases and over a hundred thousand Airmen in England alone. Most of those Airmen were very young, eighteen to twenty-two years old, and lacked the social skills necessary to mix and blend in a positive way with the English people and their culture. As it happened, a brilliant young American named John Briley was in England at this time doing his doctoral thesis. The name should sound familiar because this is the same man who would thirty years later become the preeminent biographical screen writer of his era, receiving the Academy Award for his original screenplay of one of the greatest biographies ever filmed: Ghandi. Seeing what was happening in post-war England, Briley came up with a brilliant idea: Have a mixed troupe of American and British actors play out onstage, in a comedic way, what could (and in fact did) happen on the streets and in the pubs of England. And do a new show for all forty bases every month. Great idea. Every month, a new ninety-minute review. Now all that was needed was a staff of writers to write new reviews every thirty days, a production staff to administer the internal paperwork and schedule over one hundred performances, plus a director to block, stage, and rehearse a new review every month. A staff to accomplish all these varied tasks would normally require twenty to thirty skilled professionals. Well, while in his mid-twenties and with just a couple of assistants, Briley did it all. One fateful day Ken presented himself to Briley to audition for the troop. The audition didn't go so well, but Briley immediately recognized the life force that was Ken, so he gave Ken a shot. He molded and developed Ken as an actor, and over a two-year period Ken acted in over two thousand performances of twenty different shows under Briley's direction.

His success on stage with Briley's troop had given Ken an opportunity to pursue acting as a career, so after his discharge from the Air Force, Ken went home to Philly with the ultimate goal of going on to Broadway. After all, anyone who knows Ken will tell you, not only is there always a song in his heart, but he is never afraid to let it out, and at full volume, no matter where he might be. Remember, Ken was just sixteen when he was a backstage singer for those burlesque queens belting out tunes like "Melancholy baby" and "You made me love you", so Broadway seemed the logical next step.

Ken and Millie - enjoying the cold weather at their Sun Valley retreat

Part three – Sixty-two years with the same lady

Before heading off to New York and possibly a new career, his parents suggested Ken visit his brother who lived in Phoenix. Since it had been six years since the two last saw each other, Ken decided the trip would be a good idea.

By this time in his life, Ken had seen most of Europe, but back home in America he never ventured far from around the east coast. From Philly to England and back again meant a lot of cold, sometimes snowy weather, and after a long and arduous drive from Philly to Phoenix, which was also cold and snowy, Ken was very much taken with the warm sunshine and swaying palms of Phoenix. Well, that was it! He decided then and there he was never going to be cold and snowed on again! Phoenix became his new home.

Ken would regularly spend time with his brother, almost always meeting at the local coffee shop near where his brother worked. This was where Ken first got a look at one of the most beautiful women he had ever seen. Believe me, no words could do her justice. It truly could be said that Millie was in fact one of the most beautiful women not only in Phoenix, but possibly the entire world. Practically perfect from head to toe, and there she was, working at this coffee shop. The male patrons would fawn over her and

Millie – Talk about natural beauty, how gorgeous can a woman get!

of course try to ask her out. Naturally Ken was attracted to her too, but he didn't want to be just one of the gang fawning attention on her, so he never did let on that he also felt she was the most beautiful woman he'd ever seen and certainly wanted to date her.

Well, on December 13, 1957, fate had another idea. They both happened to be at the biggest shopping center of the time in Phoenix, and happened to pass each other. They recognized one another and Ken took the chance to invite her to have coffee, and the rest, as they say, is sixty-two-year history.

A natural beauty and no-nonsense, down to earth farm gal, Millie would augment Ken's driving force. At the very beginnings of their relationship, they ventured into the restaurant business together with "Millie 'n Ken's Circle City Restaurant", located pretty much in the middle of nowhere, 35 miles outside of Phoenix. It was a good gamble though, because there was the anticipation of a new housing development soon

... and hard to believe a body can look that good at 40!

to be built called Circle City, which was expected to have an ultimate population of two to three thousand. And perhaps it would have worked if the city had in fact been built, but it was not. So it was the occasional patron from the beginnings of Circle City and the errant wildlife of the desert, like rattlesnakes and coyote, that kept things interesting for Millie and Ken as they tried to survive. One story that is a testament to Ken's marketing skills involves a stunt designed to get customers into the restaurant. Circle City Restaurant was on the main highway, which was also the main trucking route between Phoenix and Los Angeles. If the housing development didn't bring in the customers, the highway might in the form of those lonely and hungry truckers. And Ken had an idea to attract those truckers that was sure-fire. Now remember all that talk about Millie being a natural beauty? Well believe it! So Ken bought a jackass (or donkey, if you prefer) and outfitted Millie from head to toe in a gold, skin-tight lamé body suit. The truckers that had been driving across that barren desert for miles and miles without seeing anything but sand and cactus, must have thought they were seeing a mirage! Here was this beauty in skin-tight gold lamé on the back of jackass, riding up and down in front of the Circle City Restaurant. Well it worked, if only to a small degree. Needless to say, the demise of Circle City also meant the demise of the restaurant.

Through hardship and challenge, these two stuck it out and supported one another through each other's quests and adventures. Ken will tell you, the reason this relationship has lasted over sixty years is because Millie, as gorgeous a woman as she was and still is, has always been more beautiful on the inside than she was on the outside. There's no doubt that the strength of this woman has contributed greatly to Ken's success.

Millie and Ken taking time to kick back (Millie in her 80s and Ken in his 70s)

Part four – Becoming a broadcaster

After his foray into the restaurant business, Ken bounced around from sales job to sales job and ultimately landed with a new business partner and a new bedding business. Again, marketing was the key to the success of his mattress business, combining creativity with his shoe-string budget to bring customers from all over the Phoenix area to his store. Eventually he would leave Phoenix to expand to Vegas with the same business model. This is where Ken first discovered the advertising power of radio and the allure of broadcasting. He even created the character "The Smilin' Irishman" to promote his mattresses and furniture on-the-air.

Perhaps it was the allure of broadcasting, perhaps his love of performing, but whatever the reason, by 1963 he had sold off his interest in the bedding company to venture into the field of radio jingles, which were used prominently in the radio advertising of the day.

From 1963 to 1965 Ken was General Sales Manager for one of the nation's largest radio jingle businesses: Motivating Commercials Incorporated. Ken sold millions of dollars worth of airtime on radio stations by influencing his prospects that a good jingle would not only generate business, but would create an original musical signature. By 1965 he was in California, selling jingles to air on southern California's #1 country music station, K-FOX. For Ken, enthusiasm, confidence, opportunity, and success all go hand-in-hand. Ken's passion for life and his positive attitude made him a truly great salesman. He also saw the amazing opportunity that southern California presented for radio advertising, and it was here that radio advertising became his professional focus. The place to start was at K-FOX radio where he had just generated over one hundred thousand dollars in jingle sales, and was conducting his final jingle campaign. So after two years on the road Ken made the decision to settle in southern California,

In those days, radio sales people earned a commission, usually 10 to 12 percent of their gross sales, and most sales people were given a draw against that commission, and a select list of prospective advertisers. So much depended on the quality of the prospect and that prospect's potential to use radio for advertising. Here's where Ken took a different tact. He had faith in his abilities to create new radio clients from businesses that had never previously used or even showed any interest in radio. So he made an astounding offer to K-FOX: He would bring in new business that not only had never used radio, but never planned on using radio. In fact in many cases, businesses that had already been given a full sales presentation that they turned down flat. Under these conditions Ken's observation was: What could be the risk to the station? No money out of their pocket in the form of a salary or draw, and all new business creating fresh dollars the station would have never seen because these businesses had already rejected the use of radio. In other words, these were prospective clients you couldn't sell, but who Ken thinks he can. He had only one stipulation: he wanted a thirty percent commission, not the standard ten to twelve percent. The managers were flabbergasted! Thirty percent? Two to three times normal commission! But Ken saw it from a different perspective.

He reminded them this is brand new money that the station would have never seen, and the station was risking nothing. And consider this: if he generated three hundred thousand dollars in all-new business, at thirty percent Ken would make ninety thousand dollars, but the station would make two hundred ten thousand dollars in new revenue. Some might say it was a gutsy move on Ken's part, but he had confidence in the station and its loyal country music audience. Even more so, Ken had confidence in his own abilities to sell that product. So for him there was no risk, only reward. And it was a success. In his first three months he developed forty new accounts. And by the way, all of those accounts got results on radio, which made him realize the incredible power that a local station can have in getting results for its clients when you said the right thing in the right way.

Ken not only sold the radio time, he created all the campaigns, wrote all the commercial copy, and it was his voice on the air delivering the message. The response to Ken's clients was so successful that in 1968 he formed his own broadcast advertising agency specializing in the use of radio, with over ninety percent of his clients being car dealers, and which as of this writing he is still actively involved with. Through the years, we estimate he has created and written at least ten thousand radio campaigns and his voice has been heard on radio across America over ten million times. In fact, his advertising career has been so prominent that the prestigious Southern California Broadcasters Association honored him with their Lifetime Achievement Award – an award that has only been presented six times in the last sixty years.

A proud moment - Ken receiving the Lifetime Achievement Award from the Southern California Broadcasters Association

Ken at 50

Part five – Muscle man and mentor

With his physique, that big voice, and flamboyant dress, not to mention his enthusiasm, it was impossible for Ken to walk into a room and not command the attention of those present. Being physically fit past forty was a unique thing in the 1970s and '80s, up to 1990. By then Ken was almost sixty years of age and was developing a small following of people much younger who were not only attracted to his enthusiastic and magnetic personality, but impressed by his muscular presence as well. Many twenty to thirty-five years younger looking to him for advice on how to tap into that exuberance and physical strength. It always ended with the same recommendation: Hit the gym! Swim, jog, tennis, anything to challenge the body to perform better physically. Ken has always been fond of saying: You quit on your body and it's going to quit on you. He says that it is one third of where your life's main focus should be, because without a strong, healthy, highly energized body, the other two thirds; how you live your life mentally and financially, cannot be developed to their potential. As Ken likes to say, "The mind, the money, and the muscle" or "the brain, the body, and the buck".

As we go through life, we are defined and recognized for certain traits or features and of course, accomplishments. So one might say that "the muscle" is certainly what defines Ken. But that ever-present mouth will no doubt be the thing that lives on. By the time he hit his stride as an advertising icon, on any given weekend he could be heard simultaneously on over a hundred and fifty radio stations in twenty to thirty cities across the country. He could walk up to a stranger in virtually any airport, and all Ken would have to say is one of his signature slogans like "Yippie Yai Yo Kaye!" for that stranger to grin and say "I know that voice, it's you!" The way Ken phrases a statement, his special kind of inflection, his sense of interpretation, and the power behind that voice has created arguably one of the most unique, one-of-a-kind announcers ever to step up to a microphone.

His greater notoriety came in 1994 when he not only lent his voice, but also his persona to television commercials. You need to understand that Ken loves clothes and jewelry and there is little simple or understated about him. As his success grew in advertising, so did the creation of a very unique and engaging individual. With that physique, that big voice and flamboyant dress and enthusiasm, it was impossible for Ken to walk into a room, and not command the attention of those present. But remember, up to this point that voice was only heard on radio. The only people to see Ken or make contact with him were those in his life and at the gym, at a private party or any other private setting. But now Ken was on TV for the whole world to see. Up to that point, radio listeners could only build an image of Ken in the theater of their own minds, but now here he was, right in front of them on TV, where some might say his direct style, to-the-point message, powerful voice, and flamboyant appearance exceeded expectations. Ken certainly was not what viewers commonly saw in TV commercials, but the success of his formula for radio commercials easily became a part of his TV ads. Even long after his last on-camera TV commercial aired, Ken would still be stopped by strangers who remembered him from an insurance company commercial. They even remembered the character he created and would holler out an enthusiastic, "Hey, it's Solo-Man!" They remembered, even though at the time Solo-Man had been off TV for as many as ten years. These are truly some great feats among his accomplishments through more than fifty years of broadcasting.

It's important to note that almost all advertising in the agency business is a team effort. The roster for any single client's campaign included the full team: account reps, creative consultants, copy writers, producers, directors, voice over professionals and actors, engineers, editors, post production staff and the list goes on. As many as ten to twenty people. In the early days, before Dab-Row Radio grew into what some would term a traditional advertising agency, that roster was ninety percent filled by Ken himself. He was the account rep, he was the creative mind behind the advertisement, he was the one who wrote the script, and he was the one to deliver the message. Even as the agency grew to national proportions, Ken still kept his hand in all aspects of the business. And looking back on fifty years of Dab-Row commercials, whether in those early days of the late '50s and '60s, into the '70s, or at the apex of Dab-Row Radio, Inc., all told it can truly be said that his commercials have played, and his voice heard, somewhere in the neighborhood of ten million times, not only giving him the distinction of being one of the most recognizable voices in the vast world of advertising, but also no doubt making him one of, if not the, busiest commercial announcer in radio broadcasting history.

"The Old Man" popping a muscle or two at 82 – why not you?!

Preface by the author

This book is specifically for the American man-in-the-middle between the ages of forty and sixty. Even though I'm just a few months from entering my ninetieth year, I'm still one hundred percent involved with life, having the time of my life. I made up my mind during that period of forty to sixty that every day I lived, I was going to make progressively better, and that was the only way to ensure being more satisfied, accomplished, and above all, being more in tune with who I would be past sixty. And that's the feeling I'm going to try and imbue in you for your next thirty to fifty years.

A lot of people wonder how a man that old can make himself

1

believe he's still having the time of his life. Well what made me believe it, happened almost fifty years ago when I was your age. That's when I made those hard, real decisions. The possibilities and potential of my next fifty years. It was definitely decided during that twenty-year period that you are in now. Well, because of the mindset that I decided I was going to take, that is how I worked my way through and got to where I am today.

I'll assume you'd like to live well into your eighties or nineties like The Old Man. But the key to this text is living it with passion, and enjoying every waking day, like I still do. I want you to feel that kind of exhilaration and love for life, for your entire life. Because when life is lived to the hilt, when you really reach the top of anything, only one term really describes that situation: CREAM OF THE CROP - the absolute best you can possibly be. We all have so many different priorities and values. Money, sex, family, politics, religion. And each one of those general categories, could have a hundred sub-categories. So everybody has a different set of priorities on how they value things. Of course there is health and fitness. They are a very important priority for me, so naturally in those areas, I feel like the cream of the crop! Whatever your values and priorities are should make you feel like you are the cream of the crop! And it's important you know that it is not by chance, it's by choice. That will be one of the main focuses of every observation in this book: Finding it in yourself, to be the best you can be in all those areas that are of major importance to you.

The big danger during these next twenty years is going from cream of the crop, to cream of the crap! That's how critical and that's how crucial these next twenty years are. Make no mistake, they will determine the quality of the rest of your life.

Now through most of my life people have been asking me: "What's the secret to staying strong, healthy and mentally alert?" Well I'm very appreciative of all those compliments. But the answer to them, I truly believe, is right here on the pages of this book. It all starts right now, between forty and sixty, because that's the time I call THE GREAT TRANSITION. No matter how much you've accomplished up to now - you could be well educated and wealthy, truly at the top of your game - those forty years were well spent, but it's in this twenty-year time period, between forty and sixty, that you will hit your peak in all categories. It's also right about this time, all of a sudden at forty-plus, where you were fearless before forty because you thought you were going to live forever, you can let fear when you pass forty have a commanding psychological negative influence. Not a chance in hell that is going to happen if I have anything to say about it! Past forty is when most men start setting the foundation for the next forty or more years of their life. With all the success and acquisitions and all it represents having been accomplished and getting better, we cannot and we must not let those little gremlins and demons of doubt, fear, and trepidation concerning your survival step in and take over. That can and frequently does happen when you finally come to the realization that your mortality is a reality. But I'm here to tell ya, there is definitely a way to make the second half of your life, more rewarding and gratifying, and that's what I hope to share through my experiences and observations.

I have always in my mind's eye believed I was the cream of the crop, and with each passing year, I believed it even more. So as you read these pages, I hope you'll take to heart objectively the messages within them, and know that during this twenty year period, you can defeat that aging process fear-mongering demon and feel even more strongly that you are, the cream of the crop. But remember, cream of the crop or cream of the crap - always your choice, always entirely up to you!

My Creed

As a young man, over seventy years ago, like most all young men approaching twenty, for most of those twenty years we had others telling us what to do and how to think, and I for one felt the world closing in on me, restricting me, putting limitations on my potential. And like all young men way back there in the 1940s, I felt suppressed. I wanted to break out! Well I knew the only way in hell that had any chance of ever happening was for me to make the change. I knew I had to accept the fact that it was my responsibility to create a strategic thought process designed by me, to liberate me, and above all set my mind free, because I knew, then and only then would I have the opportunity to establish my values and my priorities. And make no mistake, we lived in a pretty closed, established society in those days, and that was not an easy thing to do all those years ago. Because unlike the current generation, my generation was born into a world ruled by absolutes. There was very little middle ground or gray areas in those days. Things were either black or white, or you were either right or wrong. So I sat down, pencil and paper in hand, and I created my own middle ground, and I called it very simply" "My creed."

What follows is a re-creation of those very words that helped shape my young life and create one of the most important building blocks that would form the foundation of the man I am today.

Ken's Creed

It is my birthright to be unique and to be uncommon, while all around me in this world seems so common and alike. I will seek with excitement, even at great risk, what I would consider my opportunities in life.

Above all, I do not wish to be a kept man, by having big brother look after me! Because if I did that, I would be accepting and living by the values of others most of the time.

So I will take my own calculated risks, based on my own values and my own priorities. I will strongly pursue my hopes and dreams, and I will build my entire life on them. Whether I fail or succeed, it must be on my own terms, by conditions I create.

It is my choice to pursue the challenges of the unknown, instead of living a predictable frequently boring existence. And in my pursuit of personal achievement through personal freedom, I must never compromise my integrity, my principles or my self-respect. Above all, I must never bend or concede to any other mortal's threat or will.

It is my birthright to build my own heritage. To accomplish that I must stand proud and unafraid and believe completely in who I am. Only by doing this, can I sow and reap the benefits of my own thoughts and my own creations.

This must be my human journey. To be able to say to myself with total honesty, that I have truly to my total ability, over the passage of the time of my entire life, made every possible attempt and effort to fulfill the meaning and the purpose of my life.

In looking back on those words, I'm proud that I can honestly say I gave it everything I had. I believe I did exactly what I intended to do through the course of my life, based on those words and thoughts. So know this: no matter your age - forty to sixty and beyond, even to a hundred years old and more, what I wrote at twenty can be any man's creed, who is searching with an open mind to find a way to further discover and expand his own identity and individuality, knowing that it will take his life to a higher level. Which will definitely add greater purpose and meaning to the living of the rest of his life.

100 Observations by Ken Dab-Row
-
100 ways to build better days

Somebody Who's Been There

1

I would like to think at my age I can talk about the life I've lived objectively, without sounding braggadocios or over self-serving. I want you to know that even though it's been almost thirty to fifty years since I was your age, I do remember that Great Transition into the second half of my life clearly and vividly. Think about it. Almost half a century, but I remember so well I can be specific. What I remember the most, are those constant challenges and struggles. All the ongoing changes during my formative first forty years. Like you, that's what I was thinking about. Particularly the first twenty-five years of life. Now know for sure, those were my true years of discovery and the excitement that discovery created. I knew almost every day something was going to happen. What the hell it was going to be, I had no idea. Now we both know, that's a real recipe for excitement. The term I use: paying my dues. And even though I might not have known it, that is exactly what I was doing. Hopefully you will be able to identify with that. The reason I didn't mind paying my dues? So many damn exciting things were happening and going on. My life like yours was filled with so many firsts, even my first taste of chocolate. It happened over eighty years ago, but I still remember it. What a great twenty to twenty-five years. Almost everything we experienced was a first. And it was many of those firsts, that represented the solid credentials that you will eventually judge yourself by. Then another fifteen to twenty years went by. A whole different phase of life. Family, kids, responsibility. I started, as I'm sure you did,

11

focusing on and searching for, success in business, looking for social acceptance, and still trying to be to the highest degree, an idealist. Now that's generally what I remember, from those first forty years. Learning how to live my life. Experiencing and experimenting, with excitement and energy and curiosity.

Well now that I've done that, I'd like to make a few suggestions how you, past forty, can make the next years of your life, no matter how many you have, work better, no matter how good you think you got it, I'm telling you, they can be made better. You gotta trust me on this because in ten years, I plan on hitting the one-hundred-year century mark. Well I have obviously already been through what you're going through. It was thirty to fifty years ago, but sir, I remember it clearly. My first forty? Far from perfect! But complain, not on your life. And the reason I refuse to gripe and bitch, is because by comparison, through all the ups and downs, IT SEEMS TO HAVE WORKED OUT PRETTY DAMN WELL. So let me give you my overall take on it, at this stage of the game. No matter how smart or highly educated a man is, even if he's a genius and a member of Mensa, with stratospheric qualifications up to forty years of age, those qualifications and capabilities concerning every aspect of his life, even living life to its potential up to forty, DON'T MATCH THE EXPANDED CONTENT AND CHARACTER OF YOUR HUMAN POTENTIAL PAST FORTY. Because psychologically, having been there I know this: All those people under forty, they are still going through, what you and I have already been through. You and I survived! So until those twenty to thirty year-olds steer and navigate their way through it, like you and I already have done, until they deal with all the mental

12

demons, that go with that territory before and up to forty, only then, will they have the possibility, of emerging out of that sometimes exciting but long and dark, challenging tunnel. Then they will be qualified like you and I already are. It's impossible to look back on those years until you have lived them. Only then can you reflect on them, and put them in realistic context. And once you do that, your top priority should be to use them as a means to elevate your life. Then you will be able to say with any degree of validity, that those first forty years of living, made me stronger, and prepared me well for my second forty. TO ALLOW ME TO MATURE, TO A HIGHER LEVEL.

Now that is what I feel it has done for me, and the goal of all these observations is to hopefully do the same for you. And that's what this book from many different perspectives focuses on. Now you know why that is so damned important? From here on out you have got to keep building on, and making every day, week, month, and year of the rest of your life, more meaningful, rewarding, keeping you motivated and inspired. So do not, and I mean definitely don't ever, fall into that crap-trap of thinking, that just because you're getting older, you can't make a difference in life by making it more interesting and exciting. Because that's not only something you should do, it's an absolute must-do.

So now that you've heard my story of the first forty and the Great Transition, I want you to do yourself a big, big favor. To the best of your ability, please take better care of that body! It's gotta last you for a hell of a long time - every second of every day of life! And your expectancy for living should be eighty-five to a hundred years. You can make that happen if you nourish it correctly and respect it. Now to that sometimes irrational brain of ours, that has to deal with all the aches and pains that go along with advancing years, that can if you let them, drag you down. That's why you must, on a constant basis, NOW MORE THAN EVER, expand your positive attitude so it can battle through any and all kinds of adversity. And here's another paraphrase that's been repeated a thousand times, but too often it doesn't register strong enough, but when applied personally and sincerely to you, it has tremendous value. You've probably said it to yourself a thousand times, and hopefully it has expanded meaning. You must always, for a lifetime, be willing to FIGHT THE GOOD FIGHT BECAUSE THAT'S WHAT EVERY DAY OF LIVING IS ALL ABOUT. That's why it is a must, if you wish to make the second half of your life more satisfying. Even when extreme difficulties seem insurmountable, and you want to throw up your hands and give in, that's when it's even more critical and essential to fight that good fight. And there is one more thing I know for sure, that into my ninetieth year on this planet has taught me. It is going to be one of the main themes in this book. When you exercise your willpower and power of discipline, you must on a consistent basis, make the supreme effort to CONTROL every aspect, element, and facet of your life. Only then will it be possible to live every day during the SECOND HALF OF YOUR LIFE, to its absolute potential. And from my mouth to your ears through these written words, that will hopefully give you, a lifetime full of better tomorrows.

Positive Mental Attitude

2

I know it may seem like asking a lot when you are in that forty to sixty-year-old age bracket. Well sir, not only must we ask a lot, you must use the previous years of your life effectively, during these up to twenty years you are about to live. This is a major demographic; millions of men are in your age category. But from my perspective, I don't know why all those millions of men between forty and sixty, every last one, can't accomplish every day, the power of their personal positive mental attitude. You must make this your top priority, during the second half of your life. It is an ever-growing challenge and struggle, and that is why you must make every concerted effort with every passing day, no matter how much tougher that ongoing effort seems to become. THIS POSITIVE MENTAL ATTITUDE FROM HERE FORWARD, HAS TO BE YOUR TOP PRIORITY IN LIFE. Now with that kind of practiced habit, doing it consistently year in and year out, there is not the shadow of a doubt it will not only reinforce, it will expand, elevate, and make stronger, your self-respect, self-confidence, and so very important with the aging process, YOUR SELF WORTH.

I hope we can all agree, we are talking about the most important time frame in your life. Let me use a stronger word: *Ultra*. It is ULTRA IMPORTANT this must remain numero uno, job one. You achieve that goal during this twenty year period, and like you will read in different forms throughout this book, it will make those years between sixty and eighty-plus, when most men fall into a deeper state of decline physically and psychologically, it will make the twenty to forty years that follow, sixty to a hundred, potentially the most personally gratifying, productive, and rewarding years of your life.

And now, a few phrases this book, with valid justification, almost wears out: NO <u>EXCUSES</u>! NO POINTING THE FINGER AT <u>ANYBODY ELSE</u>. IT'S ALWAYS <u>YOUR CHOICE</u>! Don't ever say to yourself: "But that's impossible." You can make the aging process, instead of a growing liability, a priceless asset. With the incredible life I have been fortunate enough to have lived, as good as it has been, I can honestly say the most gratifying years of my life, as rewarding as those first sixty were, to still be this active, involved, and motivated, has made the twenty-five to thirty years since sixty, some of the best years of my life. To the point where I still have that feeling of looking forward to a great tomorrow. NEVER LET AGE BE A BARRIER TO THAT MINDSET.

Again I emphasize, you must understand how critical these years are that you are now living in. So make no mistake, sir, if you are fortunate enough to live one hundred years, it's these twenty years you are LIVING IN RIGHT NOW, that will be the most important of your life. These are the years when you must develop and expand your own PERSONAL POSITIVE MENTAL ATTITUDE. You know, I think, sooner or later, all the millions of men in this demographic, finally wake up to the reality, that the way this planet of ours functions, as history has proven, is generally a whole lot MORE NEGATIVE THAN POSITIVE. We hear it and see it all around us all the time. And it can convince us if we allow it, that as we get older we really

16

believe we have less resistance to increased negativity. That contributes to the thinking, that older age takes men down. Well, sir, I found that to be a fallacy. I made up my mind, during this exact time frame you are in, as I got older, there was nothing in this world I was going to let take me down, defeat me or even intimidate me. And the longer I lived, the stronger that feeling got to the point now, at almost ninety, it is stronger than ever. And sir, I wish the same for you, I really do. So please now, during this so-called mid-life crisis, as you get older, make it your business to get stronger mentally, physically, and spiritually, letting nothing take you down. I'm going to keep reminding you throughout this entire text, THIS OLD MAN, IS NO BETTER OR WORSE THAN YOU. JUST ANOTHER GUY LIKE YOU, TRYING TO GET IT RIGHT MOST OF THE TIME. So whatever observation I am making that you happen to be reading, don't ever think or say *can't*. Kill that word *can't* on the spot, because if I can and did, SO CAN YOU. If I could do everything in my power to make the living of my life, regardless of my age, grow in value, WHY NOT YOU, OF COURSE YOU TOO! And you're gonna find, when you put your mind to it, it will come more naturally. Every breath you take to stay alive, breathe life into your own personal, positive mental attitude, and through that breath which gives you life every eight seconds, take complete positive control mentally and psychologically. You want these next forty to fifty years to work for you at your optimum potential, don't you? THEN YOU MUST MAKE <u>YOUR</u> PERSONAL, POSITIVE MENTAL ATTITUDE <u>YOUR</u> NUMBER ONE CONSTANT COMPANION, FOR THE REST OF <u>YOUR</u> NATURAL LIFE.

Feeble Or Mighty

3

What could be more entertaining and exciting than being a people watcher. Nothing in the world as far as I'm concerned. I think we're all people watchers. No matter how many years you live and all the thousands and millions of people you see, they almost always represent, the most interesting aspects of life. Even the best show that Broadway had to offer, no matter how great the actors and play, it would pale in comparison to being a people watcher. No doubt, IT'S THE GREATEST SHOW ON EARTH. Come on guys, I want you to look around at your fellow man, in particular the ones who are in your age group. If you have just arrived at forty, you are vital, energized, interested, and excited about the living of life. And in too many cases, just twenty years later, during this CRITICAL TRANSITIONAL GENERATION, literally thousands of those same men, at sixty, are on their way to becoming frail and feeble old men. Now why the hell should that ever happen. But it does. Open your eyes and look around, if you have any doubts. This is more than a figure of speech, this is literal fact: Thousands of men, I'll even venture to say most men past sixty, twenty years later at eighty-plus, are truly in danger of falling into that frail and feeble category. And this twenty-year period you are now in, IS WHEN THAT TRANSITION TAKES PLACE. Think about it. If you during this exact twenty-year time-frame, or whatever is left in it depending on your age, with just a little bit more of positive extra effort, in a relatively very short amount of your time, if you feel you are becoming a little physically limited, that could plant the seed of thinking it's irreversible. IT ABSOLUTELY IS NOT! There is still time to cut off that defeatist mindset, and go from feeble to getting more mighty. Don't you ever deceive yourself into falsely believing it can't be done. What's so rewarding is, having done it, I know that it has been instrumental, in helping several hundred men your age, that I have personally come in contact with. Adapt this positive mindset, so even if you are close to sixty, and that kind of negative mindset is taking hold and setting in, YOU CAN STOP IT DEAD IN ITS TRACKS, and set yourself up to make the next twenty to thirty years, strong physically as well as mentally. You can literally be as sharp as you were thirty years ago. Just as quick thinking, lucid and alert, supported by a super high energy and activity level. Feeble, my ass! Hopefully not you!

So the message is this: Don't you ever start thinking that with advancing age, your life automatically has to be less fulfilling, have less meaning, and that being left behind goes with the territory, like you can't keep up after a certain age. That is a crock full of crap! Don't you ever buy into it. YOU NOT ONLY ABSOLUTELY CAN, YOU ABSOLUTELY MUST BE THE MIGHTY MAN YOU WERE MEANT TO BE! Even past eighty, sir, don't you ever let that feeble producing gremlin or demon in. I don't want you ever to buy into that kind of mentally crippling BS. And if you are starting to think that way, no matter how mild and slight that thought might be, if you think that it is happening to you to even the slightest fraction of a degree, I want you to stop that diminisher of life, dead in its tracks. I gotta get a little more graphic. Put a screeching, grinding halt, to that kind of crappy, crippling, self-defeating thinking right now. Not for one single solitary second, minute or hour, no matter how grim the momentary environment you are in, I don't want you to ever buy into that kind of preconceived defeatist bullshit.

So clean-sweep your brain thoroughly of all that unproductive, restrictive, debilitating influence. Feeble? Frail? FEEBLE – AND - FRAIL, MY - ASS! I want you to think and believe with every fiber of your being, that this mighty-man theory is not just now and then, but that you will become, and always consistently be that mightier man. MIGHTY STRONG, MIGHTY DETERMINED, AND MIGHTILY INVOLVED WITH A POSITIVE LIFE, for the entire second half of your life. Always feed, fertilize, and enforce, then master long-term THAT KIND OF MINDSET. Now do that, and that is exactly the way your life will play out. And the rationale for that kind of thinking, through all the winning and losing we all experience in life? At this halfway point, you paid your dues, sir. YOU DESERVE IT! Now you accomplish that to its optimum, and in reality, that will mean a much more complete and fun life as you age. Every last one of these qualities I've just described, I want you to know, if they are in reverse or even neutral, get them the hell out and kick them into high gear. That's how you nourish them and keep them alive and thriving. What a great thought to know that until your very last breath, for the whole of your life, YOU ARE GOING TO BE THAT MIGHTY MAN, THAT YOU WERE ALWAYS DESTINED TO BE. Of course you are. Why the hell not? What the hell could be holding you back? Hopefully, never the guy in the mirror!

Time Immemorial

4

Just think how many years, and we're talking thousands of years, that history books have been written. In fact, every century of modern western civilization, there have been literally dozens of history books written. But it's very possible you may not be a history buff. So if the history of humankind over all those millenniums is of little interest, it's more than possible outside of your schooling, and knowing a little bit about your country's history over the last couple of hundred years, that you haven't read many history books. Nothing to apologize for. A lot of people are not history buffs. There is such a diversification of interests you could have outside of history. So that's understandable. Because when you get right down to it, our main interest, as it should be, revolves around OUR LIFE EXPECTANCY. And hopefully that will last EIGHTY-FIVE TO A HUNDRED YEARS. Simple observation: Those are the years we are alive, so those are the years that are going to justifiably pique our interest. Those are the things we're going to read, hear, see, and think about – PRIMARILY WHAT'S HAPPENING DURING OUR LIFETIME. But if you go back in recent history, and when I say recent, I'm talking about the last three to five thousand years, that is a period, commonly known as modern western civilization. It's been documented and recorded, written down. So it has tremendous validity. Sounds like a long time, five thousand years. But when you consider the planet has been here for over four billion years, it can be compared to a drop of water in an ocean of time. But it's all we got, it's our recorded history.

During that short-recorded history, I want you to think about all the thousands, and I do mean thousands, of diseases, life threatening aliments, natural disasters such as earthquakes, volcanic eruptions, tsunamis, tidal floods that happened through all those three to five thousand years. There has been a war somewhere on this planet NINETY-FIVE PERCENT OF THAT RECORDED TIME. And we're talking about wars that have literally cost hundreds of millions of lives. And in most cases, the men who fought those wars were under forty years of age.

Now to digress for just a moment, I know that every one of us has to deal with negative situations that can be discouraging, worse yet, even depressing, and in many cases hard to resolve. Now I know that personally, because I've had to battle them all my life! And I know how many hundreds of times, they got me down. In fact, as I recall, I got knocked down so many damn times, that I didn't really want to get up. THAT'S A FACT WE ALL HAVE TO ACCEPT IN LIFE, if we are going to get through our eighty-five to a hundred-year life expectancy. My point here? With all those millions who fought all those wars and died of all those diseases and natural disasters as mentioned, before forty, at least you are still alive past forty. So no matter how hard you get knocked down, you gotta get yourself up and dust yourself off past forty. Don't ever forget, all those many millions of lives that were lost over our recent history, they all died before they were forty. WELL NOT YOU, already past forty. You have the great privilege of looking forward to the next forty, so count your blessings.

So at one time or another, all of us, everybody included, nobody excluded, we are all going to have to fight that fight in the course of our life. So our greatest gift? So simple and so essential: YOU ARE STILL ALIVE RIGHT NOW, TO MAKE THAT FIGHT. FOR GOD'S AND YOUR SAKE, SIR, GIVE IT ALL THE HELL YOU GOT! You not only have this rare opportunity, you have been afforded the incentive in the second half of your life, to neutralize and discourage negative situations. You are still around to cope with them, and to keep up the fight. And if you don't give it all you got, the odds are, you won't win to the high degree you want to in the long run. Not only are these negative conditions numerous and repetitious, they are destructive bastards, that show their ugly faces in so many forms, that you gotta fight them. You know why? They seem to be all around us all the time, and if you encourage and give into them, they will become killers of your hopes, dreams, and ambitions. So always remember: About all the thousands of diseases, wars and natural disasters? YOU HAVE SURVIVED THEM, giving you the option, no matter how hard and insurmountable the struggle may seem to be, to take the God and natural given powers you have, that I know are built right in you, and use them in a constructive, productive way. So if you want to be a strong-willed person on a permanent basis, please use all your positive powers. That will be the powerful mindset you need. DON'T YOU EVER LET THAT STRONG HUMAN QUALITY GO! Always keep that positive mindset, at the forefront of your thinking. Be strongly aware of it always. You bet you should count your blessings, because now you know, having reached forty-plus, YOU ARE TRULY ONE OF THE LUCKY, RARE FEW. Just think that you have the ability and opportunity past forty, to create and execute your plan for the next forty to fifty years of your life. Literally tens of millions of people never will have that opportunity. <u>YOU DO</u>!

That's why living the second half of your life to the absolute fullest, always must be your top priority. You and I cannot permit all the bad situations and uncomfortable conditions that we experience throughout our life, to depress us. Now I want you to know, from a whole lot of long-term experience over a whole lot of years, I've seen this happen to literally hundreds if not thousands of people: THEY CAN WIND UP LIVING OUT THE LAST TEN TO THIRTY YEARS OF THEIR LIFE, WITH A BROKEN SPIRIT. Never let that be your fate, it can be deadly. A broken spirit can be even worse than a broken back, because as long as it might take and as painful as it might be, a broken back has the possibility of healing. But let me tell you my friend, if you allow anybody or anything, to weaken or break your spirit, and you don't reverse the effects of it damn rapidly, that negative impact on your spirit, will if you let it, ultimately cripple you mentally. The only thing you should and must say is: NO THANK YOU ... NOT ME. You must always think: I will never have anyone or anything break my spirit. Always know in your conscious mind, you have too much self-pride, backed up by a wealth of willpower. Say: "I will resist every destructive and negative influence." That's how I expect you to think! And not just as you are reading this page or these words, and not just for a day or two or a year or two. THIS IS THE MINDSET YOU MUST MASTER AND MAINTAIN, FOR THE SECOND HALF OF YOUR SENSATIONAL LIFE. Tell yourself at the start of every single day: "That sure as hell is not going to be my destiny. I deserve a better fate, because that is definitely NOT WHO I AM." You must do that and that spirit of yours for living, will stay stronger and solidly intact.

Your Old Pops here wants every little bit of this to sink in. All these words and thoughts and observations on all these pages, are coming from a man, and I will repeat this several times in this read, who is no different than you. Just a hell of a lot older! What I have already done, is well within your capabilities. Am I a strong-willed man? You bet your ass I am! Are you a strong-willed man who is going to get even more strong willed? You bet your ass you are! But know this: with all the complexities of life, that I will refer to and comment on, I'm a man of simple needs, who appreciates every sight, sound, touch, taste, and smell of life. I make it my business to relate to almost anybody and everybody, and sincerely show an interest in who they are, and what they are going through. THAT'S MY VALUE SYSTEM. That's why I'm telling you, that right now, that strong, powerful, positive mindset, so necessary to maintaining a strong spirit, YOU MUST RECOGNIZE IT IS NOT ONLY IN YOU, IT ABSOLUTELY IS WHO YOU ARE. But you must bring it out and keep it elevated for the balance of your life. Make that willpower you have so damn iron clad strong, that all those negatives you will run into all your life, simply cannot penetrate. Your biggest blessing? YOU ARE STILL FULLY ALIVE, while millions of people, since recorded TIME IMMEMORIAL, lost their lives before they were even forty. Fate and destiny never gave them the advantages and opportunities, that you are just embarking on during this, THE BEGINNING OF THE SECOND HALF OF YOUR LIFE.

25

Life After Forty

5

It can be a rude awakening, but something you cannot be self-deceptive about. In this case reality has never been more important. In this observation, there will be no compromises. Once you hit forty, you must accept it's a whole new ball game. We become astutely conscious that we are not going to live forever. When you wake up to the reality of your mortality, it will probably be there every day for the rest of your life. Well there's a figure of speech: Life begins at forty. Fortunately for you, that's a reality. YOU ARE JUST STARTING THE SECOND HALF OF YOUR LIFE. During the next twenty years, wherever you are in it through sixty, will come all those dramatic, ultra-important and relevant, continuing changes. And once you become aware of that psychologically, that indicates you must definitely rearrange your values and priorities, concerning most probably every aspect of your life. So know when you do, IT WILL DEFINITELY DETERMINE THE OUTCOME OF THE REST OF YOUR LIFE! And the better you adapt to this second half, the better chance you have of improving the quality of this forty to eighty year-plus phase of living.

Now we all know life is simple enough, when you break it down to common denominators. And you are going to see repeated in this book, the primary common denominator is THE THREE SEQUENTIAL PHASES OF LIFE. Of course there must be a beginning, then hopefully a very long middle, and more frequently than not, a relatively short end. I don't know about you, but I found that my first twenty years was my beginning. Traumatic indeed. Think about the dichotomy of that period. You go from total, COMPLETE DEPENDENCE on your parents, then without any preparation or preconceived concept of responsibility, you are TOTALLY INDEPENDENT. That was my experience during my first twenty years. Then comes the second half of what I still call the beginning, the next twenty years, where after acquiring your education and independence, it's now time to accept that responsibility, for not only supporting yourself, but the family that can become a reality in the near future. That's where most of your accomplishments as an adult, will come into play. And that will be your life up to forty years of age. You are so actively busy, you have so many hopes, dreams, and ambitions that you want to accomplish. And because some of them seem so far out of reach and so distant, as much energy as you commit to them, you can't seem to see the end of them. YOU ARE SO PREOCCUPIED, you somehow think you're going to live forever, because in your mind, that's how long you think it may take to ACCOMPLISH THEM ALL. You know what your thinking was at that time, it's only a few years back. From twenty approaching forty, you never thought about your mortality, because of all those preoccupations and responsibilities that consumed you.

Then we hit the middle. We're at the halfway mark: forty-plus. Well, that's where you are right now, sir, maybe five to ten years into your second half. I believe if you lived a hundred interesting, highly active, fully rewarding years, these will be the most important twenty because now, sir, you are truly that man in the middle, your highly vulnerable, pivotal period. We go from being that ambitious, driven family man, and before you know it, your kids are finally grown up. And if you are still married at that time, you become empty-nesters. Then all of a sudden, like overnight, you know, YOU ARE MIDDLE AGED. Well what the hell is wrong with that? Too many guys take and make that a rude, depressing awakening. When you maintain that way of thinking, you are playing directly into the hands of that DESTRUCTIVE DEVIL CALLED NEGATIVITY. And if you give that son of a bitch license, your insecurities and self-doubts will increase exponentially. Believe me, I know, I've lived through them. I admit openly, many of those same challenges, I faced during that potentially demonically-controlled time frame. It did seem insurmountable at the time. Just keep your guard up to fight them off like The Old Man did. You gotta be assertive and self-assured every day during this twenty year period. Because God knows I know, that man-in-the-middle condition can, and will if you allow it, create a variety of psychological endless problems, that can easily cause CONFLICTING AND CONFUSING THOUGHTS.

It was long ago, but I remember it clearly, it was a fragile time in life. You must stabilize those shaky psychological underpinnings, if they exist, and exercise YOUR AWAKENING POSITIVE POWERS, act on them, and you will continue to realize your hopes and your dreams are still very much alive. MAYBE EVEN MORE ALIVE THAN YOU THOUGHT. Once you make that discovery, and minimize that potentially negative state of mind, only then will you recognize you have made it to REAL MANHOOD! Facing and accepting fearlessly this reality, is a sure sign of real maturity. Well my friend, that's where and what you should be: MATURE AND SECURE. That was the most important and main purpose, of why you spent those FIRST FORTY YEARS GROWING UP AND OUT OF BOYHOOD. You must capitalize on those first forty, then exponentially make every year after forty up to sixty, much more ENRICHING AND REWARDING. A real tried-and-true experience is speaking to you, sir. So remember, every page you read, I am you and you are me. There will be no political correctness where my opinion is concerned. You can rest assured, that I am going to express my opinions, evaluations, and experiences with total, sometimes brutal honesty, to convince you, that what I just said is completely true, about your second forty. IT CAN AND SHOULD BE LIVED BY YOU IN SPECTACULAR FASHION.

So right here as you begin your journey through all these following pages, I want you to know for damn sure, YOUR TIME HAS NOT PASSED. Passed, my ass! The most valuable times of your life are just arriving, YOU ARE RIGHT AT ITS THRESHOLD. It will keep getting, and you will keep making it more valuable, with each passing day. IT'S YOUR NATURAL POTENTIAL, BE INSPIRED AND UPLIFTED BY IT. Now you do that, and you will be setting yourself up to be the most COMPLETE, CONFIDENT, AND SELF-ASSURED MAN, YOU CAN AND WILL BE FROM THIS DAY ON!

Man In The Middle

6

When I was in high school, about seventy-five years ago, maybe there were twenty men in this whole country past the age of one hundred. Well with modern medical technology and improved nutritional methods, we are so much more knowledgeable about good health, and how to delay the natural decline that comes with age, there are literally THOUSANDS OF MEN LIVING PAST THE CENTURY MARK. This leads me to believe as technology gets even better and more highly developed, the majority of men between forty and sixty right now, should have little trouble making it to a hundred, if they live their lives physically, mentally, and spiritually to their optimum, and I don't mean sometimes, but always by seeking out the highest levels possible, of those three great qualities of mind, body, and spirit. Just think how great that would be. Sitting there right now at your age, you being the man in the middle between forty and sixty. How inspiring, and what a great opportunity and source of encouragement, IF YOU CAPITALIZE ON IT. All these positives that advanced technology can now provide you. To know you have more than a fifty/fifty chance to make it to a hundred or more. And not just living a hundred years, but to make those hundred or more years INTERESTING, EXCITING, PRODUCTIVE, POSITIVE, PASSIONATE, AND REWARDING! And all you have to understand, not just through this Great Transition, but through all the remaining years of your life, is how to tie all those years together, keeping them ORGANIZED, STABILIZED SO THEY SUPPORT AND

STRENGTHEN EACH OTHER, and further establish your identity, during this most important second half of your life.

Now let's talk about what I consider the first phase of your life, it lasts up to forty years from the minute you are born. Then there's that second phase you are living in right now, forty to sixty. And of course, sixty to infinity, the one I'm living in.

As we will share extensively in so many other observations, during that first phase, it seems we spend the majority of it SEARCHING, FINDING, DISCOVERING, AND LEARNING. And that really constitutes the majority of our mental focus up to our late teens. Because up until that time, pretty much everything is being done for you. Think back, during that period of your life, you were almost completely dependent on others. You are listening and learning. And it is coming from all directions on a daily basis, as mentioned in so many other observations. Between your parents, teachers, and religious influence, not to mention the strong input of the media, movies, and now the world wide web, the internet. And all that was coming at you, having an audible and visual impact on essentially, ALL YOUR VALUES AND PRIORITIES. That's a pretty heavy long-term load to lug around. All that absorbing, while you are still so young in the process of growing up. So through it all, you didn't give much thought to the future, or the man you would need to become. That was the farthest thing from your mind.

And of course during your teens, it was during that time that you made that big discovery. YOUR HORMONES KICKED IN WITH THE FORCE OF A HURRICANE! What a revelation! All the changes, confusion, and conflicting messages. But with

31

that first erection, your focus is totally different. And for the next few years, even with all the hormonal interference, somewhere in your late teens, you start to think about your future. You vaguely begin the formulation of the kind of man, you think you may want to be.

So now let's put it all in context. The most important aspect of searching, discovering, finding, and experimenting, after being told what to do, and being essentially dependent on others, now the time has come for YOU TO DEVELOP YOUR OWN INDEPENDENCE, which would not only allow you to learn, but would prepare you to put into motion, plans for your future.

And that was your focus as you left your teens behind, and transitioned into your twenties. Now came, in most probability, the most important word for the next twenty years of your life: RESPONSIBILITY. You, in just those few years, going from very little, if any, responsibility, to almost total personal responsibility for the conduct of your life, in just a few short years. My God, man, what an agenda you had to develop. The completion of your education to get a job, whatever that education was going to be. And all the hundreds, even thousands of choices of profession or vocation that existed. You needed the training to acquire the chosen job, that would provide the money to support a family. Over seventy-five percent of us get married and have children. So you keep working, you keep progressing, and you generally raise those children up to eighteen years of age before they can leave their home. That is a major long-term commitment you have to make, but you made it because YOU FELT YOU WERE UP TO IT.

Then all of a sudden, it seems like overnight, your children are grown up. You were so busy and active during those eighteen to twenty years of being a parent. And that all takes place somewhere in your middle or late thirties to your early forties. So the first major phase of your life is just about finished. It was a challenge, it was a struggle, but those first forty years represented A REAL SENSE OF ACHIEVEMENT. Think about it. What a row you had to hoe, what a mountain you had to climb. So don't you ever forget, sir, YOU MADE THAT HAPPEN. Through all the trial and error, all the ups and downs, YOU SURVIVED IT ALL. One hell of a giant-sized, long-term accomplishment.

Then you hit that critical point where you suddenly became the MAN-IN-THE-MIDDLE. Then came what most men would consider the unknown factor. You were so busy keeping life going with the job and the kids and the house payments, you didn't even notice what was obvious, right in front of you, that had to be dealt with: After two exciting and interesting generations, you have now reached YOUR GREAT TRANSITION. It's funny how all this works. Like I just mentioned: at twenty, you essentially knew where you wanted to be at forty. But once that first phase is completed, it's almost like HITTING A PSYCHOLOGICAL BRICK WALL. A lot of men don't know exactly where they want to be, in the next two to three years, no less at sixty. Hence, those very descriptive words that describe that condition: Male menopause. Because if there is such a thing as male menopause, it can certainly identify and be described as our midlife crisis. I wasn't exempt, I know the experience. Just like any normal struggling emerging man, I spent those first forty years searching, finding, and experimenting. Using good and poor judgment in essentially equal proportion. But the primary key to my growth during that period of time, WAS NEVER BLAMING ANYBODY ELSE, OR RATIONALIZING AND JUSTIFYING MY POOR JUDGMENT. I knew I had to learn from my experiences. At that critical point, I was the man in the middle. I can picture it so clearly, it's hard to believe it was almost fifty years ago, that I faced tremendous self-doubts and insecurities. I could easily become RUDDERLESS AND MISDIRECTED through my insecurities, or become MORE PRECISELY FOCUSED, WELL DIRECTED, and more in charge of my life. I had a choice. The latter conclusion was my true turning point in life. I made damn sure, to use the purpose and experience of those first forty years, to aid in my maturity. I was acutely aware during this great transitional, I had to take it and elevate it to a higher level, which would create the reality to CULTIVATE GREATER SELF PURPOSE AND SELF WORTH.

Now you know why this second phase of forty to sixty, WILL BE the most critical time of your life. The time where you definitely will establish, how these oncoming years of the rest of your life, will play out. It's during this transition that you can easily get CAUGHT UP IN IDEAS, CONDITIONS, AND SITUATIONS THAT ARE POTENTIALLY PROBLEMATIC. Then instead of recognizing their negative nature and eliminating them, you can expand upon them, allowing them to produce greater insecurities and self-doubts. If that's how your next forty to sixty years play out, it can easily lead to bad decisions affecting adversely your mental, emotional, and physical well-being. This can be a more than probable pitfall IF YOU

34

DEVELOP A NEGATIVE PERSPECTIVE IN THE PROCESS OF AGING. Don't do it!

In your twenties, you were just finding yourself. You would see a successful, forty-five-year-old man, polished and on top of his game. And just learning about life at that tender age, you would look with admiration at this accomplished forty-five-year-old man. And we had a great term for that kind of guy: WHAT A CLASS ACT. And you thought to yourself, BOY, THAT'S WHAT I WANT TO BE. And of course that kind of thinking was understandable and justified. Who wouldn't want to be a polished, mature, sophisticated man. That's what you aspired to. But here's the contradiction: why, when you finally entered your forties, and arrived at all those desired goals, WOULD YOU EVER ALLOW the awareness of your mortality, over these next twenty years, to become a potential negative with damaging ramifications.

Those first forty years served one purpose and one purpose only: TO GROW YOU UP. And that means it will be right now, during this phase of life. But here's the good news: It's never too late, to get your values in order and keep them organized. YOU MUST SET TRUE, REALISTIC, BELIEVABLE, SENSIBLE GOALS FOR YOURSELF. Always handle intelligently and realistically, your psychological transition of this aging process. Make it a priority to take better care of yourself. Elevate your natural God given assets, by making yourself stronger not just mentally, but physically.

When you do that, you'll be laying the rock-solid foundation needed, for that long exciting and successful final phase of your life. Like it did me, YOU WILL BE REWARDED BEYOND YOUR WILDEST EXPECTATIONS OR IMAGINATION. No arrogance intended, but in this case, I really know exactly and precisely what the hell I'm talking about, when I say to you, if this half-smart tough kid from Philly could do it, YOU BET YOU SURE AS HELL CAN TOO. Your best years are still ahead of you, sir, not behind you. Right now, I am in the final phase of my final stage. SO WHAT? Sure, I'm still mentally and physically strong, but I know where I am in my journey - halfway down the home stretch, headed for the finish line. So I feel a responsibility to everybody in my life, including you, to make every remaining day I live A CONTRIBUTING AND INSPIRING FACTOR FOR OTHERS, so that you and they can create positive options on a consistent basis, concerning every element in their life, during this very important twenty year period. Please do everything in your power, to make these changes right now. And if you've already started down that positive road, don't ease up on the throttle, keep the pedal to the metal! Make it all fit even more efficiently into your very confident value system. If you are realistically and always objectively practical in your beliefs, THEY WILL ALWAYS WORK FOR YOU! Do not bankrupt your present and your future, by living in the past, trying to be something you've already been. At this stage of your life, to guarantee improvement, YOU CAN, WILL, AND MUST TAKE THIS SECOND HALF OF YOUR HUMAN JOURNEY TO A HIGHER, MORE MEANING LEVEL OF FULFILLMENT.

Descending

7

There are specific circumstances where the word *descending* has a positive meaning, but it has many more negative implications. Of course if you are riding a bicycle, it's a whole lot better to be going down the mountain than up the mountain. But not in the framework of this observation. For every man in this age group, who just might think they are in a psychological state of decline, evaluate that kind of unsure frame of mind, no matter how slight it may seem to be. TURN IT AROUND. Don't ever think getting older is more of a liability than an asset. It sure as hell is not, as proven by this time-tested old-timer. I still hopefully can instill and demonstrate to the best of my ability, how unnecessary it is as you get older, to be DESCENDING INTO A NEGATIVE STATE OF DECLINE. That must never be any part of your permanent mindset. From personal experience, be forewarned, this is not easy. It's a long-term tough task, and as years pass you must work harder still to achieve results relating to your POSITIVE AGING EXPERIENCE. Believe as personal truth, you must make that steadfast effort psychologically to know, YOU ARE NOT DESCENDING BECAUSE OF YOUR AGE. Now let's get to the crux of the matter. Heads or tails, yes or no. Descending or ascending. EVERY DAY IN EVERY WAY YOU SHOULD BE ASCENDING WITH A CAPITAL "A"!

No one knows better than your Old Pops, wear and tear goes with this long-term journey. I have been playing the aging game longer than most men live. I knew all these years, no matter how tough and turbulent the undertaking, it was a very small price to pay for what I determined would be, my even more rewarding and sensibly sensational SECOND HALF OF MY LIFE. So know as you advance up the aging ladder, no matter how tough, how hard, or how long that uphill climb, when you get to where I am now, you will know how small a price you paid, for the euphoric feeling you will have received, for this very long and arduous, but immensely gratifying life you are continually embarking on.

Understand, when it comes to you being more of a quality human being as time progresses, at this relatively early middle stage of your long life, you must believe and feel even better about who you are. Now you do that day in and week out, and you will absolutely objectively realize, that you are not, I repeat, YOU ARE NOT DESCENDING, YOU ARE NOT IN A STATE OF DECLINE. That is the biggest load of convoluted, misleading crap ever conceived. With the purest form of core-value honesty that I can muster up, know this: I believe no younger person, had any advantage over me when I was twice their age, as long as MY FRAME OF MIND STAYED UNSHAKABLY POSITIVE, AND I ALWAYS REJECTED AS UNACCEPTABLE, THAT STATE OF DECLINE MINDSET, no matter how STRONGLY ESTABLISHMENT VALUES IMPLIED IT. This was the proud stamp of self-approval I personally required and needed, to maintain my confident, competitive ability to feel secure in who I was going to be on an expanding basis, with the passage of my time.

I don't think I can make it any clearer, how damn important and totally relevant this observation on descending is, to the elevated quality of the rest of your life. YOU MUST GIVE THE FULLEST PURPOSE AND MORE MEANING, TO EVERY SINGLE DAY YOU LIVE *REGARDLESS* OF AGE. I hope these words plant the seed for your mind to fertilize and feed on, so no matter how well you are currently handling it, you can ASCEND TO AN EVEN HIGHER QUALITY OF LIFE. You must reject and diligently rise above any and everything that suggests DESCENT in the process of your aging experience. You must maximize the quality of your life at this stage of the game. In life there is not a chance in hell you'll ever lose, if you know this as you grow older: kind sir, play these years FAIR, SMART, AND REAL. Then know absolutely, being a winner don't make you a sinner - it's never a sin to win! Now you do that, and you will constantly be soaring, not sinking! DEFINITELY ASCENDING, NOT DESCENDING.

So think back, and validate your long, interesting journey. All those tough-to-take tasks and challenges THAT THROUGH DOGGED DETERMINATION, YOU OVERCAME AND RESOLVED. They were the tools you needed to survive and prosper. It was Y-O-U, who shouldered whatever burden came along. You are now more than ever before qualified to expand on that reality. You came all this way and paid this big of a price, DON'T EVER LET YOURSELF FALL VICTIM TO DESCENDING. ASCENDING? YOU BET YOUR ASS! No maybes, should or could bes. THIS POSITIVE WAY OF THINKING IS A MUST if you want the quality of your life to improve. That's how you take everything positive, tangible and intangible in your life, TO AN ELEVATED LEVEL.

Every Day Is Different

8

So I've heard, except it's not a figure of speech, know that every morning from the moment you wake up, you are faced with a different day. Every day is going to be different in some way. No matter how similar you might think it is, no two days of your life will ever be totally identical. You may go to the same job, have the same responsibilities and the same basic conversations with the same people, but there is always that element of difference. So what you've got to ask yourself in the course of living this day, is that difference going to be negative or positive. Is it going to be an asset or a liability. We have to keep this in the realm of broad generalization, but understand, no matter what influences, responsibilities, and conditions of that day are, you and only you can determine, what kind of day you are going to live in. AND THAT'S ALWAYS GOING TO BE YOUR PLAY, YOUR DECISION, YOUR CALL. So right here right now, this is the day you are living in. An hour or two from now, you may be doing something different. Right now, you are reading this book, but here is what's important: I want you to play this only living day of your life right, with CLARITY OF POSITIVE THOUGHT AND OPTIMISM. I know adversity is all around you. But why the hell would you pick the downside and the gloomy way of looking at things, when with just ONE POSITIVE THOUGHT, you can adjust and change that direction, one hundred eighty degrees to the upside! KNOW YOU ALWAYS HAVE THAT OPTION. Now it's nice when the sun is shining. But even if there's clouds and the skies are gray, what you have to know is the sun is still shining right behind them. Have the mental power to penetrate that psychological cloud-cover.

If you look at it any other way, particularly if you let negativity prevail, that would be foolish and misguided. Stop and think about it, why would ya throw away a potentially good day. And with all the foolish things this older man has done, I'm no fool, and neither are you, sir.

So, make this day a winner. If you do that every day, day in and day out, week in and month out, always thinking most of the time like a winner, which means being positive more often than not, then this very day you are living in, and all the tomorrows that follow, YOU WILL HAVE THE REST OF YOUR INTERESTING LIFE to win the day, every day, and always feel like the winner you are. ONLY YOU, CAN STOP YOU.

You Are Unique

9

I know as you look around, everything in this modern era seems so similar, like general categories, and each one covers millions of people. A good example of that is clothing styles. Some famous fashion designer comes up with a new concept of dress, and within a matter of weeks or months, millions are wearing it. That's why so many people, because of those conditions, DON'T REALIZE HOW UNIQUE THEY ARE. Even cars, SUVs and trucks. They are beautiful, they are reliable, but they are relatively similar in design. So therefore, the one thing we don't think we are, because all the products we're so involved with, are so much alike, WE VERY RARELY THINK OF OURSELVES AS BEING UNIQUE. Think about the meaning of that word. The actual dictionary interpretation and description of the word *unique*. Of course you want to be unique, who doesn't? But, kind sir, that is exactly what and who you are. Right now, at this very moment, YOU ARE THAT ONE OF A KIND!

So always be aware of your uniqueness. You have your own truths, your own realities lined up, in the exact order that you want them. Now you know as you think back, that's an absolute truth! So let's take a look at the real picture and the real numbers. Most people are aware of our planet's population – well over seven billion, representing over two hundred countries. Think of all the cultures and ethnicities involved. Let me put it this way: if there were actually two of the most identical twins on this planet, THEY WOULD NOT BE EXACTLY ALIKE. But this next thought I'm about to share with you, is one hundred percent true every time all the time. It is impossible, and would be a display of ignorance, to even argue an opposite position or point of view. And it is one of the rock-solid cornerstones of "Age, My Ass!" Your valid, precise reality is: YOU, ARE UNIQUE! Of course you are one of the masses of that over seven billion people on planet earth, but I want you to know for damn sure, your truest of all truths, you are an ABSOLUTE ORIGINAL!

When you accept that realization, being a one-of-a-kind, you might feel a little isolated. Just don't be intimidated by it. Don't you ever think of your uniqueness and your originality, as a burden. IT IS JUST THE OPPOSITE AND MUST ALWAYS SERVE AS THE SOLID FOUNDATION THAT INSPIRES YOU. With all those things that are on the plus side of your ledger, at the very top should be you being numero uno. Be conscious of it always, specifically that one-of-a-kind identity you definitely are. You bet your ass, you are unique! That positively will always be YOUR MOST STRATEGIC AND GREATEST ASSET. But you must accept it, as your reality. When you do, you will find the value and purpose of your life, EXPANDED BEYOND YOUR CURRENT COMPREHENSION.

And a few points to remember: No one on this earth, no other person has your exact face, fingerprints or your thought processes, and definitely not your DNA. Always revert to and fall back on that great unique quality. And it's going to be needed, whenever something challenges your self-confidence or has the potential to cultivate insecurity. REVERT ALWAYS TO YOUR UNIQUENESS. That is the only way you will even know, how

EXTRA SPECIAL AND EXCEPTIONAL OF A PERSON YOU ARE. I want you to know as a mathematical fact, that can never be denied. You are that ONE OF A KIND. Am I getting through to you? Know for certain YOU DEFINITELY POSSESS TRUE INDIVIDUALITY AND ORIGINALITY. Please, kind sir, activate, recognize, and accept it, because it absolutely lives in every cell of your body and soul, every day of your life.

So whenever those defeatist gremlins and demons of insecurity try to slip into your psyche, kick their asses firmly out! Show them who the hell is the real boss - YOU! Expressing your UNIQUENESS in every possible way. This is not a now and then or every once in a while happening. This is today, tomorrow, every day, every week, for the rest of your natural life. So I want you to light that unique fire of that one-of-a-kind individuality, that burns so strongly and deeply in the belly of your soul and spirit.

Just undeniably knowing that, it should and will increase and fortify your self-confidence and security. So I want you, for every breath you take, to appreciate and be grateful, for your uniqueness.

YOU ARE A ONE OF A KIND, AND DON'T YOU EVER FORGET IT!

Beginning And End

10

Well, the title says it all, and one thing is for sure, every beginning, including the life expectancy of the whole universe, has an end. Now some guys find that hard to take. Well what we are really talking about here is the TRUEST OF TRUTHS, and it's one I am going to make sure you recognize and acknowledge: When it comes to life, the living of it and how full you make it, if you are fortunate enough to have a long life, seventy five to a hundred years, that short beginning and that long middle, leads to the reality of those words nobody wants to hear: the end.

My friend, as sure as there's a beginning, you should know that implies by its very meaning, there is going to be an end, or there would be no need for the word *beginning* no less *middle*. At forty to sixty you should still be forty to sixty years away from your end. Well, sir, your Old Pops here is in the home stretch, nearing the finish line, the final phase of the final stage, and absolutely, TOTALLY THRILLED AND GRATIFIED TO HAVE HAD SUCH A LUCKY AND LOADED WITH GOOD LIVING, LONG, EXCITING LIFE. Now of course as we get older, we all naturally focus more on the end than the beginning or the middle. Well the fact is, anybody's life, at any age, could end at any time. It happens tens of thousands of times every day. So here's the point of reality I want to make: Imagine being over forty years old, approaching or into these very important middle years, and spending the next thirty to forty years, or more, FEARFULLY WORRYING about how it's all going to end. Most likely when that time comes, for all of us, it's going to happen, relatively

45

speaking, pretty damn quick. But now my young friend is not the time to worry about it. Not when you have so much more time to be fully alive, and so many PRODUCTIVE AND EXCITING OPPORTUNITIES, TO ENHANCE AND EMBELLISH THE LIVING OF IT. These should, could, and will be the best, most fulfilling years of your life, BUT ONLY IF YOU BY CHOICE, MAKE THEM THAT WAY. And if I'm not worried about it at my age, and you still got at least thirty to fifty years more to live, why in the hell would you RESTRICT AND LIMIT, all that positive potential development of the second half of your life, when that end is still decades away.

Think of what I just said, and how relevant and realistic it is, for you to have a FEARLESS, POSITIVE STATE OF MIND AS YOU GET OLDER. Why would you be preoccupied to even the smallest degree at this stage with your mortality, when these should be your FINEST FIFTY MOST FANTASTIC, FASCINATING, AND FULFILLING YEARS. You see, all that really counts, is to fearlessly put into the substance of your life, everything you have learned from the beginning. Don't worry or even think about the end, because from your viewpoint, IT WILL NOT AND CAN NOT CONTRIBUTE ANYTHING POSITIVE OR PURPOSEFUL.

So from a common-sense perspective, why wouldn't you live every day of life to the fullest? THAT'S WHERE YOUR WHOLE FOCUS SHOULD BE DIRECTED! Being preoccupied with your mortality, is a total WASTE OF YOUR CURRENT PRECIOUS TIME, and can fill your life with negativity, trepidation, fostering insecurities and self-doubts. So no matter how little your preoccupation with your mortality is, I implore you, sir, REORIENT AND ALTER YOUR MINDSET. Search and find your most positive, constructive meaning of life. That will ALLOW YOU TO SELF INSPIRE, EXCITE, AND MOTIVATE. You want your fair share of life's rewards? I found that to be the most positive path.

We all know too well that mortality has always been, from mid-life on, man's greatest struggle. FACT: Every beginning will have an end. So you must put in place, a strategic, positive mindset, that makes every single day of the rest of your life A NEW BEGINNING. I'm telling ya, pal of mine, it works, and I've got the track record to prove it! IT IS ONE OF MY TRUEST, DEEPEST, AND MOST PROVEN BELIEFS. And if I can somehow get you to think that way at this stage of your life, not one minute of your entire human journey will be UNNECESSARILY wasted. There is no greater feeling at any age, especially those middle years between forty and sixty, than to relate to life FEARLESSLY, with passion, energy, and animated purpose. If that's happening, fine. If it has any chance of happening, fine again. But I want you to fight as hard as you can, to make progress. The next step is, you must reduce and hopefully eliminate, as many negative preoccupations concerning your age as possible. Because they have the power to take away, even void, all those outstanding positive assets you have. I'm doing that right now, nine full decades down life's rough and tumble roads, and my mindset is: I CAN'T WAIT FOR TOMORROW, because tomorrow is going to give me the opportunity, to make a better day than the day I'm living in. Let me tell you how far The Old Man's gonna take this: even on my last day of life, I sure as hell will do everything in my power, NOT TO WASTE IT. So please, sir, exercise with all your mental might, those forces in you that put purpose, passion, excitement and thrills into every day, that you have left to live on this Earth.

DON'T EVER BE AFRAID TO EXPRESS YOUR EMOTIONS TO THEIR FULLEST. Just don't over-do it, and become uncontrollably emotional. I didn't say hold those emotions back, if they contribute to making a more valid positive point or decision. In fact, if you play it smart and keep it real, you'll give very little meaning to the words *beginning* and *end*. They both represent a very short period of time, of your very long eighty-five to a hundred-year life expectancy. The only thing that really counts for the likes of you and me right now, that's of any real value is what's going on BETWEEN, the beginning and the end. I'm telling you, that's the only sensible way to look at it. I call it wisdom at work! You must make every remaining day of your life, PAID IN FULL. Every word you just read, is absolute truth, lived and carved in stone by Yours Truly. So do me a big favor and forget about the end. For you it's a hell of a long way off. It will take care of itself when the time comes. What really counts, is the life you are living right now. Inspire, excite, and motivate yourself, and watch everyone around you REACT, APPROVE, AND RELATE TO YOUR POSITIVE PERSONA. You want your fair share of rewards in life's second half, then always believe you'll find the best in life, all your life, and pal of mine, if you pursue hard enough, you sure as hell will find it, and you, Mr. One-Of-A-Kind, WILL MAKE IT HAPPEN.

Reality Check

11

Let me tell you when reality really sets in, and it's something you become acutely aware of when at thirty-five to forty, you know you could be a little bit out of shape. Almost all of those years up to forty, you were basically in good shape, in most cases. Of course there are people that are born fat, and they are fat even when they are young and active. But I'm going to assume, more than likely, that's not you. It's possible you reached a certain point of good condition, worked at it real hard, or at least harder than most, to optimize your state of physicality. But then comes the day, as I repeat to near exhaustion, when your mid-section may start to spread, those love handles get a little bigger, and you feel a little heavier on your feet. Just nature at work. Not quite as bouncy as you were! If that's the case, IT DIDN'T HAPPEN OVERNIGHT. It's an insidiously slow process. And we can't forget, what most men consider their most important body part. Of course, up to forty, that power-packed, always ready for action penis, that somewhere between forty and sixty, every once in a while, seems to be a little less ambitious.

Been through it all over this long life of mine, I learned that no matter how good I took care of myself, I discovered what I just described to you was going to be a part and parcel, of all the twists and turns a long life seems to impose, ESPECIALLY FOR THAT MAN IN THE MIDDLE, WHICH WAS ME, AND IS NOW YOU. Let's add a little flexibility here. These years you are living in right now, are smack dab in the middle of your life. Now having lived this long, I'll assume you've had many successes. A lot of good things in life came your way. But when you are the man in the middle, these years can seem to be a little unjustifiably cruel. Again, no Superman here. I was adversely affected by all that stuff. I truly had to face up to it. I learned that many of those mental and physical changes that I was experiencing, that seemed at the time to be a letdown, even depressing, IF I HAD LET THEM, COULD TAKE CONTROL AND COMMAND THE CONDUCT OF MY LIFE FROM THAT POINT ON. That would not only have created self-doubt and uncertainty, but it would have over the long term gotten worse, as I was getting older. Well, let me tell you from personal past experience, NOT A CHANCE IN HELL THAT SUPPOSED DOWNWARD SPIRAL WAS GOING TO TAKE ME DOWN WITH IT. And I sure as hell hope, NOT YOU EITHER. So from this day on, no feeling sorry for yourself, like everybody but you is doing just wonderful, and only you during this time-frame are going through this annoying change. You got a hell of a lot of company! In fact, I've got many friends, that are ten to fifteen years my junior, and every last one had to face up to this purely psychological tricky challenge, which is exactly what it is. So know for sure, no man is exempt. Every single living man on this planet in that middle forty to sixty age group, will go through it, and to be very frank, there's only two outcomes: THEY WILL PSYCHOLOGICALLY EITHER WIN THE BATTLE OR LOSE IT. And that will depend on how strong willed and disciplined they are in the long run. PLEASE, SIR, BE THAT WINNER.

Now of course the rudder in life at this mid-range time frame, can get a little loose. Is it possible to temporarily lose a little direction? Even be a little misguided as a result of having your brain play games with you, which it usually does? And how well I know. But here I am, all these years later, having experienced the whole purpose of what this MID-LIFE STRUGGLE SHOULD BE. It should be you exercising all your inner strengths that you have developed, cultivated, and fortified over that first forty-year-long life period. THAT SHOULD HAVE PREPARED YOU TO WORK YOUR WAY THROUGH IT.

Now some more reality. Does the fight get tougher the longer we live? Let's not pussyfoot around here, of course it does! It's a growing challenge which implies, YOU GOTTA FIGHT A LITTLE HARDER. That's what I'm doing even at this late stage of my life, where the wear and tear is extensive. So I expect you to fight that good fight every day, getting a little tougher to prepare yourself for the years ahead, TO MAKE THAT DECLINE A LITTLE SLOWER. Then when you complete this challenging time of your life, you will emerge mentally victorious, and remain at the very top of your game. ANYTHING LESS *YOU SHOULD FIND* TOTALLY UNACCEPTABLE. What you have just read, I have said dozens of times in dozens of different ways to thousands of men your age. Please, sir, let it sink in deeply and permanently, and you will understand this reality to be clearly positive: It is one hundred percent possible, to make your life more rewarding, right to the last breath of life your lungs suck in. WHAT A BENEFIT, TO KNOW YOUR LONGER LIFE, CAN RETAIN ITS HIGH QUALITY!

Control Your Emotions

12

What a struggle I had. I gotta tell ya, I'm pretty uninhibited and not afraid to express myself. But sometimes my emotions got out of control. And when they did, I never once blamed the situation, condition, or person on the other end. The key: I always took personal responsibility, when I lost control of my emotions. I UNDERSTOOD there were certain things I alone had to definitely deal with. Finding your fulfilling upside of life just will not be attainable, IF YOU DON'T CONTROL YOUR EMOTIONS.

Let's assume this is true for every one of us: we have something on our mind associated with being over-emotional, that seems to be a constant preoccupation, but in reality, IT LITERALLY IS NOT AS IMPORTANT, AS YOUR VANITY AND PRIDE MAKE IT. Once you become sure of yourself, and that self-assuredness is a higher priority than your vanity and pride, you will instinctively and confidently give whatever that negative preoccupation is, a lower priority. Better yet, justify discarding it altogether. And why wouldn't you do that? The more you think of it, or other preoccupations like it, the more you are building on a negative thought process, which could morph into a permanent lifestyle. Don't make sense to do that! So know from a position of objective evaluation, exactly the situations you are living in. If you blow them out of proportion, you will surely have a loss of emotional control. And how well I know that out-of-control experience. I overcame it, I conquered it, I REFUSED TO BECOME A VICTIM OF IT, because I knew what the consequences would be.

I want you to look every potentially over-emotional fact that concerns you, straight and fearlessly in the eye. You should, with objectivity, practically ponder your thoughts every day of your life, IF YOU WANT TO BEAT THAT OVER-EMOTIONAL MENTAL BOOGIE MAN. As we get older, if we don't do that, not only do we become more emotional, we become less capable of securely handling it. So if you will, sir, here's what I recommend you do for all the years ahead of you: Commit to organizing your thoughts accurately, in ACCORDANCE WITH THEIR REAL IMPORTANCE. Instead of taking something that controls you emotionally, and blowing it way out of proportion! I love this word, it's one of my favorites: FEARLESSLY! You must deal with every overly-emotional outburst fearlessly, from a position of real strength and knowledge during this twenty-year transition. These are the most important years of your life, and The Old Man is telling ya, that's how you mentally control your emotions, and GET OFF that self-doubt and insecure old-age treadmill. Treadmill, my ass! If you are smart, bold, and proud, you are going to be moving straight ahead, making your life more secure and solidly grounded, because the one thing you are probably aware of, which is going to be repeated again and again in this book, and I know it's tough love, but it's my reality, it's your reality, and it's common knowledge: TIME WAITS FOR NO MAN, NOT YOU, NOT ME. So why the hell would you waste one minute of it, when you know it is an absolute limited commodity, as frequently stated throughout this text. Every day you live no matter your age, IS A DAY LESS YOU HAVE TO LIVE. You must make the most of it every minute of that never

53

again to be lived day, the most valuable of any truth you will ever hear, read, or see. The odds are, BEING EMOTIONALLY OUT OF CONTROL, WILL PRODUCE JUST <u>THE OPPOSITE</u>, denying you precious time, that could and should have been more productively utilized.

It's this simple: you want to be happy, you want be fulfilled? Like you just read, get off that treadmill. Treadmills are for hamsters, not for positive thinking human beings! I want you to move forward, upward. Make every moment of your life from here on out, as positive as it can possibly be. And by the way, no matter what your support system is, no matter who encourages you, NOBODY BUT <u>YOU</u>, CAN DO IT FOR <u>YOU</u>. All that support will mean very little, unless you assume and take total responsibility, for all your actions. By design, your emotions are intended to be under your control. You must, with advancing age, definitely keep your base instincts under emotional control. Now I'm not trying to play "Joe Perfect" here. Every man past forty still has all those appetites, and by the way, I still do. So why would you short change yourself or compromise ANY OF YOUR APPETITES, URGES, AND DESIRES. They are there to be totally enjoyed, as long as you keep them under *emotional control*. But keep this in mind, and make it a constant in your life: Very little satisfaction will be found, if you let any of your strong drives and instincts, take control of your emotions in life. <u>YOU</u> MUST GOVERN AND CONTROL, <u>YOUR</u> EMOTIONS. That will allow you to operate and conduct all of life's most rewarding activities, from a position of mental, physical, and psychological strength. I want you to also know for damn sure, I AM STILL ENJOYING EVERY LAST ONE OF THEM AT

MY AGE.

So I'm telling you loud, clear, and realistically, you, from a position of self-confidence and self-worth, must take COMPLETE CONTROL OF YOUR EMOTIONS. When that becomes your reality, WHATEVER DESIRE OR URGE YOU HAVE, CAN NOW BE FULLY SATISFIED. The same drives you had at twenty to thirty, you can still experience with equal gratification from forty to eighty-plus. So let's see if we can agree on this: most of your natural urges and drives will become less rewarding and unproductive IF YOU LOSE CONTROL OF YOUR EMOTIONS. Now, can you accomplish that all the time? Hell no, of course not. You must make, with conscious determination, that effort every day of your life. Only then will YOU FIND THE TRUE, VITAL, ENERGIZED, SELF RESPECTED YOU. And it will last for the rest of your PROUD, PRODUCTIVE, AND DAMN EXCITING LIFE.

In Charge Of Your Life

13

It's not just nice, it's a wonderful place to be! In fact, when you think of it, you have the option to do it most of your life. Now of course, being in charge of your life is not easy to accomplish. There are so many challenges, obstructions, and unknowns that exist. But when YOU are in charge of YOUR life, there is no feeling in the world that even comes close. Now there will always be compromises we have to make, in dealing with other people and situations. At work you have a boss, and there's always a chain of command in business. Even life in general, where there is give and take and ebb and flow. Of course, if you are married and have a wife with a strong personality, that requires give and take. But that does not mean you cannot use your STRENGTH OF MIND to always be IN CHARGE OF *YOUR LIFE*. Now what I mean by that is being IN CHARGE OF YOUR THOUGHTS. You must own them one hundred percent. Which will allow and encourage you TO BE IN COMMAND OF YOUR PERSONAL ACTIONS.

When you think exactly that way, and this is an absolute, there is no in-between. With that kind of positive mindset, you will be headed in the right direction. Even with all the adjustments you're going to be confronted with, on a day to day basis, many of them are not only going to be challenging, but quite a few EXASPERATING AND DIFFICULT. Well when you are fundamentally in charge of your life, your main responsibility IS TO YOU. Come on, my friend, open up that mind of yours in an objective, fair, and just manner. Of course somebody else's advice and knowledge could be beneficial. Everybody knows something you and I don't know. But that doesn't mean you can't clarify in your mind, and visualize for yourself, only the best of things as YOU EVALUATE THEM. The majority of your thoughts every day, should be on things, tangible and intangible, that bring you gratification. But keep in mind the word *consideration,* so that it's never unjustifiably at the expense of somebody else's mental or physical comfort. You make this moment that you're living in right now, and the minutes and hours that are going to follow on this day, MAKE THEM YOUR OWN <u>AND YOU WILL BE</u>, FULLY AND AUTHORITATIVELY IN CHARGE OF YOUR LIFE. That thought with time will grow stronger and ultimately cultivate a deeper belief in who you are.

Please, if you will, remember what I have said time and time again, and know it as absolute fact beyond the shadow of a doubt, the ability to handle and take full charge of your life is built right in you. For that to fully evolve, you must always live in compliance with, and trust your TAKE CHARGE ATTITUDE, when it comes to the things that are of vital importance to your values that you consider of the utmost importance. DON'T EVER COMPROMISE THOSE CONDITIONS. Please, sir, do not run from it, do not lose control by giving in and surrendering to a tough situation. Now, if you have already started down this positive path, fine. But don't you ever forget, YOU WERE BORN TO BE, <u>IN CHARGE OF YOUR LIFE</u>.

Live With Your Thoughts

14

Every second of every minute of every hour of every day of my life, even when I was sleeping and dreaming, I had to live with my thoughts. So obviously this is a theme that I'm going to discuss with you, several times in the course of this read. I am going to tell you, how YOU ARE THE MASTER AND THE MAKER of your thought processes. You can always choose to change your thinking, in as many ways as you wish, so let's keep it uncomplicated. You should choose frequently as possible, positive trains of thought. It is that fundamental and basic, even more importantly, essential, when it comes to you starting off your day. Positive or negative: YOUR CHOICE! I just described on the previous pages, why nobody is in charge of your life but you. Because only you, no other human being on this planet, lives with the thousands of thoughts you have every day for as long as you live. Now I know we all have moments, where those little tidbits of self-doubt, start creeping into our psyche through adverse thinking. When that takes place, we are creating negative thoughts that could impede and dominate our positive progress, AND DIMINISH OUR SELF CONFIDENCE. Let me give it to you straight. I want you to definitely kick that kind of crappy compromised thinking, completely out of your thought processes, and do it right now, because that's exactly what it is: crap. We must cultivate and activate our will and our mental strength, which when utilized affirmatively and decisively, will allow us to stop them dead in their tracks.

I want you to take charge of this day and every day hereafter, particularly during these critical transitional years. I want you to keep growing and getting mentally tougher and stronger, by constantly picturing and visualizing, THE VERY BEST OF WHAT AND WHO YOU <u>THINK</u> YOU ARE. Then with passion and purpose, I want you to take that giant leap right into it, and live it out all the way up to sixty, establishing the valid premise of being able to live the next thirty to forty years of your life beyond sixty, with an ongoing, STRONGER, CONFIDENT SELF BELIEF. You must execute with powerful purpose, THE MOMENT YOU ARE LIVING IN. That will be the only guarantee you have, that you will be providing yourself with the most, of whatever it is you want. Any less of an effort will minimize your capacity, during this crucial transition. Being that you are going to have to live with your thoughts, with every breath you breathe, make damn sure YOU MINIMIZE THE ONES THAT PROMOTE SELF DOUBT, AND MAXIMIZE THE ONES THAT <u>ENSURE YOUR SELF WORTH</u>.

The Second Forty

15

You know, this time of your life does not have to be dominated by a conflicting and confusing state of mind. In fact, with a little bit of positive purpose, you can change the potentially fearful forties, into the fantastic OPPORTUNISTIC FORTIES AND FIFTIES. It is a whole new change of life psychologically, and to accurately coin an old phrase, IT'S A WHOLE NEW BALL GAME, a game you can surely win. So during this great transition, a lot is going to depend on how intelligently and realistically you arrange or reorganize, in the CORRECT ORDER OF IMPORTANCE, your values and priorities. Then get ready for those more rewarding years that are going to follow. They should not, and you must not allow them to be, the compromised second forty. If you play it smart and real, THEY WILL BE THE SENSATIONAL SECOND FINE-AS-AGED-WINE FORTIES. And hopefully more confidently satisfying, than the experimental first forty. But, a lot is going to depend on how effectively, YOU ARE WILLING TO CHANGE AND REARRANGE YOUR VALUES AND PRIORITIES. That will be the positive key that you have to turn, to unlock and determine a greater lust for the living of your life.

You are going to find sprinkled liberally, through all these observations, what The Old Man calls THE THREE PHASES OF LIFE. It's fundamental and easily understood. You had a BEGINNING, you are living in the MIDDLE, and we're all going to have an END. And every aspect, facet, circumstance, and condition of your life, that is going to be covered in this entire text, will be what you can make happen between the beginning and the end. I'M TALKING ABOUT YOUR LONG LIVED, MAGNIFICENT MIDDLE OF LIFE. So we're going to keep it very uncomplicated. Chronologically, you are smack dab in the middle of your life.

So let's put those three phases of life in their correct context. We'll examine them individually. I like to believe the beginning is not just when you are a kid, but a time frame that encompasses your first twenty years. To be specific, the most formative years of your life were those TEN YEARS BETWEEN TEN AND TWENTY. Then we have twenty to forty. That is the time where you are so busy with building the meaning of your life, I don't think one in a million men that age are ever thinking of the end. And why in the hell would ya?! Just starting into your twenties. My God, man, all the ventures and adventures that you are about to go on. So many preoccupations and obligations, and of course all the unknowns that are going to come your way. AND THE REASON YOU NEVER THINK OF THE END? Because with all that in front of you, you really think you almost have to live forever, to accomplish whatever you choose to undertake in life. So I believe it's realistic, that from twenty, almost all the way up to forty, would you ever think of the end. It's way too far off when your mind is that preoccupied.

BUT THEN WE HIT THAT MID-WAY MARK, those critical years between forty and sixty. *Your Great Transition*. You are truly there now, you are that man in the middle. And although it took forty years, when you finally reached it, it was like an epiphany, an awakening. All of a sudden, almost like overnight, you go from all those boyhood thoughts, about all those wonderful tomorrows, most of which as young men, we have seen come to fruition, then like out of nowhere, staring us right in the face, MIDDLE-AGE. And too many of us, make that a somewhat disappointing, even depressing discovery, WHEN JUST THE OPPOSITE SHOULD BE YOUR TRUTH. We have to understand, and learn from our experiences, that the price we paid during those first forty years of accomplishments and successes to varying degrees, was for a profound and positive reason. It was during those first forty we felt almost indestructible. Then middle-age arrived. And if we allow it to, IT WILL PLAY DIRECTLY INTO OUR INSECURITIES AND SELF DOUBTS, having the potential of creating big psychological battles and problems, and through negative thought interpretation, can and will grow and expand, if you let it. If you DON'T LET IT, not a chance in hell it can. That's why you must develop an even more positive mindset. And if you are in your fifties, and you've been on this gradually declining psychological mindset, know for sure YOU CAN ABSOLUTELY, WITH CHARACTER AND A POSITIVE VISION, *TURN IT AROUND*.

The door is always open during this twenty-year period, but, and this is another big "but", you must believe thoroughly and completely that the first forty-year period, SET YOU UP TO SPRING-BOARD YOURSELF INTO AN EVEN MORE ELEVATED MATURE MANHOOD. This will allow you to cope with and handle much more efficiently, the challenges and struggles that you must face up to, and overcome during your second forty. THAT'S WHERE YOU REALLY ARE. That's what going from forty to sixty, the first twenty years of the second half, SHOULD BE ALL ABOUT. Let me tell you what it's not about. It's not about backing off, or quitting a little bit at a time. That could happen if you start feeling sorry for yourself, or letting yourself get mentally boxed in. That's what I call BECOMING A MORTALITY FATALITY. Please, sir, don't fall victim to it, don't do it. The price is far too great when you have so much longer to live.

What I've just described can be done, sir, because I'm still doing it, and I'm humbly proud to say, pretty damn successfully. So know this is not just some empty theory. I also want to keep reminding you, because of my many already lived years, IT'S NEVER TOO LATE. So you can bet your sweet, wonderful, and worthy ass, it's anything but too late for you, kind sir. This older man will do and say everything in his power throughout these many pages, to convince you how WONDERFULLY DIFFERENT THE SECOND FORTY YEARS OF YOUR LIFE CAN BE. Even assuming you are positive about your second forty, which you probably are, I hope my words, at my stage of the game, increase your positivity, inspiring you to make it more abundantly gratifying. Know for sure, when it comes to real manhood, real maturity, God, man, please understand and recognize, YOUR TIME HAS NOT PASSED. Passed, my ass! IT HAS JUST ARRIVED. So if you are past forty, you are only a few years into it. If you are in your fifties, you've been living with it for ten years or more. I WANT YOUR CONFIDENCE TO CONTINUE TO GROW WITH YOUR AGE to ensure the rest of your life will be a SELF-FULFILLING SUCCESS.

Natural High

16

How sweet the thoughts, and with the passing of years, how easy it is for us to embellish and expand on those younger years. Of course youth was a NATURAL HIGH. One that every young man is going to experience the excitement of. Raging hormones, at their absolute natural maximum. But we were all so naive! Before we could recognize all the flaws in the world that existed, we were loaded with idealism, pushing the passion level to a new high. Always ready to strongly, emotionally express ourselves. High powered hormones didn't just make you screw a lot, they make you talk even more. What we were really doing was looking and searching, sometimes blindly, for the ANSWERS TO LIFE. So let me ask you this: Why in the hell in the name and the honor, of everything that you lived through during those first forty youthful years, why would the thought even cross your mind, that you should or would have to give up anything exciting or interesting, just because you are over forty? (Easy for me to say, almost fifty years after the fact!) Now I understand, because I've been there. When men become middle aged, and that body may be less strong and efficient, that can negatively affect you psychologically. But, know you still have complete and total flexibility, in search of your natural high. YOUR CHOICE SHOULD BE OBVIOUS, because YOUR <u>MIND</u> IS NOW STRONGER AND <u>MORE</u> EFFICIENT, than it was during those first forty! Now I have been pretty fortunate physically. Of course I don't have the muscle mass I had thirty or fifty years ago, but I still have my fair share. But those muscles, they sure as hell cannot do what they did fifty years ago! So here's how I handled that, and it will hopefully serve as an example to you. Instead of losing confidence because of A LITTLE LESS LIBIDO through my middle years, I used my mental muscle, and all those accumulated past experiences, not only to be bolder and more expressive, but to absolutely be more self-assured, KNOWING EXACTLY where I was, at any given age and stage of my life's journey. That's why you, with all you've been through, you have earned the right, you deserve the opportunity, to develop to its fullest your greater self-confidence.

Now let's get to the physical. After over seventy years in the gym, I am always going to make the supreme effort, to sustain and maintain the highest level of physical condition that I can. And even though I'm in year ninety, and know there are compromises, I REFUSE TO LET THIS ADVANCED AGE, GET IN MY WAY. So certainly, if you are pushing fifty to sixty, where your strength and health are concerned, with so many more years to live, I don't want you to think, no less assume, the next ten to twenty years have to be a period of slow decline. You want that STAY-STRONG, PHYSICAL NATURAL HIGH? You can still, WITH AMAZING RESULTS, do something about it! There is no doubt that the stronger you are, the more energy you have, the better equipped you will be, to highly increase all those mental and psychological strengths, so you can take on with even GREATER EFFICIENCY, ALL THE CHALLENGES THAT ARE GOING TO BE THERE, EVERY SINGLE AGING DAY OF YOUR LIFE. So of course it's going to be helpful and beneficial to you, to do some kind of exercise. I can tell you from past experience, even fifty years ago, when you get past forty, the expectation is that your physical prowess can naturally, as time passes, be diminished. So if you knew for sure the opportunity was there to prove just the opposite, why wouldn't you willingly and enthusiastically make it your reality, when you now know you can. You will definitely feel that extra surge of strength, creating even greater energy and excitement, THAT YOU MIGHT HAVE THOUGHT WAS DONE AND GONE FOREVER. Well you're gonna find out just like your Old Pops here did, it will be just the diametrical difference of what you expected, because you somehow might have thought that losing strength just naturally goes along with getting older. Well obviously it doesn't. Like me, you will feel a new natural high so literally euphoric, it will represent more than you thought you could ever POSSIBLY PHYSICALLY ACHIEVE.

Well that almost says it all, sir, if you choose to capitalize on it! So even if you're past fifty, that kind of potential life force still resides in every single cell of your body. Don't settle for just being alive. Keep getting more and MORE alive with each passing year. Keep fighting and clawing to take it to the highest level you possibly can. We're talking about YOU RE-GENERATING YOUR INNER AND OUTER STRENGTHS, that you thought for sure, you were NATURALLY losing. WELL, SIR, YOU ARE NOT. Again, this old man is living proof. It is one hundred percent there, if you CHOOSE TO CAPITALIZE ON IT. Now, if you have started down that path and are living it, that's great! But if you feel that flame slowly diminishing with the passing years, you must re-ignite it! AND YOU SURE AS HELL ONE HUNDRED PERCENT CAN. And once you have it in your grasp and utilize all of its assets to your benefit, then watch your life fill up with MORE POWERFUL MEANING AND PURPOSE, than you could ever have imagined.

So know for sure, that natural high you took for granted during those first forty years, you not only gotta work extra hard for it now, but even harder as you get older. SO WHAT! *DO IT*! Think about it, if this old well-worn war-dog is still doing it, what the hell would or could be holding you back? I have absolutely not a single doubt in this old but bold brain of mine, knowing you sure as hell can make this an absolute, and have that COMPLETELY ALIVE FEELING, ongoing and growing at this stage of your life.

Now, to close off this observation, I know you've heard or even said: it ain't rocket science or brain surgery. Well when it comes to your physical well-being, from your personal perspective it should be just as important AS ROCKET SCIENCE OR BRAIN SURGERY. And IT HAS NEVER BEEN MORE VALID THAN IT IS RIGHT NOW, concerning all the natural ingredients we have just discussed on what a natural high is. THERE IS NO SPECIAL TALENT OR ABILITY NEEDED HERE. All it's going to take on your part, is you getting YOUR ASS AND ALL YOUR OTHER PRECIOUS BODY PARTS IN GEAR. Then, man, get the hell out there and mix it up with life. And do it IN A BIGGER, BOLDER, SOMETIMES MORE BOISTEROUS WAY. And I do mean you must always make THAT EXTRA HIGH ENERGY EFFORT. Work at it hard, and your highs will feel natural, FOR ALL YOUR MANY YEARS TO COME.

Disparaging Way

17

I think the number one priority, and I'm talking top value, that every guy past forty needs to face up to, and know as a fundamental fact of his life is this: It is your personal self-saving obligation, to be concerned with the SURVIVAL OF YOUR DIGNITY AND SELF RESPECT, during this, the second half of your life. Never, and I do mean never under any circumstances, allow anybody, not one single person, don't you ever give license to any of them to ever refer to you or about you IN ANY SUGGESTIVE, DISPARAGING, DISRESPECTFUL, OR DEROGATORY WAY. And this includes the full spectrum of people in your life, friend, foe or anyone in between.

If you ever sense for a second and your instincts indicate, no matter how subtle that's on course to happen with anybody, CUT THEM OFF. You know, it's a sad situation, generally speaking, to CRITICIZE, PUT DOWN, AND DISRESPECT, which seems to be so very prevalent nowadays. That kind of thinking, in general terms, is thought to be the product of generational change. But is it? I know I was bull-headed when I was young. Somehow always associating older people because of their age, with having more flaws, shortcomings, like they were outdated, and therefore automatically assuming, they were out of touch. I can say in all honesty that was a big part of a not fully mature, insecure me, up to my early thirties. I, like most men my age, thought I had all if not most of the answers. Well the reality is, I HARDLY HAD ANY ANSWERS! So at this stage of the game, your midway mark, don't let anybody try to impose that kind of miserable, crappy mindset on you. AND I KNOW BECAUSE THAT'S EXACTLY WHAT I WAS GUILTY OF. Don't let them inflict that on you. If you permit that kind of creeping disrespect, even at a perceptively slow rate with advancing age, that may influence you to start believing YOUR LIFE WOULD BE MORE USEFUL AND VALUABLE, IF YOU WERE YOUNGER. That is not only a falsehood of major proportions, but a complete fallacy. The time has come to leave those youthful, insecure, false manifestations of the mind behind you. Let me be totally politically incorrect on your behalf. That is a MILE-HIGH MOUNTAIN of the most unadulterated BALDERDASH, POPPYCOCK, AND BULLSHIT, *B-U-L-L-S-H-I-T*, ever visited on middle-aged mankind!

Keep your guard up, but do not let false pride play a major role. Never let intimidating negative elements seep in, and have a major impact, just because you are getting older. Don't live the rest of your life thinking younger was better. THAT WOULD BE A FRUSTRATING, ENDLESS ROAD TO NOWHERE. The proverbial Lost Highway. What a sad fate, because that means you may possibly never know why, who, and what you really are. That past identification is what you were, NEVER TO BE LIVED AGAIN. YOU MUST BOLDLY, PROUDLY LIVE IN YOUR PRESENT MOMENT, CONSTANTLY LOOKING AHEAD TO YOUR MORE REWARDING TOMORROWS. Father Time never loses, big guy. He'll be there to tell ya when your time is up. So don't waste it, be the man you were meant to be, and right now that's you LIVING COMPLETELY AND COMFORTABLY WITH THE AGE YOU ARE.

Detours, Bumpy Roads & Dead Ends

18

In every man's day-to-day life, there are what I call DETOURS, BUMPY ROADS, and DEAD ENDS. Not just some of the people most of the time, this is all people. Where you are concerned, everybody you meet in your lifetime, is going to face those detours, bumpy roads, and dead ends. No one is exempt. So know, in your life as in mine, EVERY SINGLE DAY OF OUR LIVES WE ARE GOING TO RUN INTO, A DETOUR, GO DOWN A BUMPY ROAD, OR HIT A DEAD END. And if I remember correctly, and I do, I found more of them from forty to sixty, than at any other time in my life before or since. First on my part came a little "why me" bitching and griping, but I ultimately faced up to my reality. Let me tell you what I did with all those detours, bumpy roads, and dead ends. Knowing they were going to be there, I finally woke up and realized my responsibility, was to navigate and handle them to the best of my ability. *Me, nobody else!* What I learned, because they were there every day, was the challenge to OVERCOME AND RESOLVE THEM. Result: IT MADE ME MENTALLY STRONGER, MORE DECISIVE, AND CONFIDENT. Because of it, I became a more spontaneous and resilient man. I decided I was going to see the plus-side of the picture, by NOT AVOIDING, but accepting them as my ongoing reality. So of course I stopped bitching, complaining, and looking for something or somebody else to blame. I used every bumpy road, every dead end, and every detour as a learning, growing experience. If they were going to be there every day of my life - and they were - you can bet your sweet ass, THEY WERE GOING TO SERVE ME A VERY POSITIVE PURPOSE. Hopefully that is what you are doing or soon will be. You must use those dead ends, detours and bumpy roads in a constructive way. If you do, your physical, mental, and psychological powers will become more highly developed. I can't think of a better way to handle it from forty to eighty-five. But in spite of all this passage of time, I remember very clearly, right up to this day I'm living in now, I was faced with many difficult to navigate detours. I rode on a lot of long, uneven, bumpy roads. And I sure as hell hit a lot of dead ends along the way, MANY OF MY OWN MAKING. Just do what The Old Man did, sir, DEAL WITH IT ... HANDLE IT.

Nothing to apologize for, no escaping it. Your choice: QUIT ON YOURSELF, OR TAKE THEM ON. To be honest, during my mid-life crisis, I thought about quitting many times. I thought it was the easiest way out, when a task seemed like it might contain a little too much turmoil. I could have said "The hell with it, it's not worth my time or effort." Well in fact, sir, that would be a contradiction, exactly opposite to the truth. Young brother, I want you to know that no way on your life was that going to happen to Ken Dab-Row. I knew if it did, I COULD DEVELOP A DEFEATIST ATTITUDE. The consequences would have impacted and affected negatively the rest of my life. QUITTING WOULD HAVE BEEN TOO DAMN EASY. Those detours, bumpy roads, and dead ends had already taught me LIFE WAS NEVER, EVER MEANT TO BE EASY. I knew if I didn't effectively attempt to get around those detours, smooth out those bumpy roads, and bust right the hell through those dead ends, EVERY DAY OF MY LIFE I WOULD BE SOWING THE

71

SEEDS OF SELF DEFEAT. So of course, with an assertive, fearless, forceful, show-me-what-the-hell-you-got attitude, I took them all on! What a feeling of accomplishment, to make them a POSITIVE PART OF MY *PAST*. Kind sir, as an absolute I'm telling you, if I didn't learn how to smooth out my bumpy roads, I knew what the consequences would be. Now did I smooth them all out? Hell no! But the majority of them? Hell yes! I expanded most of them into bright, open roads of opportunity. I realized, at your age, this was one of the MOST IMPORTANT REALITIES of my long human journey. And the same kind of positive impact applies to all those dead ends and detours.

I hope these vibes are coming strongly and sincerely through to you. It is one hell of a terrific, life-long uplifting, confidence-building feeling.

So there you have it. You will not have to look very far, because there is always going to be waiting around every unknown corner for you and me, ever day of life, a detour, a dead end, and a bumpy road. ATTACK THOSE MISERY MAKING BASTARDS WITH POSITIVE POWER-PACKED CHARACTER AND COURAGE. And I do mean with a real assertive, take-no-prisoners, no nonsense attitude. Then exercise complete authority over them with deep belief. Say to yourself: "No way in my life from here on out, is there a detour, dead end, or bumpy road that will EVER HAVE HALF A CHANCE IN HELL OF SLOWING ME DOWN, NO LESS STOPPING ME!"

Upper Head/Lower Head

19

At forty, all men bar none, enter what the concept and theme of this entire text is all about: *Your Great Transition*! Now if you are just around forty, look at all the time you are afforded, because this process is going to take up the next twenty years of your life. For this whole generation, or however far you are into it, it is literally, truly, based on potentially, with all our advanced medical technology, YOUR ONE HUNDRED YEAR LIFE EXPECTANCY, and you should expect to live that long. And why the hell not, with all this modern medical science. But let's get back to the present. Right now, you are the man in the middle. And here's how I want you to think about that: You have all this time, forty to sixty years, TO SERVE AS YOUR ALLY. So when you think back to your first forty years, it's most important you be realistic. It's so easy to exaggerate or OVER-GLAMORIZE those youthful years. Of course those were the years, that so many things that we saw and heard and done highly ignited our genes, turned us on in so many different ways. My God, man, not just every day, almost every minute of every hour we were making new discoveries, or were vividly thinking about them. And of course, all the excitement they created around us. Naturally that was due to our raging hormones, fueling most, if not all our drives FOR ALL THE UNKNOWNS YET TO BE DISCOVERED. It was our top priority. It arrived at about thirteen years of age, and continued right through to where you are now. The way I like to describe it, tongue in cheek to create a little levity, it was the upper head - you know, the one with all the billions of brain cells in it - being controlled during that long period of time, by your overactive lower head WITH ABSOLUTELY NOT ONE SINGLE BRAIN CELL, but a very insatiable appetite! It is simply amazing, how during those first forty years, THE DOMINANCE ONE HEAD HAD OVER THE OTHER.

Now the Lord knows I'm not knocking it, I loved it! But I didn't over-glamorize it. I kept it within the realm of reality. And that's the kind of objectivity you must exercise, during this great transition, where you must REARRANGE YOUR PRIORITIES. Because nature is going to serve up the same menu for you, like it does everybody else, during your mid-life mystery of a miracle. So don't expect the numerous erections at forty to sixty that you got at fourteen or fifteen, because even if you could come close, sir, it is just a natural fact of life that every man in the middle is going to have a few less erections. Now to add a little humor to it, let's assume that you are fifty to sixty-five, and you were still getting eight to ten erections a day. And you're thinking, wow man, wouldn't that be the greatest. I would just about walk through fire to FIND THAT FORMULA! Well, good buddy, I don't think so, because at this stage of the game, you probably wouldn't know what the hell to do with four or five of them! Come on, Mr. Man-in-the-middle, life from here on out is a whole lot more than a hard-on. The reason your single-focused libido slows down is TO MAKE ROOM TO GET THE OTHER IMPORTANT PRIORITIES IN YOUR LIFE IN ORDER.

So realize, you have reached that time in your life, where nature tells you: adjust. But know this for sure, kind sir: IT DOES NOT

MEAN YOU HAVE TO GIVE UP ONE DAMN THING! Life can, will, and should smell and taste just as sweet and delicious, as it ever did at any time in your younger life. Just keep your boundaries realistic. So, after forty years or more of living and learning, DON'T YOU THINK IT'S ABOUT TIME THE UPPER HEAD DID A LITTLE MORE THINKING FOR THE LOWER HEAD?! Getting this old and wise, hopefully you have learned, if you keep living through your schmuck, that's what you could become: A schmuck! Schmuck, my ass! Not you, or any man reading these words, WORTH HIS SALT AS AN INDEPENDENT, STRONG-WILLED, SECURE, MATURE MAN.

Even me, a man my age, give up sex? Not this old boy! But maybe and hopefully, your upper head (you know, the one with the brains, but too much pride, and a vivid, overactive imagination) finally wakes up, where you will hopefully be in control of your lower head. Because that is the only condition, that in every respect of your middle-aged life, will put you WAY AHEAD OF THE GAME. So there's no reason why you or any man in that forty to sixty age bracket SHOULD BE AFRAID OF THIS TRANSITION. When you get thirty to fifty years down the road like your Old Pops, life should and will still be sweeter than ever. And that, sir, is exactly what it will be, as long as your UPPER HEAD becomes the decision maker, thinking for and steering the LOWER HEAD out of HARM'S WAY. That's the SMART WAY, during the second half of your life, to make sure YOU STAY WAY AHEAD OF THE GAME.

Peak Years To Compete

20

I know it sounds like a contradiction in terms, when on the one hand I say this twenty-year period, from forty to sixty, is more relevant than when you were twenty to forty, while on the other hand, those are truly the years you built your life on. Expanding family, advancing on the job, compete, compete, compete! AND YOU DID IT. Feel good about that, in spite of all the setbacks and so-called insecurities of all the unknowns you were working your way through. More likely than not, you competed, and more often than not succeeded. And here you are in that forty to sixty age range, and I'm telling you, in spite of all those things I just said and you just read about zero to forty, *these* are your peak years to compete with even greater success FROM A PSYCHOLOGICAL PERSPECTIVE. The CHALLENGES AND ACCOMPLISHMENTS, if you keep that mindset of yours in a positive mode, THEY WILL BE EXPANDED.

Naturally past forty years old, no less at sixty to seventy, it's impossible to be as physically competitive as we were at twenty to thirty-five, up to forty. Those were our peak physical years to compete. Emphasis on *physical*. And nature knew what it was doing, because that was the time you needed it, those were the years you were driven, almost compelled to compete and climb the ladder of life, which required optimum stamina physically. So naturally, NATURE MADE THOSE OUR BEST PHYSICAL YEARS.

So taking that into consideration, just because it's impossible to be as strong physically past forty, just the opposite can and should be true when it comes to your MENTAL MUSCLE. Now is the time, for every little bit of strength your body loses physically, TO WORK AND CONCENTRATE WITH AS MUCH MENTAL ENERGY AS YOU CAN. Understand, I am not talking about learning power, or about the intellectual switches in your brain working that much better. As I see it, this time frame is about something of much more relevance: THE STRENGTH AND RESILIENCE OF YOUR WILLPOWER. Having the will to work your way through, whatever personal obstacles you are faced with, and maintaining the constant mental powers to push that will forward. IT'S CRITICAL TO THE SUCCESS OF YOUR LONG-TERM SURVIVAL! Make no mistake, sir, if you let the aging process discourage or distress you, just the opposite can and most likely will occur. From my personal experience, at your age, I knew the journey I was about to embark on, was going to make me TWICE AS SMART AND RESOURCEFUL, as I was from twenty to forty. I just knew it. I could almost semi-consciously sense it. Look at your own life, and realize how obvious and practical this evaluation is. In the second half of your life, you are just starting that journey to live twice as long, WITH THE HOPEFUL RESULT, YOU WILL BE TWICE AS EFFECTIVE AND EFFICIENT. But make no mistake, it's a narrow but straight and long physical and mental road. But it will only be possible as long as you keep positive purpose in your life, and to maintain a strong healthy body IS A NECESSITY. Not an easy task with all the negativity that can, if we let it, infiltrate and influence us during this great transition. That's why I said although the road is narrow, it is straight. But that straight, narrow, and clear road can only be yours by choice.

If you want the overall quality of your life to get better as you get older, you MUST CONSTANTLY BE ADJUSTING to the ever changing psychological and physical environment. Of course physical muscles are nice. They serve many purposes. I have found their presence profound and beneficial. That's why I want you to be as physically fit as possible, at this stage of your life going forward. But know this for sure, sir: that mental strength of yours at this mid-life stage just may be A LITTLE MORE IMPORTANT THAN THE PHYSICAL. It is a total necessity to your successful survival, as a self-confident man, through these middle years and beyond. But no maybe, should, could, or would here, sir. I'm telling you as sincerely as I can, this is an absolute one hundred percent must do. EVERY DAY OF THE REST OF YOUR LIFE, MUST BE LIVED WITH YOU, PUTTING MORE POSITIVE PASSION AND PURPOSE, INTO EVERY THOUGHT AND ACTION OF YOUR EXISTENCE. You must keep your lust for living FULLY ENGAGED AND ENDLESSLY ACTIVE.

So keep this in mind: Don't envy younger generations when THEY SHOULD BE ENVYING YOU. You have already completed what they must go through. Know in no uncertain terms, not one of them half your age, HAS HALF YOUR MOXIE OR HALF YOUR KNOW-HOW. Now that should be your true valid mindset and identity. With positive purpose, keep embellishing and building on it, YOUR VERY DO-ABLE DESTINY.

Energized Mind

21

So let me ask ya, how do you do that? I assume that you already believe you use up a lot of mental energy, but every time you do, you may think, maybe, just maybe there's more. No more maybes where your mental muscle is concerned. Let's focus on one of my favorite words: MUST. And, sir, I do mean YOU DEFINITELY MUST, adapt to and optimize the age you are, and in the process you must keep ENERGIZING WITH PASSION AND POSITIVE PURPOSE, YOUR THOUGHT PROCESSES. I'm talking about the exact year you are living in, as the exact marker you must use to recognize and accept THE AGE YOU ARE. Let's break it down to this day, this moment, or how about EVEN YOUR NEXT BREATH. So know this, where an energized mind is concerned, it makes no difference if you are forty four, seventy four or even one hundred four years old, as long as YOUR BRAIN IS FUNCTIONING NORMALLY. You must have your thoughts organized, so they can be spoken affirmatively and accurately. And even though we are decades apart, sir, you and I both know that there is no better time than now, to search and FIND THAT MORE MATURE AND SECURE ENERGIZED MIND.

Yours Truly knows that sure as hell is not easy. At your age, I would look back when I was younger and rationalize, which made it unrealistic. You know what I call that? STRETCHING THE TRUTH. Even in the glamorization of our youth, you have to fully understand that right now is not only the RIGHT TIME, it's the very best time to build for yourself, an even higher level of life.

Though said frequently, in this case, there is no purer truth: YESTERDAY IS HISTORY, TOMORROW IS A MYSTERY. So realize the importance of the day you are living in, and make it a superior experience. Know for damn sure you possess all the component parts: PASSION, AUTHORITY, AND CONFIDENCE TO ENSURE AND GUARANTEE YOUR ENERGIZED MIND. And I don't want you to forget, that this is a minute to minute proposition, right down to the breath you are taking, and the moment you are living in through that breath.

Of course look back at fond memories of your first half of life. It was a hell of a lot of fun, but kind sir, it's over and done. But here we are on page 80. FROM THIS MOMENT ON, keep actively energizing that positive mind of yours. Do that with consistency and the vast majority of your life's experiences will be IMMENSELY ELEVATED. It's the results of that kind of thinking, that will keep your spirits upbeat and active, and keep your mind HIGHLY ENERGIZED. Think that way with EVERY BREATH YOU TAKE.

Thoughts And Ideas

22

Absolutely amazing when something comes natural, how we take it for granted. A good example of that is not our physical tangibilities, but what essentially can be considered an intangible. You really can't touch it or see it, but you can certainly feel its presence every second you are alive. The non-stop human mind! WHAT A COMPLEX, INCREDIBLE DEVICE. It has capacities that are nothing short of astounding. From the very beginning of your life to the very end, no less between forty and eighty, do you realize that not just every day, but almost every fraction of every second of every minute, you are THINKING OF SOMETHING, and that something, no matter how subtle and slight, just may HAVE AN IDEA RUNNING THROUGH IT. Every waking hour you still have for as long as you live, will be motivated by connected thoughts and ideas. So I guess we have to ask ourselves this question: Ideas - chance or choice? YOU MUST HAVE IDEAS THAT ARE IN ACCORDANCE WITH, AND DETERMINED BY YOUR *POSITIVE VALUES AND PRIORITIES*. If the subject content is negative and conflicts with your fundamental sense of values REJECT IT. In that way, you will be hopefully keeping the majority of your thoughts and ideas optimistic. That is exactly what will happen when the thoughts you formulate are pleasant and productive, make you happy, and you find personally gratifying. This is of the utmost importance, when it comes to building your confidence and reassurance.

Now here's what I believe you shouldn't want to do, and it's so easy to get trapped into: going one hundred eighty degrees from your positive thoughts, to allowing negative thoughts to dominate, diminishing the prospects of positive thinking. If you allow NEGATIVE THOUGHTS, they will create and build NEGATIVE IDEAS. That's a condition that can geometrically EXPAND and cultivate A LIFETIME HABIT. And, sir, that could unknowingly turn into a curse. But when it shows its ugly face, don't walk, run as far away from it, as you possibly can. You and I both know, negative thinking is a fact of life. THAT'S HOW YOU REDUCE ITS IMPACT AND EFFECT.

So from my perspective, in accordance with my value system, I have to ask: why would you leave to chance, the destruction this mental monster can cause, when you can make positive thoughts and ideas your PRODUCTIVE CHOICE. I'm serious, why would you or any man in his right mind, make a negative choice of THOUGHTS that result in expanded negative IDEAS, when you recognize that just the opposite is so easily possible and attainable. So on this long remaining human journey, if negative thoughts keep trying to edge their way in, and outweigh the positive, take your conscious, focused, strong-minded stand, AND TURN IT AROUND WITH AUTHORITY AND DETERMINATION.

Now of course that's not easy in this mostly contrary, negative environment, where things around us on such a consistent, daily basis, are so unfavorable. ALWAYS, EVERY WAKING MOMENT, BE AWARE OF ITS PRESENCE. I want you to exercise the positive upside of your life, with every thought and idea you can. And I want you to fight off with all your mental might, THAT CORROSIVE, DIRTY DEVIL OF MENTAL

82

DAMAGE, called negativity. Now we both know that is not an easy task. IT IS A CONSTANT, SECOND TO SECOND, OPTIMISTIC THOUGHT AND IDEA PROCESS. It's not only tough, it's a strategically long-term undertaking.

Know for damn sure, my better than good man, when you have real earned self-pride and self-worth, that you have worked a lifetime for, and it represents the most valuable and meaningful purposes of your life, YOU DO NOT AT <u>ANY EXPENSE</u>, SURRENDER YOURSELF TO <u>ANY KIND</u> OF CONSCIOUS INTERNAL NEGATIVE THOUGHTS AND IDEAS. Please, sir, make yourself fit this mold. And that means you don't ever, let any kind of outside mental force, that isn't in line with your positive way of thinking, penetrate and enter your mental wheelhouse.

Only positive thoughts and ideas, CAN AND WILL ELEVATE YOUR SELF WORTH. And self-worth means SELF CONFIDENCE, SELF REWARD, AND SELF RESPECT. So, young brother of mine, ALWAYS KEEP YOUR MENTAL GUARD UP, because negative thoughts and ideas are always going to intrude and try to dominate your thinking. That is why you must build your own strong mental barrier to keep it out. The only sensible solution: encourage positive thoughts and ideas to OUTWEIGH AND OUTNUMBER THE NEGATIVES. Sir, that is still my every day goal, try to make it yours.

Three Kinds Of Getting Older

23

We all should, and hopefully you will, particularly when you pass the proverbial half-way mark at forty, be acutely aware of your year-to-year aging process, BUT ALWAYS FROM A POSITIVE PERSPECTIVE. First, let's go back to, without question, the most formative years of your life, between the ages of ten and twenty, when there is very little thought of your mortality. At that young life-forming age, which covers ten years of your life, you are always going to be so busy formulating your life, that the farthest thing from your mind, is the end of your life. Then in just two short decades, when you enter at forty, that second half of your human journey, you become vividly conscious that ALL LIFE, INCLUDING YOURS, HAS AN ENDING. So in whatever period of this twenty year time frame, that this epiphany takes place, you go from very little if any thought, to being absolutely, totally aware, of your mortality, AND THAT CAN BE THE SEED YOU FERTILIZE AND NOURISH, THAT CREATES WORRY AND PREOCCUPATION. Certain fears and insecurities seem to set in, when we become aware of our mortality. Now look, I know it's not easy, it's going to be a lifelong challenge BECAUSE I'VE BEEN IN IT FOR FIFTY YEARS. But you gotta play those fears down. You must devote all your efforts to reducing mentally, the troubling impact fear creates. If you don't, with that kind of negative mindset, you will have established a growing criteria, which will accentuate your own limitations. IT WILL FOCUS ON ALL THE SO-CALLED NEGATIVE ASPECTS AND

EFFECTS, OF THE AGING PROCESS.

I believe that's a pretty accurate observation for many men past middle age. So we all know, at this stage of the game, it's something we have to face up to and deal with. Look at all the variables here, but there is one reality we must recognize with a positive and realistic attitude. As the years start to pile up, the aging process for all of us, not just men, women too, IT CAN BECOME A MAJOR OR MINOR PREOCCUPATION. I have fortunately handled it all the way up to this late stage of my life successfully. And again, let's keep it simple because it really is not complicated or confusing. All those negative mortality mental conditions I just described, they only become progressively complex and confusing, if YOU ALLOW FEARFUL THOUGHTS AND INTENTIONS to dominate. So once more we get back to one of the core themes of this book. Make the smart choice - DON'T LEAVE IT TO CHANCE!

To me, there are only THREE KINDS OF GETTING OLDER: CHRONOLOGICAL, PSYCHOLOGICAL AND PHYSIOLOGICAL. Now with chronological, you have no choice. Not a damn thing we can do about that, as so often written in many pages of this thesis. Every day we live is one day less we have to live. We all know that. That is as much a mathematical fact as two and two being four. NOBODY BEATS FATHER TIME AT HIS GAME. That old taker and giver of life always wins. So every time you celebrate a birthday, you have lived that year completely, and it is time to start another year. A year older. YOU CAN'T CHANGE THAT. This not only applies to everybody on the planet, it applies to every species. Once you've used up a year, that year can never be lived again. But hopefully the way you lived that year, will have had a positive impact on the rest of your human journey. Now, if you are blessed with good genes, supported by a progressively positive attitude, there is absolutely no reason in the world, YOU SHOULDN'T HAVE NINETY TO A HUNDRED SATISFYING, PRODUCTIVE, AND FEARLESS YEARS. Come on, my good man, in your case, there's tons of time left. So if it's there, you must diminish, even conquer, whatever FEAR you might have of your mortality. You must be very realistic and face up to fear, FEARLESSLY. The battle is on, so you must take it head-on, meet and beat its potentially intimidating influence. You can do that, and when you do, it will lead to a PERMANENTLY POSITIVE ATTITUDE, ABOUT THE PASSAGE AND PURPOSE OF YOUR PRECIOUS TIME. Let me make it clear. In the entire universe, of which planet earth is less than a grain of sand on a mile-wide beach, even the most powerful, massive, and vast forces of the cosmos CANNOT STOP TIME.

Now let's get to the good news when it comes to aging. This must be your personal commitment because YOU AND ONLY YOU must be strong-minded and prepared, to focus on and change the psychological aspects of your life, particularly if you are not fully satisfied, with its current state of being in dealing with your mortality. You must embellish and enhance all tangibles and intangibles, that are HIGHLY RELEVANT and of great importance to you. Then, kind sir, exercise the term I use so frequently in this book: DIG YOUR HEELS IN, AND DON'T TAKE ONE STEP BACK. Take the offensive with aggressive confidence. Elevate all thoughts to the highest possible positive level where the aging process is concerned, for the entire second half of your life. If you let your guard down and there's any slippage CONCERNING YOUR FEAR OF MORTALITY, THAT MISERY-MAKING BASTARD WILL SEEP IN, ATTEMPTING TO DOMINATE YOUR THINKING. KEEP–IT–THE–HELL–OUT!

Now let's talk about your physical self. Now there's something, with a little more effort, raising it to a higher priority, you can HONESTLY, EFFECTIVELY CONTROL. How healthy, strong, and energized you are, is definitely a matter of your choice. That health, that strength, and energy you have, at your age, IS NO ACCIDENT. This is an infinite proposition. Even at this advanced age, I am still trying to make gains physically. So maybe you should just ask yourself (this is you talking): "AT MY AGE, HOW DO I EXPAND, AND HOW FAR CAN I TAKE MY PHYSICAL POTENTIAL?" God, man, the answer is obvious. That will be totally up to you! With all the meaningful words in the English language, it's hard to find one strong enough to describe the difference, PHYSICAL ACTIVITY HAS MADE IN MY LIFE. Sir, I can't encourage and implore you strong enough: YOU MUST RESPECT YOUR BODY EVEN MORE NOW THAN YOU DID IN YEARS PAST. Because now, past forty, your need is even greater. Of course you should commit to making your body the best it can be for this second half of your life. Guys, I am dead damn serious. There has been no more important of a truth for me in my life, and hopefully just a little of it will rub off on you. Get on board, young brother, get with the program, and you will absolutely produce LONG-TERM

REWARDS, THAT YOU WILL FIND BEYOND
MONUMENTAL AND STRATOSPHERIC.

And of course as mentioned, psychologically, that same kind of
thinking applies. Two little two letter words say it all: DO IT. DO
IT! It will be the biggest damned favor you've done for yourself.
JUST TRY TO IMAGINE THE ADVANTAGE THIS IS
GOING TO GIVE YOU. Whether you look in a mirror or your
mind's eye, it will always be the real you. You will be the most
positive, passionate, and productive person possible. Then those
two little, two letter words - do it - will become, to your benefit,
two four letter words: DONE DEAL! Guys, that's the real math.
Two out of three ain't bad, because it's those two that will
improve upon and expand greatly, THE VALUE TO YOUR
LIFE. Of course everybody's chronological path, not for one
minute can that be changed. But, the physical and psychological,
YOU CAN AND SURE AS HELL SHOULD ALTER IF
NEEDED. When you highly develop those qualities, they are all
you will ever need, to fight off and minimize, any kind of
chronological negativity.

So, no matter your chronological age, you can always be as
highly motivated as you want to, when you keep a major focus on
the PHYSICAL AND THE PSYCHOLOGICAL. Again, that's
how you MINIMIZE THE EFFECTS OF THE
CHRONOLOGICAL. Make that your long-term commitment,
kind sir. Accept this philosophical change, it will become the
POWERFUL, POSITIVE CORNERSTONE, for your entire life.
Instead of fear dominating your thoughts of mortality, you will
develop a feeling of greater personal peace of mind with each

passing year. That will progressively provide the powers needed, to overcome whatever fears you might have thought you had about your chronological journey.

What a great, positive way to think. Assuming you are somewhere in your forties or fifties, feeling better about your physical and psychological life than you did ten years earlier, that will elevate you to an unexpected high, higher than you ever thought possible. JUST DO IT! Don't rationalize that being victimized by fear is a chronological must of your human journey. YOU MUST BE REALISTIC, YOU MUST BE FEARLESS. Of course all of us are all eventually going to run out of time. That's why you must realize, that as time passes and the less time you have THE MORE VALUABLE YOUR TIME BECOMES, THE MORE YOU MUST MAKE THE MOST OF IT. You must keep that in your control. Only you can make your allotted amount of time more valuable and more meaningful. And not just for you, but for all those you come in contact with.

Sir, wherever you might be at this stage of your journey, keep that body strong. I want you to be as strong as you can possibly be. And then when you've achieved that, don't be a quitter, KEEP IMPROVING UPON IT FOR AS LONG AS TIME ALLOWS. With all your powers of will and discipline, when you do that, it will absolutely produce an energy level so high and so self-inspiring, it will literally amaze you. It will be more than you could ever have imagined or anticipated. And I'm telling you, THIS CAN ASSUREDLY BE YOURS. I want you to fill your life up with abundantly rewarding activities. Always keep in correct perspective, those two words that are present every second of every day of your life: Negative and POSITIVE. So here's what you SHOULD EXPECT FROM YOU: no matter what kind of negativity enters your life, I NOT ONLY WANT YOU TO WILLINGLY TAKE IT HEAD-ON, I EXPECT YOU TO ATTACK IT AND DOMINATE IT AND KNOW, ALL THOSE SUBCONSCIOUS EVIL SPIRITED DEMONS, OF THE <u>SO-CALLED</u> FEARFUL AGING PROCESS, *ARE DEFINITELY DEFEATABLE*. So do it. MEET AND BEAT THAT DESTRUCTIVE, SOUL DESTROYING, GOOD FOR NOTHING SON OF A BITCH CALLED FEAR, and do it big time, all the time, for your entire lifetime.

So there you have it, your three kinds of getting older. Chronologically, Father Time is in charge all the time, ALL THE WAY. I want you to cope with that fact, from a strong position of willpower and courage. But, physiologically and psychologically, where those two powerful forms and facets of your persona are concerned, YOU CAN BE YOUR OWN MASTER, ONE HUNDRED PERCENT IN CHARGE OF YOUR OWN DESTINY.

Manhood

24

Without a doubt, or fear of contradiction, one of the most reassuring words to any member of the male gender is MANHOOD. Manhood is something all men should aspire to, because one thing is for sure, when you are born, you are far removed from being a man. We start off life entirely dependent as a baby. Then after a year or two passes, we start to walk and we mutter a few words and become a little boy. Then a few years later, when you reach your teens, you become a bigger boy, and you remain that big boy for six to seven years, up to twenty or twenty-five years of age. And as discussed so often in this book, THOSE ARE YOUR EXPERIMENTAL YEARS, where you struggle and strive to go from that big boy phase, to becoming a young man. Anything where you have the opportunity to relate to being more of a man. Then you finally finish whatever schooling or training you need to do, to get that better job. Well if that job affords some security, a family usually follows, and that is not a temporary commitment, because now, after so many years of very little responsibility, you have entered the realm of FULL RESPONSIBILITY. Finally, after fifteen to twenty years of being the head of your family, you should feel realistically that you have reached and accomplished, REAL MANHOOD.

So now it's time for you to examine objectively, in a very fair and balanced manner, what is, or what should be considered, the REAL MEANING OF *MANHOOD*. Ask yourself: "How many ways do I interpret and describe my manhood? Is it going to be possible for me to express my manhood the WAY I WANT TO?"

Boy, what a variety of choices you had and still have. So many ways in which that word can be used, that are connected to your state of mind. This is even more psychological than it is physical, and in many ways, subconscious. You know what I'm talking about here, that underlying feeling you have of *manliness*. Always trying to the best of your ability, to live your life in a *manful* way. Then there are those high-sounding words that associate themselves with manhood. *Brave* is one. Being brave is a proud feeling. Then there's what I consider the most important word associated with manhood, *fearlessness*. Being fearless! Then another word we hear so frequently today, *heroic*. Those words and all aspects of them, are how we associate and identify with manhood. What is fundamentally important in connecting yourself with real manliness, are the authoritative qualities IT REPRESENTS. You having true self confidence, physical strength, and of course virility. Those are qualities generally recognized, as manly. And a few other takes on this relevant word, that can produce long-term positive results. How about *man-sized*, *man-power*. Those are the variables, of what MANHOOD <u>SHOULD</u> BE ALL ABOUT.

But only when your accurate interpretation of all these words, becomes a permanent part of your mindset, will you have a TRUE BELIEF IN *YOUR* MANHOOD. Now you do that consistently and YOU WILL HAVE EARNED THE TITLE OF REAL *MANHOOD*. Make no mistake, keeping that manhood is a lifelong endeavor. But know this, once you have strengthened and established that MANLY STATE OF MIND, and feel that word literally describes who you are, THEN AND ONLY THEN, WILL IT BE POSSIBLE, FOR YOU TO BE THE MOST

COMPLETE, SELF CONFIDENT <u>MAN</u>, YOU CAN POSSIBLY BE.

At this stage of your life, that's the feeling you should have in abundance, in EVERY POSITIVE INTERPRETATION OF THAT WORD. That is exactly what you should be, after forty-plus years of living and learning. It's a feeling you will find stratospherically satisfying, totally reassuring, and confidence building. When you truly believe you have arrived at that point in your life, it's like a MENTAL COAT OF ARMOR.

Now let's get one thing straight, and also establish as undeniable fact: not only must your age never be a barrier or obstacle to your total manhood, but FROM THIS POINT ON IN YOUR LIFE, you must always be FORTIFYING GREATER BELIEF IN YOUR MANHOOD. Truth be told, when you examine it closely, not because of age, but only with age, and the passing years of experiences they represent, is it even possible for you to establish with confidence and permanency, YOUR GROWING ONGOING MANHOOD. Too many men settle for being half a man. Why in the hell would any man with an ounce of common sense even consider letting that describe him? Sir, it is so damn important, that you honestly believe in your heart, your soul, and spirit, that from head to toe, that is exactly what you, Y-O-U have fully achieved – UNDENIABLY, REAL MANHOOD. So here you are, Mr. Man In The Middle, getting older. But not for one second of your life, should you ever think that means, becoming less of a man. I'm here to tell ya, IT ABSOLUTELY DOES NOT. And don't you ever allow anybody to imply or suggest that it does. Then in these oncoming years, you will be afforded the

93

opportunity, to become even more of a man. I can't say it enough: You have finally paid your dues in full, sir. You have fully earned and deserve that title: AUTHENTIC MANHOOD, in every one of its many meanings. So don't you ever let negative thoughts where your manhood is concerned, EVER ENTER YOUR THINKING. And don't buy into the bullshit that THE AGING PROCESS MEANS A DECLINE IN YOUR MANHOOD. That is an absolute fallacy. Proof? Hello - here I am! Ninety years after sucking in my first breath of life. Just make it your choice to take charge, and know that will be your CONSTANT CHALLENGE. Never, under any conditions, do you ever let aging in any way, shape, form, or fashion diminish your manhood, and kill the courage needed for you to maintain it. ALWAYS FOR ALL YOUR LIFE, *EVERY DAMN SECOND,* BE THE MOST FULL AND COMPLETE MAN YOU CAN BE. So know as you age, you must be not less, but even MORE OF A WISE, PERCEPTIVE MAN AS YOU GET OLDER. That means YOU BEING THE MOST COMPLETE MAN. Only then will you be able to be MORE OF A MAN in EVERY SENSE OF THE WORD, during this, your sensational second half of life.

Procrastinating

25

Talk about a human habit that we're all afflicted with, that occurs every day of our life. And the reason I say "our" life, not just your life, every man's life, including your Old Pops here at this late stage, almost on a daily basis, this little demon tries to creep in, and his name is *Procrastination*. Now I understand, we all procrastinate and we all hesitate. Not just a habit, this is a state of mind of every human being. But if YOU ALLOW IT FREE REIGN, IT COULD TAKE OVER YOUR WHOLE PERSONALITY AND VALUE SYSTEM, and that more likely than not would be a downer. So let me tell you how I fight it. I told myself, almost fifty years ago, that this is for the young and insecure, those who are not in the know, those who were still learning to play the game of life, and at every turn they could PROCRASTINATE OR HESITATE OUT OF YOUTHFUL INDECISIVENESS. I decided during the second half of my life, that was not going to be my fate. After living those first forty years, I made up my mind, I was going to LIMIT THE NEGATIVE IMPLICATIONS, of procrastinating and hesitating. That's what that first forty years was suppose to have taught me. Well it did, and hopefully that's what it taught you.

Procrastination, in many respects, was immobilizing when we were young. Procrastinating restricted and put limits on us, and our good timing. Although that seemed to go along with the youthful territory, let's face it, WE ALL PROCRASTINATE. But I found as I got older, to be perfectly honest, I realized I can never completely eliminate it, but in the course of aging, I have effectively reduced the limiting effects of procrastination successfully. I knew I had to MEET AND BEAT THIS MISERY MAKER OF INDECISION AND INACTION. It was a long, hard fight that paid off. So at this mid-point of your life, it's a fight YOU MUST WIN. Remember, procrastination and hesitation can lead to STAGNATION. Not a pretty picture, in fact, an ugly word, sir. And if you allow stagnation to take hold, it could be a constant, for thirty to fifty more years. That kind of LONG-TERM LIMITATION could be CRIPPLING, when that kind of thinking dominates. So of course, procrastination, hesitation, and stagnation, were understandable when you were young, facing so many unknowns. But not now, my good man. The time has come to know YOU ARE IN CHARGE OF YOUR ACTIONS AND DECISIONS, THEY MUST BE STRONG, DECISIVE, AND TIMELY.

Be that complete, most decisive man, that you know you are capable of being. The time is now to get and keep your life in high gear, then, as I like to say, hit the damn throttle, and hit it hard, always STEERING YOUR LONG AND ENLIGHTENING HUMAN JOURNEY, IN THE PRECISE DIRECTION YOU WANT IT TO GO.

The Climb

26

No matter how hard, high, or difficult your climb in life is, let me give you my take on how to deal with this issue. What you don't do, is worry about multiple choices. Simplify it! When I say "The Climb", we'll use a mountain as a comparable analogy. All your life you are hopefully climbing higher up your mountain. And the whole goal of your efforts is to REACH THE SUMMIT, no matter how high or steep the climb may be. And forget about how long it takes, it's a lifetime project. And there are only two choices! EITHER YOU QUIT, OR YOU TAKE ON THE CLIMB! Sir, no in-betweens. At some point in your great transition, you either STOP CLIMBING, or you KEEP CLIMBING. And brother of mine, that will be your most critical turning point of life. Get discouraged and STOP IN YOUR TRACKS, or no matter how steep and tough of a climb your mountain represents, WITH TENACITY AND UNSTOPPABLE DETERMINATION, YOU CONTINUE ON. That's why at being past forty, working your way into the second half of your life, knowing you are getting older, you must ask yourself: WHICH ONE IS GOING TO BE ME? Do I quit or not quit? And your answer should unequivocally be: "Hell no, I AM NOT A QUITTER!"

So let me tell you what your Old Pops does. Every morning when I wake up (and boy, I hope that keeps happening!), the first words out of my mouth on that only day of life I'm living in, you know what I say to that day? "DAY, SHOW ME WHAT THE HELL YOU GOT IN STORE FOR OLD POPS! I CAN'T WAIT.

Then, throw every damn bit of it at me, from all and any angle you want to". And, sir, you can take it to the bank, as sure as grass is green, this older man is going to take it all on! There is not an obstacle big enough, or person influential enough, or any adverse condition, that has any chance to reduce the meaning and purpose of ANY PART OF MY POSITIVE DAY. I am drop dead, stiff kick in the ass serious, sir. When it comes to the high value I place on my time, no matter how many extreme challenges come my way, unexpectedly or unknowingly, I will definitely do what the hell it takes, to overcome every last one. THIS IS MY DAY, IT COULD BE MY LAST, SO I WILL MAKE IT WORK FOR ME, BECAUSE TOMORROW HAS NO GUARANTEE.

So, as long as you are pulling a breath, and have one ounce of life left in that body of yours, you must take all your heart and soul has to offer, and FIGHT LIKE HOLY HELL, to make sure you make every day of your life, LIVE UP TO ITS POTENTIAL. Now imagine how gratifying that's going to be, to know you have thirty to fifty more years to activate that kind of positive thinking. MAKING THAT CLIMB TO THE TOP OF YOUR MOUNTAIN A TOP PRIORITY, EVERY LIVING DAY OF YOUR LIFE. Don't you ever use or think, of that ugly f-ing word *quit*! You keep clawing, climbing, knowing, THAT AGE WILL NEVER BE YOUR BARRIER OR BREAKING POINT. Please keep busting your ass every day trying to REACH YOUR SUMMIT. Remember, this is a test of YOUR COURAGE AND CHARACTER, to confirm, a higher level OF A MORE COMPLETE LIFE.

Supreme Lifestyle

27

I don't think there's a man I've ever met, from forty to a hundred-four, who don't want a supreme lifestyle. That should be every man's quest in life: to find his real superior reason for living. But many men don't always achieve that goal. Well there's not a chance in hell that a supreme lifestyle will be any man's reward IF HE DOESN'T MAKE HIS MOST *SUPREME* EFFORT! Boy, my friend, I hope these words and thoughts hit home. No matter your accomplishments and how elevated they may be, you always have the opportunity to be more exceptional, and expand the meaning and purpose of your life. You know, negative situations are always going to present themselves, trying to invade your thoughts. SHUT THEM OUT, DON'T LET THEM IN. You've got to know and accept, the older you get, the more negative forces there are going to seem to be. Which means you must make a more concentrated effort to keep your spirits up, never letting negative forces dominate your thinking and TAKE YOU DOWN. This is every man's battle every day, but during this great transition, it's of even greater importance. It's one you must make during this time-frame TO MAINTAIN AND ENSURE A REST-OF-LIFE SUPREME LIFESTYLE.

During the second half of your life, you must intensify your effort to reduce the impact and effect, of your day-in and day-out MOSTLY NEGATIVE SURROUNDING ENVIRONMENT. Ramp up and focus your willpower to MINIMIZE ITS EFFECT. When you've accomplished that, and you must believe you can, only then are you going to know and feel, the quality of almost every facet of your life taking a quantum leap. But make no mistake, my good man, that will be unlikely if you don't exercise YOUR PERSONAL POWERS OF WILL, DISCIPLINE, AND COMMITMENT. You want a supreme lifestyle? THAT'S THE PATH YOU MUST TAKE. Never in the course of the rest of your life, quit on that concerted, day-to-day persistent effort, to encourage and promote endless positive results.

Now if I may, I'd like to recommend: first - you physically stiffen that back. Stand as straight and tall and confident as you can. Then you make willpower, discipline, and commitment your most POWERFUL MENTAL TOOLS. Never let vanity or false pride, which were the normal products of your youthful insecurity, get in the way. YOU MUST HONESTLY LIKE AND RESPECT YOURSELF FOR WHO YOU ARE. Think about the high degree of meaning and purpose that statement has. What good, or of what benefit is it, having other people like or praise you, IF YOU DON'T RESPECT YOURSELF IN EQUAL PROPORTION. So here's what I've asked myself every day of my life, and what you have to ask yourself: In your pursuit of a supreme lifestyle, HAVE YOU TAKEN IT TO ITS LIMIT? Is it possible for me to take my positivity to another level? And of course, with confidence, your only answer should be: "I ABSOLUTELY CAN AND WILL WITHOUT A DOUBT, MAKE MY SUPREME EFFORT TO TAKE MY SUPREME LIFESTYLE TO ITS OPTIMUM LEVEL!" Now say that to yourself at least once a day.

Because once that premise is established and solidly locked in your mind, when those conditions are met and psychologically in place, then ask yourself with confidence and inspiration: "WHAT IN THE HELL IN GOD'S GOOD NAME COULD POSSIBLY HOLD ME BACK?" You must firmly, believe there is no force of nature strong enough to do that!

Everything I've just said about you making that exceptional supreme effort, IS NOT COMPLICATED. And I want you to know now, as I knew at your age, IF THERE WERE EVER ANY BARRIERS TO WHAT KEN DAB-ROW CONSIDERS A SUPREME LIFESTYLE, <u>KEN DAB-ROW CREATED THEM!</u> That's right, I built those barriers, and I knew, I was the only one who could tear them down. Well thankfully I did, and I'm still doing it to this day. So if any barrier to that worthy goal EXISTS IN YOUR LIFE, tear them the hell down and GET THEM OUT OF YOUR LIFE. That is the only way you will create ROOM TO EXPAND, sustain, and retain your SUPREME, LIFELONG, POSITIVE LIFESTYLE.

Self Loving Way

28

You should never feel selfish or arrogant when it comes to being proud of yourself. DESERVED SELF PRAISE, is fine and should be the result of your positivity and honesty. These fundamental qualities are a must in order to love yourself. You must live every second of your entire life with yourself. Not hard to figure, it sure feels a whole lot better to love yourself than not. That is the only possible way to enhance and enjoy, THE SECOND HALF OF YOUR LIFE. Know in your heart of hearts, that you are, in YOUR OWN RIGHT, a most VALUABLE HUMAN BEING. If you lived a hundred more years, every single second of that hundred years, you must live with everything tangible and intangible you are, THE GOOD, THE BAD, AND THE UGLY (the title of observation 93). Just make sure there's more good than bad and ugly, so you can justifiably live your life in a SELF LOVING WAY.

Now that being said and making that a certainty, is not automatic or a natural instinct, because each and every last person on this planet, must also live with their liabilities. And boy, are there some libelous words that we use and feel almost every day of our lives. Words like *worry*, *resentment*, *distrust*, *anger*, even *hatefulness*. So here's what you have to do: DON'T MAXIMIZE AND LEND VALUE TO THE MEANING OF THOSE UGLY WORDS. Just minimize their use. Just remember, almost always, certainly more often than not, those words produce negativity, creating liabilities that serve NO POSITIVE PURPOSE in your life. That's why your order of business at the start of every day?

Don't ever let all those problematic words I just mentioned, get in the way of how you start every single day. Those words can breed and lead to thoughts, that will put you into a joy destroying rut. And when you start communicating with people who you know are going to be more negative than positive, DON'T OVERREACT TO THAT KIND OF PESSIMISTIC PERSON. Now I know it's near impossible to control that completely, because sometimes in the workplace, where you spend most of your waking hours, people have that kind of mindset most of the time. Always keep them at arm's length, or better yet, completely out of YOUR PERSONAL LIFE. This is it, kind sir! The food you taste, your personal feelings, WILL ONLY OCCUR AS YOU ARE DOING THEM RIGHT NOW, THIS MOMENT. Remember, right now is THE MOST IMPORTANT PART AND TIME OF YOUR LIFE. The less negativity on this day, the better. Tomorrow has yet to be lived. Sure, have high hopes and dreams for it. The wonderful memories you are making right now WOULD NOT EXIST IF YOU WERE NOT LIVING THIS DAY, MOMENT TO MOMENT IN A SELF-LOVING WAY. Well the one quality that guarantees it, is you wearing this and every future day of your life exactly like that. You have to know and believe that's the kind of positive power living in every cell of your body. Please, sir, take this time-proven tidbit of advice from The Old Man: find it, focus on it, activate it, and use it to its full capacity, every blessed day for your own personal self-loving way. Just down-play those ugly thoughts that produce and generate ugly words like *spiteful*, *harmful*, *anger*, *despise*, *detest*, and *hate*. Don't let that sick kind of thinking to be your fate. Let the opposite of everything they represent BE YOUR DESTINY.

Love Every Minute

29

Wouldn't it be great if the world around us, created an environment for us to love every minute of our life. Now this is an extension to the previous observation. Every day consists of fourteen hundred forty minutes. So in this frequently negative world, it's almost an impossibility to love every one of those minutes every day. But, if you LEARN TO LOVE YOURSELF at least as much as anything else in this world, you will wind up LOVING MOST OF THOSE MINUTES. No matter what other comparison you would consider, I personally have found in my life, no more effective way. Nobody should know better than you, when it comes to growing up, maturing, and becoming a more complete, mentally balanced, and sophisticated man, at this, the midway mark, you have accomplished that mission. Always be conscious of that fact. Not maybe, possibly, or probably, KNOW FOR SURE THAT'S WHO YOU ARE, one-hundred percent of the time. Only then will you know clearly, better than ever, how to love even more, every one of those fourteen hundred forty minutes, you are smack dab in the middle of on this day.

When it comes to covering the second half of your life, from age forty, right down to the finish line, you must definitely MAKE THE MOST OF EVERY MINUTE OF EVERY DAY. Always having that desire to prosper and fill up every moment to its optimum. Now with all these fancy descriptive words I've just used, you know what the most important word is? MUST! Not maybe, not perhaps, not can I, not will I or should I, but must! The word *must*, must always be prefaced by that one letter word:

I. And that's you, sir! Always saying "I must", and always say it with meaning, that consists of positive sentences and paragraphs, which result in total MINUTE-TO-MINUTE SELF INSPIRATION. And know this: When you inspire yourself, it radiates. It's a vibe you're throwing out. YOU ACQUIRE THE POWER TO INSPIRE! That's what the word "must" will always make happen, when used in a positive context. Now look, I know that's not an easy thing to do, with all the negative and contrary ways in this world. But every day of my life, in spite of most of the world around me, those are exactly my intentions. BUT IT ONLY GETS DONE WHEN I MAKE IT A <u>MUST</u>. So young brother, whether you are as few as twenty or as many as fifty years my junior, if I can still say "I must" at this stage of my life, with only a few short years to go, and you still got thirty to fifty, THERE'S NOT ONE VALID REASON FOR YOU TO THINK ANY OTHER WAY. If I can still keep my spirits this highly elevated, during my tenth decade, I sure as hell don't want to hear any excuses from you, sir. Be that *must* guy you were meant to be. SEARCH AS HARD AND BE AS HELL-BENT AS YOU POSSIBLY CAN BE, EXPLORING THE POSITIVE POTENTIAL OF LOVING EVERY MINUTE OF EVERY DAY OF YOUR LIFE. Looking, searching and discovering, every last one of your more rewarding roads, if you want an enriched, exciting second half, TRAVEL THEM PROUDLY AND FEARLESSLY.

Now that's the psychological. Let's slightly alter our direction and get with the tangible and visual. I want you to look in the mirror, and I want you to know and feel from nose to toes, that every square inch of what you see reflected back, is ONE KICK-ASS,

MOUNTAIN OF MANHOOD. When you are in front of that mirror, THAT'S THE ONLY THING I WANT YOU TO SEE. And you could be skinny or fat, four foot six or six foot four, that should make no difference. I want that image you see to create such a high degree of positivity, that it will INSTANTANEOUSLY DIMINISH ANY KIND OF SELF DOUBT OR INSECURITY. Right there at that moment, boldly open your mouth and you tell yourself in the spoken word: "My search is over, I HAVE FINALLY FOUND THE REAL, POSITIVE ME AND I LOVE WHAT I SEE!" All it takes is five to ten seconds every morning when you wake up. JUST DO IT! And keep saying it until it becomes one of your most deeply seeded beliefs. Only then will you be able to open that door to your mind wide, and TRANSFER IT INTO YOUR REALITY. And once that psychological mental door is opened, YOU STEP BOLDLY AND PROUDLY THROUGH IT. Having the determination to stay with it, will produce the big rewards that come in getting it done, which means YOU STAYING AND REMAINING THAT WAY EVERY DELICIOUS DAY, FOR YOUR ENTIRE LIFE, from eighty to a hundred and beyond. That's the lifelong challenge. You must make it one of your top lifetime priorities. SO EVERY DAY FROM THIS DAY ON, YOU KEEP THAT COMMITMENT OF REAL PRIDE IN YOURSELF. You will find yourself getting stronger in every respect. Just know you MUST LOVE EVERY MINUTE OF LIFE POSSIBLE.

Challenge Yourself

30

If there's one word that is always in your life, more often than not in the forefront of your thinking that seems bigger than life, staring you right in the eye every day you live, is the word *challenge*. Brother of mine, you can't escape it. Life is always a challenge. You are always faced with so many, it's almost like breathing. They seem to be around every corner of your life. And here's the important fact at your stage of the game: EVERY CHALLENGE THAT COMES ALONG NOW, SEEMS TO BECOME A <u>LITTLE BIGGER</u> AND MORE CHALLENGING AS WE GET A <u>LITTLE OLDER</u>. We gotta be careful not to let our thought process turn into an ongoing negative narrative, where you are constantly saying to yourself: "Lord, man, how many challenges can I accept and handle with advancing age?" Just maybe implying you can't handle them all, or even quite as well. Well, sir, the greatest, most important challenges of your life, ARE STILL AHEAD OF YOU <u>PAST</u> FORTY. I can still remember when I was twenty to thirty-five, approaching the big four-o, there could be endless challenges on a day-to-day basis, but they were coming at me from a different angle, all with a different meaning. And at that time in my life, I had the youthful stamina and capacity to handle them efficiently, even easily. But between forty and sixty, my challenge became different. IT WAS ME CHALLENGING ME. And that's what you are going to find. The challenges become a little tougher. You know, so many challenges in the first forty years of your life, can almost be handled sub or semi-consciously with ease. Well all the challenges from here on out, that are still going to arise every day in abundance, for the balance of your life, just may require a little extra effort to handle. So know this for sure: who you are going to be during these next twenty years, not to mention the thirty to fifty that are going to follow, will be DETERMINED by how well you HANDLE THE CHALLENGES right now during this, your great transition. You must handle them in an assertive, secure, and fearless fashion. If you do what I'm recommending, and work more diligently and confidently in handling all the challenges in your life, I assure you, every day of your life will get substantially and abundantly that much more fulfilling.

This is what you must sincerely believe: YOUR HIGHEST HOPES AND DREAMS ARE NOT TEN OR TWENTY YEARS BEHIND YOU. They are not a thing of the past, if you CHALLENGE YOURSELF WITH INTENSE POSITIVE PURPOSE, motivated by self-respect. You do that every day and they will be right in front of you, ready to be contested and conquered, in these critically important next ten to twenty years. I want you to imagine and visualize this: LIVING THIRTY TO FIFTY MORE YEARS OF HAVING YOUR FAVORITE DREAMS COME TRUE. Once again, sir, there's only one way that's going to occur: You, every day of your life, elevating your attitude to new heights, so you have a clearer, broader, more spectacular outlook on life in general. THAT'S YOUR OVERALL CHALLENGE. So whatever I will be doing today, or this week or this month, even in the years ahead, that I will hopefully be fortunate enough to live in, you can bet your ever lovin' ass, I'm going to make every effort possible, to handle my challenges with as much energy and committed action as I can humanly muster. Because only in that way does the possibility exist, that all of my tomorrows will provide me with GREATER GRATIFICATION.

I can't make this point strong enough. It is absolutely damn critical, that you accept assertively, aggressively, supported by self-worth and self-confidence, EVERY SINGLE WORTHWHILE CHALLENGE THAT LIES AHEAD OF YOU. I have searched in my mind and my imagination, and I have not found, in almost a century of living, any other way that has guaranteed me the VALID MEANING OF A BETTER TOMORROW. The rest of your life, and all the challenges it presents, can definitely, IF AMBITIOUSLY AND FEARLESSLY ACCEPTED, allow you to live every remaining minute to YOUR HIGHEST POSSIBLE LEVEL.

Staying Fulfilled

31

This particular observation really gets to the core of the theme and purpose of this book. It's important you know that to lose any of life's meaning after forty, is based on pure myth. It is a total misconception. I'll take it even a step further, it's a CONTRADICTION OF WHAT SHOULD BE YOUR REALITY. Well hopefully in your case, this observation will reverse or at least alter, what I consider a FALSE AND FLAWED PERSPECTIVE AND PREMISE. Many men in this forty to sixty age group, actually believe they have already lived the best years of their life. Sir, I cannot emphatically enough make the point, how far-fetched that is from the truth. I sure as hell hope you are not under the false impression, that your first forty years were so fantastic, they can never be equaled as you get older. If that kind of crappy, crippling standard of thinking is creeping into your mindset, do this older man and yourself a big favor: I want you to, WITHOUT OVER-EMBELLISHMENT, think clearly and realistically, about those first forty years of yours. Of course there were a whole lot more rock-hard erections and hot new discoveries, that's a given. That was a part of your youth, and of course, again, that was great stuff. But if you are going to be realistic, think about ALL THE PROBLEMS AND INSECURITIES ALL THOSE HARD-ONS AND UNKNOWNS CREATED. Now of course it was exciting, everything seemed so new to you. But we both know the game we were playing at that age: TRIAL AND ERROR. Now let's try to be even-handed and level-headed and look at it realistically. If you look back and focus accurately on your youth, you will realize that not knowing and sometimes blindly searching, could create a big load of unknown negatives to lug around, DURING THAT FIRST HALF OF YOUR LIFE.

Let's evaluate the stages of life. First stage, puberty. WOW! Boy, what an experience! You were between twelve and fourteen years of age, just two short years, but the impact of that hormonal change, when you finally found out your penis served a whole lot bigger purpose than just peeing. Talk about intense - THAT WAS OVERWHELMING! Every man living knows, in those two or three years, almost all your youthful life force, was a result of that total preoccupation, your hormonal awareness and your new found weapon – your penis, went from a BB gun to a double-barrel shotgun. That made those two or three years, if not the two to three most important years of your life, certainly more stimulating. It all happened so quick, your priorities totally changed for life. That was a critical, mind-blowing awakening, and you know it! It led you into what would become, the biggest part of life's first half, all the way from fifteen to forty. During that twenty-five-year period, you essentially stay in that generally high hormonal gear. The only thing that changes as you acquire more experience as you get older is, you'll be more discreet. BUT IT WILL BE THE DRIVING FORCE BEHIND ALMOST ALL YOUR THOUGHT PROCESSES.

Now at this stage of your game, although still gratifying, that hormonal discovery from twelve to fourteen is not quite as consuming and overpowering. You have had enough time and forethought to figure things out. But then this great transition comes, this twenty years between forty and sixty, and the power, or the lack of it, gets even MORE CRUCIAL AND CRITICAL TO THE BALANCE of your long human journey. And know it sure as hell is going to be a whole lot different during the coming years, than the years between twenty and forty. That also was a given, NATURE AT WORK. There will be hundreds of physical, mental, and psychological changes that you must go through. And to put it mildly, they are going to seem a little tougher task at this stage of your life.

Let me tell you what the two most important choices that will present themselves to you are, during this twenty-year period: You can let that almost imperceptible creeping negativity build up, which could result in you slowly giving up on yourself BY CREATING LIMITATIONS. Or, referring to one of the main themes of this book, *chance or choice*? It's really just that simple, sir. And that's what The Old Man did, I made a positive choice. And because I STAYED WITH THAT CHOICE, I'm still staying fulfilled all these decades later. And I want you to know I will continue to do it to my fullest capacity, for all my remaining years. So let me simplify what I think you must do, and you must do it WITH ALL THE ASSERTIVENESS AND SELF CONFIDENCE YOU CAN MUSTER. To coin a figure of speech, you must GRAB LIFE RIGHT BY THE BALLS and do it with a highly motivated state of authority! Make that the foundation of who you are. Then, every other action you will ever take, and every decision you will ever make, will be infused with a greater feeling of exhilaration and YOUR OWN PERSONALIZED POWERFUL PURPOSE. This will allow you to breathe that rarefied air, waiting for you at the very top of your mid-life mountain. If you haven't already, when you accomplish that, you will find the overall feeling of well-being superior and longer-lasting than your big hormonal awakening. Now I'm not knocking a good hard-on, which sure as hell contributed to that overall feeling of being fully alive. It was a fantastic, life changing experience. So let me ask you this: WHY IN THE HELL WOULD YOU GIVE IT UP? You can still exercise that hormonal, sexual arousement, but now your life should have an even broader, MORE VARIED, AND FULFILLING MEANING.

So all you have to do is KEEP THE PURPOSE OF YOUR PENIS IN PERSPECTIVE, and you will be more gratified in a greater variety of ways, during the long living-out of this, the diversified and intelligently directed second half of your life. This twenty-year period offers you the opportunity to cultivate a greater, mature potential, to build A MUCH MORE MEANINGFUL EXISTENCE. It's right out there in front of you, just waiting to be rediscovered by you, ready to produce new forms of satisfaction. So, kind sir, if the shoe fits (and it sure as hell does!) what the hell could possibly be holding you back? Wear it well! If that's already your story, keep writing more and better chapters, and live them out for all they are worth for all your life. Only then will all your mental and physical strength and energy, play itself out for all it's worth, TO PRODUCE A MORE FULLY REAWAKENED YOU, EQUIPPING YOU FOR A MORE FULFILLED AND REWARDING REST OF YOUR LIFE.

Super Human

32

Of all the action heroes, I guess the most popular one would be Superman, and the main reason for that popularity, everybody strives to be super in one way or another. And of course, we all would literally say, there's no such thing as a TRULY AUTHENTIC, SUPER MAN. Well, my friend, there absolutely is! And any time you want to see that super guy, he'll be right there IN THE MIRROR looking back at ya! You must believe right now in this moment, that super human power is in you. I'M AS SERIOUS AS AN AVALANCHE. And all you need is to take positive possession of, and believe deeply enough in your elevated self-purpose. So know, and know for damn sure, by any measure of the imagination, you don't have to be an exceptional athlete, or a near perfect physical specimen. That is not the established criteria for YOU TO FEEL LIKE A SUPER HUMAN who gets SUPER RESULTS, in the everyday living of his life. That ability, to take the quality of your life to a super-human level, as I like to say, IS BUILT RIGHT IN YOU. Now it's not going to happen overnight or in any short order of time, but once you visualize it and believe it, you will be literally, THAT SUPER EXAMPLE OF A MAN.

You possess all those basic elements, characteristics, talents, and abilities, that are definitely and without question in every way, EXCLUSIVELY WHO AND WHAT YOU ARE. But you must identify them, expand on them, optimize them, believe and understand that is the true you. Make no mistake, sir, and don't ever question yourself, WE BOTH POSSESS THOSE SUPER

QUALITIES RIGHT NOW! I made sure I acquired them during my great transition. And now in your case, they are pleading and begging to be fertilized and fed, and grown in strength by you, TO WHERE THEY ARE INDESTRUCTIBLE.

Now gauging perfection on a scale of one to ten, if there were ten billion men on this planet, not one would be a ten. PERFECT IS IMPOSSIBLE. Don't expect it, but for sure don't be intimidated by it. But ask yourself: "Why the hell would I settle for being a four or a five, when with a little extra effort I can increase my own self-confidence and strengthen my discipline." Don't you know, sir, that automatically leads to you showing a little more character, leading to an increased belief in yourself, then staying for your entire life an eight or nine! Come on, pal of mine, no matter how close you are to that description in pursuit of a higher energized level of life, just keep raising the bar. IT'S ALL RIGHT THERE INSIDE YOU, JUST WAITING AND WANTING TO BE DEVELOPED EVEN FURTHER.

I want you to TOUGHEN UP PHYSICALLY AND SQUARE UP MENTALLY. Stand tall and think straight. THAT MEANS HONEST AND FAIR. Being proud of the man you are, as long as it is REAL PRIDE as a result of accomplishments, and not FALSE PRIDE. Just thicken that hide and control that vanity. What you are going to be in this second half of your life, is not yet fully established or determined. ONLY YOU CAN TAKE THAT DETERMINATION, TO A HIGHER LEVEL. You know how I feel about that mountain we all have to climb. Some get to the top. But the real truth is, about half way up, if the climb gets a LITTLE TOO STEEP, and the effort required gets a LITTLE

TOO TOUGH, as we get older, instead of making the full climb, too many men in the middle of their life settle for going half-way. And sadder yet, some even quit in the foothills. Please, sir, bust your balls to not let that be you. NO MATTER THE OBSTACLES OR HOW STEEP THE CLIMB, NEVER, *NEVER* QUIT. Keep clawing, scratching, exerting every bit of mental and physical energy possible, regardless of the struggle or how long it takes. DON'T EVER STOP IN YOUR PURSUIT TO REACH THE TOP OF YOUR MOUNTAIN. If you have that hell-bent-for-leather attitude, you are going to get a hell of a lot CLOSER THAN YOU EXPECTED TO YOUR SUMMIT. Make that your natural normal way of thinking. Of course it's a long hard haul, but let me tell you what I do know, having had all this time to make that climb: only with your strength of character and courage, do your chances of reaching your summit REALISTICALLY IMPROVE. It's a positive psychological part of your life. When you reach it, you will look down with such a sense of satisfaction and proud accomplishment, which will generate the feeling that EVERYTHING IN YOUR VISION IS YOURS. What a real confidence builder and psychological breakthrough. An astounding, unique feeling. Why? BECAUSE YOU MADE IT ATTAINABLE. YOU WILL NOW HAVE WITH PROVEN BELIEVABILITY *JUSTIFIABLY BECOME YOUR OWN SUPER MAN.*

Play It Smart

33

I know it's only a figure of speech that some people don't take very seriously. Well with me, those years between forty and eighty, I took damn serious. So wherever you are at this stage of the second half of your life, you not only need to get the message, you must place ENORMOUS IMPORTANCE on that little catch phrase *play it smart*.

Now if you are under forty, it still applies, it can fit any age. We all like to play it smart all of our lives. But you are going to find out when you pass that forty mark, playing it smart becomes a whole lot more relevant. You must, at this mid-way junction in the process of aging, be very serious, with a sharp, clear focus on THE ULTIMATE MEANING OF YOUR LIFE. Well, if you don't keep it real and play it damn smart, that will have very little chance of happening. You know something, that's worth repeating. Say to yourself on a daily basis: "I'M PLAYING IT DAMN SMART AND KEEPING IT VERY REAL". And the foundation needed for that, is your ability to confront and face up to your reality. Anything less should be unacceptable. Now, what that means is you winding up with twenty to fifty more years, of you living life at a HELL OF A LOT HIGHER LEVEL. Now, with all your challenges at this age, it's not a cinch. But I'm telling you, kind sir, it is worth more than you can imagine. If you do it right and play it smart, it's like a royal flush. You are going to love the results.

Now let's you and I take another approach on how to play it smart. Don't ever think *work* is a dirty word, because the most valid connection to that word: LIFE IS WORK! Love and appreciate what it produces, and you'll keep working at it harder, PRODUCING A MORE POSITIVE ATTITUDE TOWARDS IT.

You know why so many men past forty set themselves up for defeat? More often than not they evaluate and relate the word *work* as more negative than positive. You have to realize, that only when you're WORKING AT LIFE can it or will it, contribute anything that's fruitful and meaningfully worthwhile. Most people associate the word *work* mainly with making a dollar. And let's face it, some of the things we do to make a buck, in the minds of so many, they associate the word *work,* with being a *burden*. THAT'S THE NEGATIVE SLANT. But if you diametrically juxtapose the word *burden* with the word *reward,* YOU UNCOVER THE POSITIVE, PLAY IT SMART SLANT. In fact, you feeling productive in life, will only happen when you are working at something constructive and meaningful. You want a fulfilling, satisfied life? WORK AT IT! And here's another slant, as referred to frequently, DON'T LOOK FOR A SHORT CUT, don't look for the easy way out, because not only will you not find it, IT ISN'T THERE, NEVER HAS BEEN. If you want your best possible results, show you got the guts and determination, to make every effort absolutely necessary to accomplish whatever those goals are. All those people looking for that short cut, that lazy, easy way, WILL NEVER REACH THEIR OPTIMUM GOALS. As previously described, that's the reason so many men remain in the foothills of life, and never even start the climb up their mountain. I know this is a whole lot of tough love coming at ya from a whole lot of different angles,

118

but allow me to take it a step further. Not only should you not look for the easy way, accept the fact and reality, that to accomplish complete success, in all things that are of the most importance to you, THERE IS NO EASY WAY, NEVER WILL BE. So please take those two terms: *Shortcut* and *easy way*, and remove their negative influence from your thought processes. They are NOT YOUR ALLY, THEY ARE YOUR ENEMY. I have found out in my long human journey, not only are those two terms destructive, they are the devil in disguise. EASY WAY? SHORT CUT? MY ASS!

You knowing no matter what you're doing, that upbeat path to a better life, work or play, whatever project you're involved in, you need to stay productive and be rewarded by its results. You bet it is no easy trip. THIS IS A ROUGH, TOUGH, HUMAN JOURNEY YOU ARE ON. But if you play it smart, you will be greatly gratified. And you'll never feel lonesome, because that can be every man's destiny, and it should be. And I mean every man worth his salt, in that forty-plus category, is going to be faced with ever increasing uneven and unfair twists and turns. Well, kind sir, make no mistake, it's those twists and turns, that absolutely must be traveled, IF WISDOM AND MATURITY ARE TO BE FOUND. You must constantly climb the ladder of life, IF YOUR MOUNTAIN OF MEANING AND PURPOSE ARE TO BE FOUND. You bet, there's a time to play and be a boy, but right now you are at a turning point in time, where the most important personal content of your life, must be played smart. So welcome it with enthusiasm by playing it JUST THAT WAY. Don't you ever run from a challenge you consider worthwhile. Not only take it on with enthusiasm, pride, and grit, but always accept willingly the struggle that goes along with it. And no matter how many there are, you just line them all up one by one, and as you approach each one of these perceived overwhelming struggles and conditions, do what The Old Man has been doing, particularly during this second half of my life. With your mental and physical prowess and life force, YOU TAKE THEM ALL HEAD-ON WITH A GUSTO AND BOLDNESS OF ATTITUDE and you will ALWAYS CONQUER and NEVER CONCEDE. Now of course during this hard, long, challenging journey, you just might get knocked down a couple of dozen times. Well you gotta keep getting up off your ass, and take them all on again, HARD AS HELL, letting every difficult situation know in no uncertain terms, YOU CANNOT BE DEFEATED. If you want your life to be lived in unbeatable fashion during your next fifty years, this just may be your formula. One thing is for damn sure at this stage of the game, sir: if you don't play it smart, there will be VERY LITTLE <u>REAL</u> SENSE OF ACHIEVEMENT. And always remember, when that deceiving devil of temptation, tells you to take the short cut and that easier way, YOU'LL PLAY IT SMART BECAUSE YOU'LL KNOW YOU ARE DOING IT THE RIGHT WAY!

Emotionally Mature

34

I want you to know as a matter of fact how important it is as you get older, to have your head screwed on right. Only then can you understand the advantages created by the aging process. But this has to be your one hundred percent personal journey. DON'T LOOK FOR OUTSIDE HELP. Take control now, and know you are accurately headed in the right direction. The first major reality and one you must accept, is THERE ARE SO MANY OPPORTUNITIES YOU HAVE THAT DIDN'T EXIST WHEN YOU WERE YOUNGER. And that is no exaggeration, rationalization, or contradiction in terms. And no, I am not blowing wind up your ass! I'm telling you from a lifetime of experience, that's a factual, actual reality. God, man, from fifteen to thirty, we were so idealistic. THEREIN LIES YOUR REAL CONTRADICTION IN TERMS. We all associate idealism with our selfless concern for the world, while at the same time, our youth was our MOST SELF-SERVING TIME FRAME. We thought the world belonged mainly to, and revolved around, us. So it's understandable, that every generation finds for itself what are its values, and that's what younger people think now. So their mindset is going to imply the world, if not entirely, mainly belongs to them. Simple evaluation here: If we let them think the world belongs to them, that means to some degree, WE HAVE SACRIFICED OUR INFLUENCE, EVEN DIMINISHED OUR OWN VALUES AND PURPOSES. That's where that kind of thinking will take you. If you sacrifice your influence as years pass, you will be conceding power and authority, which would indicate a weakening willpower. Let me tell you what your attitude should be: YOU MUST CONSTANTLY KEEP YOUR POSITION OF AUTHORITY IN THIS WORLD. Make damn sure it is kept at its absolute highest level. If you don't do that every day of your life as you get older, you will be implying by virtue of your conduct, that you are suppose to live your life at a lesser, more antiquated criteria as people half your age. Are you f-ing kidding me? Not for one God damned second of your aging process should that be considered, no less allowed. Because your Old Pops is here to tell ya, and state as clearly as he can as a matter of personal fact, the EXACT OPPOSITE has been true for this old war dog.

Just think of all the years of experience you've had – forty-plus. Look back, concentrate and locate any period of your younger life, and think of all the circumstances that you had to stand up to. You know they were in the hundreds, even thousands. So many different difficult situations you had to deal with. IF YOU WEREN'T GOOD AT IT, SIR, THERE IS NO WAY YOU WOULD HAVE GOTTEN THIS FAR SUCCESSFULLY. That is why you must never underestimate your worth, because of your age. At this stage of the game, you are SUPREMELY QUALIFIED to turn every aspect of your life in the right direction, and keep your priorities in their correct order of importance. Now you do that, and watch your life springboard and catapult to NEW HEIGHTS OF SATISFACTION.

Just maybe as you're getting older, you may think certain things in life are going sideways, even downhill. Again, you belong to a big, big club. THOSE ARE THOUGHTS THAT OCCUR TO

ALL OF US AS WE AGE. Yours Truly is no exception. But remember, they are only thoughts, YOU AND I HAVE THE POWER AND CHOICE TO CHANGE OUR THOUGHTS, redirect them if that's what's needed. I am talking about every single thought process in our life. No category excluded. Sex, work, politics, religion, money, and whatever their relationship is to all this new technology. Quite an undertaking, but one you are totally capable of. Now here's what I don't want you to think: just because we are ALL IN THE PROCESS OF AGING, don't you ever think you are SLIPPING BEHIND. That is such a misguided, misconceived giant pile of bullshit! BANISH IT COMPLETELY FROM YOUR BRAIN. Your insight, your vision, perception, and experience, are now your highest developed qualities. Concentrate on and cultivate even greater INSIGHT, sharper VISION, and more precise PERCEPTION. Three fundamental essentials that will help develop YOUR GROWING SELF CONFIDENCE. Qualities you possess in abundance. For God's sake young brother of mine, organize and execute them wisely and frequently. And never forget the title of this observation, KEEP THEM ALWAYS UNDER EMOTIONAL CONTROL.

So no matter how rapidly this world seems to be changing, or how much more informed younger generations are with current technology, that is not a negative. It's a positive fact of life. I have no doubt that if this current technology is used correctly, in a FAIR AND JUST more often than not manner, the results could be beyond amazing, when it comes to all the achievements, this advancing science is capable of providing. To fight it would be a losing battle. But, let's not forget what is just as or may be of

123

even greater importance, when it comes to your everyday living of a full life.

THEREIN LIES A COMPLETELY DIFFERENT STORY. It's about you knowing totally and completely, that you are now qualified to become a leader in life. All those years you just lived QUALIFY YOU TO BE THE TEACHER. Now if you don't already feel that way, develop that kind of AUTHORITATIVE THINKING. You've earned it. Make no mistake, all you have to do is look back ten to twenty years or more, and you'll be able to identify that, even with all their information, the younger generation? They are now YOUR STUDENTS in the process of learning the real meaning of life. So here's my recommendation: WHY IN THE WORLD WOULD YOU GO TO YOUNGER PEOPLE FOR SOMETHING THEY HAVE NO CONCEPTION OF, HAVING NEVER EXPERIENCED IT, BY LIVING THROUGH IT. That statement is valid beyond question. Look at all the obstacles, struggles, and challenges that you have been through, and not only survived, but conquered, THAT THEY HAVE NOT. You must never forget your elevated place in this world, and know precisely and exactly the proven values it represents. Those younger people should be flocking to you, for obvious reasons, because at this stage and age of your life, they are not and you are EMOTIONALLY MATURE, solidly grounded, aware, and much more in charge of the facts of life. THOSE ARE YOUR GREAT ASSETS, and they only came with the experience age provides. Let me put it this way: numbers don't lie. All those years lived give you, the great quality and the rare ability, to more CLEARLY DEFINE REALITY. That will not be found in any member of our gender, twenty years or more our junior. I DON'T CARE IF THE KID IS A GENIUS WITH A MENSA IQ, and nobody should know this better than you: the longer you live, the more you learn, the better you evaluate and perform, and apply more accurately, your acquired information. Please, sir, always display that kind of wisdom and maturity. YOU HAVE DAMN WELL EARNED AND DESERVE THAT KIND OF CONFIDENCE AND SELF WORTH. *THAT'S WHO YOU ARE*. If there is even the shadow of a doubt, focus and force your mental muscle to eliminate that negative concept, because IT CAN ONLY EXIST IF YOU ALLOW IT TO.

So there it is my young, fantastic, emotionally under control brother. Know for sure you have truly reached that point in life, where you take your mid-life and elevate it to a high-life every day, for the rest of your life. But remember, this is all based on your staying EMOTIONALLY UNDER CONTROL, AND PSYCHOLOGICALLY MATURE AND STABLE.

A Thread Runs Through It

35

There's and old expression that people like to use called "a thread runs through it", which I think more or less means, one thing being closely associated with, and definitely corresponding to another thing. So you should know, there's a thread that runs through every aspect of your thinking, and that connecting thread is definitely and constantly there. You know what that constant should be? You knowing the wonderful human experience of the advantages you have, of LIVING EVERY DAY OF YOUR LIFE, TO ITS FULLEST. Now of course, many things can interfere with that. It's more than possible you can overreact emotionally and have your judgment disoriented, even distorted in the process. Things can go south. In many cases they do, for a variety of reasons. We are all EMOTIONAL CHARACTERS, no matter how cool, calm, and laid-back we appear to be. THAT'S WHAT BEING ALIVE IS ALL ABOUT, and that's what long-lived experience taught me. So as a result of our very nature, we can often become emotional, and that's OK. Out of control, over emotional? DEFINITELY NOT OK. That's when emotions can generate big problems and obstructions. When you are out of control emotionally, you can, and more than likely will, MAGNIFY, EXPAND, AND ENLARGE NEGATIVE THOUGHTS. So whatever the situation is you are going through, whatever the experience is you are having, that seems overwhelmingly consuming, unless you feed and strengthen and let it dominate, IT CANNOT AND WILL NOT STAY THAT WAY. You must use your mature, positive persona to overcome it, and reduce its effect.

Now let's put all that in a formative, clear, fully transparent perspective. Under any and all human conditions in the living of life, when you are depressed or crying, even deeply disappointed or in a state of desperation, DON'T YOU EVER THINK YOU ARE ALONE. No matter the almost uncontrollable anger that you may feel, not only are you not alone, you are experiencing a FUNDAMENTAL CHARACTERISTIC OF EVERY MAN'S BASIC NATURE on a recurring basis. We are all going to have to deal with those kind of circumstances, and that's where your discipline and your willpower come into play. Because YOU DO HAVE A CHOICE, so make it the right one, and expand on it by letting the THREAD OF YOUR POSITIVE THOUGHTS not only run through it, but dominate it. There's always going to be things happening in your life, negative and positive. There's no escaping that. Hundreds of conditions and situations created by other people, with different or opposing views and opinions, that they think might have the best outcome, can in fact HAVE JUST THE OPPOSITE EFFECT ON YOU, get you down and put you in a real funk. Well I'm here to tell you from a long lifetime of personal experience, I've had thousands of things in my life go sideways, even south, and rarely, but at times go into free-fall. And it wasn't easy for me, because by nature I'm a pretty emotional guy. BUT COMMON SENSE SPOKE TO ME. Why the hell would I add negativity to my emotions, and then stupidly expand on it. That would be the dumbest thing I could do! IT WOULD BE AN EXERCISE IN FUTILITY ON MY PART. So I'm telling you, DON'T LET THAT KIND OF NEGATIVE THINKING GET THROUGH AND CONSUME YOU, because if you allow it to cook too long in your brain, it can become a strong part of your permanent personality. The right thread to run through your thinking is the power of your love, and the strength of your appreciation of life. That is the only way to lift your spirits. That's how YOU TURN NEGATIVE CIRCUMSTANCES POSITIVE, AND CONVERT LIABILITIES INTO ASSETS. When you expand on negative thoughts, they can be OVERWHELMING AND OBSESSIVELY DISTRACTING. Please, sir, with all the powerful mental muscle you possess, you must keep that to an absolute minimum. Because if you don't, you may have just taken the first step in starting to quit on yourself. Somewhere on that dark twisting road, you will possibly reach the point where you quit on life. UNACCEPTABLE! UNNECESSARY! A COMPLETE AND TOTAL WASTE OF YOUR PRECIOUS TIME, AND HIGHLY VALUABLE LIFE. You have to fully believe, you are made of a hell of a lot better stuff than that.

So from every positive perspective, wrap your arms, your mind, your heart, and your soul around every moment you have. Of course life is not easy, never has been, never will be. BUT MOST IMPORTANT TO YOU, DON'T YOU EVER EXPECT IT TO BE! Do everything you can to KEEP THAT THREAD OF POSITIVITY RUNNING THROUGH YOUR MIND. I'm telling you as sincerely as I can, young brother, it is the only way to ignite the light that will brighten YOUR LOVE OF LIFE. Only then will you give life the opportunity TO LOVE YOU RIGHT BACK.

A Decade At A Time

36

Forty to fifty, fifty to sixty, seventy, eighty, ninety and beyond, we can live our life and break it down generally, IN DECADES. Each one of those ten year periods, constitutes NUMEROUS BIG CHANGES AND DIFFERENT GROWING EXPERIENCES. Each one of those decades represents a whole lot of water over the dam. During any given ten-year period, your life has changed in so many ways, that you are in many respects, A DIFFERENT MAN THAN YOU WERE TEN YEARS EARLIER. The living of a long life, and staying strong and consistent throughout it, must be your rock-solid foundation. Its PURPOSE SHOULD BE A FEEL BETTER, LOOK BETTER, PROUDER, BOLDER MAN WITH EACH PASSING DECADE. The passage of time does not necessarily have to impose an expanding psychological liability and burden. I'm telling you from long-lived experience, with each passing decade, that kind of high-flying energy and positive attitude, DOES NOT HAVE AN AGE LIMIT ON IT.

And let me give you something else to think about. As those decades keep passing by, and you keep going higher up on that aging-ladder, when you've worked hard and managed your life efficiently, well know without question or doubt, you have earned and justified every right, AFTER FOUR VERY DIFFERENT, CHALLENGING DECADES, to improve upon THE NEXT FOUR DECADES. You must make every decade you live, better than the previous one. Now you still may work for twenty to thirty more years at your job for money, but at this point you have more than earned the right, to REFLECT, looking back with a real secure feeling of accomplishment. Sir, there comes a time when you've really got to smell the roses, AND THIS IS IT! Because you and I and the Lord know, you sure as hell have it coming. And hopefully now, the load is a little lighter, as it should be. SO OF COURSE YOU DESERVE IT. Allow me to put it this way, kind sir: at whatever age you were, or are going to be, when you finally finish doing what you do to make a buck and pay the bills, you must never, and I do mean damn well never ever RETIRE FROM THE LIVING OF A FULL, COMPLETE, AND DIVERSIFIED LIFE. You must continually keep it filled with even more passion and purpose, with each passing decade.

That thread we spoke about runs though all my thoughts, and I've said this hundreds of times, you must continue to keep dreaming your dreams and scheming your schemes. NEVER LET THEM FALTER, always keeping them VIVIDLY ALIVE, no matter how many decades pass. That's the only way you keep your life promising, interesting, and fulfilling with age, continuing to chase that dream, decade after decade. As long as you are pulling a breath, my friend, you must, and I do mean MUST always reach HIGHER AND WORK HARDER FOR THAT DREAM. Not for one single minute of your life do you ever let that DREAM DIMINISH. If you do, it will eventually fade into obscurity, possibly taking you with it.

What I'm hoping to prepare you for and make you aware of, is when it comes time to stop working, and you retire from whatever it is you were doing to make that dollar, *DON'T YOU*

EVER RETIRE FROM BEING A PRODUCTIVE HUMAN BEING. By the way, that word *retire*? RHYMES WITH *EXPIRE*. Sir, that is the lowest road you can take when it comes to aging. So let's turn this decade to decade observation in the opposite, upbeat direction, and make sure each decade of your life gets progressively more rewarding. Once you are on that positive path, with four to six decades yet to be lived, that's how you go from retire to SELF INSPIRE. That's the high road you belong on, for the balance of this great gift of life you have been given. Look at all the time you still have remaining, for a potentially higher quality of life. So play it smart and real. Travel your own gratifying, totally fulfilling road, that leads you to a HIGHER LEVEL OF INSPIRED LIVING. And don't question yourself, because, after nine full decades, your Old Pops is still doing it! Develop that kind of inspired mode, and it will become your permanent mindset. That is your guarantee of a completely gratifying total lifespan. Please, sir, don't you ever stop reaching for and chasing that dream ONE DECADE AT A TIME. You will not only never waste a day, without question you will know YOUR LIFE DOES NOT NEED LIMITS ON IT, PAST FORTY, NO LESS EIGHTY. Let others establish your limitations? NEVER! Limitations, my ass! Living an expanded, broader, more meaningful existence, decade after decade, ALWAYS!

Keeping Score Every Twenty-four

37

You know our theme here? Well it's not just a theme, it's an adage, it's a constant, and I wish I could say it on every page. You must live your life ONE DAY AT A TIME. You and I know why that makes sense, because where time is concerned, we have no other choice. Life is most precious in the now, this very moment. The air you breathe, the scenery you see, the food you eat, are experiences you can only live one day at a time. It is only in this day you have the touch, the taste, the feel, and the smell of that day. THERE IS NO OTHER TIME YOU CAN BE AS FULLY ALIVE, as during the day you are living in. That's why this little observation has such a big meaning: Keeping score, every twenty-four. Now what you need to do in this day, even if there's something on your mind, that may be a little negative or slightly disturbing or even depressing, you must accept that particular condition, CHALLENGE IT, AND OVERCOME IT if you wish TO LIVE THIS DAY OF YOUR LIFE TO ITS FULLEST and make this twenty-four, YOUR WINNING SCORE. You must establish in your mind, the action required to make this day produce more positive than negative results. We all know they are both there. But it will definitely be your DEFINITIVE SENSE OF CONSCIOUSNESS, to maintain a mindset, where your positive content ALWAYS outweighs the negative, BY THE PROVERBIAL COUNTRY MILE. Then, at the end of this twenty-four, you will have produced a winning score. Let's face it, on a long-term basis, that is a heavy, hard to sustain undertaking. It's never automatic or easy. If you expect it to be, DISAPPOINTMENT WILL BE YOUR DIRECT RESULT. All those unexpected things you experience don't happen by accident. So not only do you have to work at being positive about yourself, to be very blunt and realistic, you have to work at it every single day, as hard as you damn well can. And what you are going to find out is it's more than worth the effort. Why? THIS IS THE ONLY DAY YOU ARE ALIVE. That's why, you should never willingly accept negativity. Then every priceless positive minute of this twenty-four-hour day, you will naturally make a fully concerted effort, that you find personally rewarding and fulfilling. Again, why? You created it, it's YOURS, 100% YOURS!

Think, as you read these words, how great it would be if you could have that kind of mindset, every single day for the rest of your life. Knowing with vivid reality, EVERY DAY OF YOUR LIFE IS SUCH A PRECIOUS, ONE-TIME-ONLY GIFT. To know, you have made your supreme effort, a winning score, at the end of every twenty-four. And it all starts with that six to eight inches between your ears. You may have big biceps and a wide back, but YOUR MENTAL MUSCLE, must always be THE STRONGEST MUSCLE in your body. And you have to believe, you've got a hell of a lot of it. Use it ever twenty-four in the most powerful, positive way you can, to make much, much more of your HIGHLY VALUABLE TWENTY-FOUR. And no matter how strong you may be mentally, you just may be UNDERESTIMATING YOURSELF. When you focus and concentrate optimistically and affirmatively, your mind is tremendously powerful. Your will and determination can absolutely be made stronger. But that will not come to pass

UNLESS YOU EXPRESS YOURSELF COMPLETELY, ASSERTIVELY, UNABASHEDLY, IN A POWERFUL, POSITIVE WAY. Sir, do not ever hold back on your thoughts and feelings, as long as they are not hostile or damaging to anybody else. Let them come fully alive, and you will have opened the door, to your SUPER SATISFYING TWENTY-FOUR, producing an indestructible sense of profound and impenetrable positivity. That, through constant practice, will express the AUTHENTIC YOU. Please try to lock this in your brain: Don't ever forget that nature gave you a mouth to fully express yourself vocally. And in expressing yourself, DON'T EVER BECOME LIMITED OR INTIMIDATED AS A RESULT OF POLITICAL CORRECTNESS. And may I suggest, kind sir, thicken that skin a little. Then you won't have to worry about trivia or nonsense producing a negative influence on your feelings and decisions. Then, when something is of great importance to you, high on your priority list, make sure you say it precisely HOW YOU WANT TO SAY IT, and of even greater importance, saying it *WHEN* YOU WANT TO SAY IT. I have found that's the kind of mindset it takes to stay strong and confident in this, THE MOST IMPORTANT HALF OF YOUR LIFE. Be self-assured and your timing will always be right. That's how you make every twenty-four, YOUR *PERSONAL* WINNING SCORE.

Don't Be Ashamed

38

I want you to know you're not perfect. I'm not perfect. Even Albert Einstein wasn't perfect! PERFECTION IS AN ILLUSION. Of all the billions of people on this planet, not a single one is perfect! We all constantly question our judgment, but know that's OK, if you do it in an honest and objective way. Ken Dab-Row, perfect? Even after a lifetime of living and thousands of experiences to smarten me up, I'M AS WROUGHT THROUGH WITH FLAWS AS SWISS CHEESE IS WITH HOLES. So know for sure, that is the status quo for every human on Earth. That is the math you must accept. But if you haven't, until you do, SELF IMPROVEMENT WILL BE DIFFICULT.

Which brings us to the title of this observation. If everybody who wasn't perfect was ashamed of themselves, every living human would have to bear the burden and carry total, unnecessary, excessive, TIME-CONSUMING SHAME AROUND. DON'T YOU EVER BE ASHAMED of your actions, as long as your intentions are fair and just, knowing that every human being, don't always use and exhibit perfect judgment. And here's another very VERY important point: After you overcome self-imposed shame, don't ever allow anybody, even those close to you, who care for you, whose thoughts towards you are well intended, ever suggest, imply, or ASSIGN SHAME TO YOU. GRANT NO ONE THE RIGHT TO CROSS THAT LINE. Be ashamed of yourself because of what others think you are? Not on your life for all of the rest of your life should you ever let that happen. If you allow someone to assign you shame, that will GENERATE

A FEELING OF LESS SELF WORTH, making you feel more insecure. Nobody has that right, it is one hundred percent wrong. You should never tolerate that kind of conduct for even one minute of your human journey. When I say be proud of who and what you are, I'm implying be proud of the good things you do. Obviously I'm not talking about breaking laws, hurting other people, being a bad person, or betraying a trust. The penalty for that kind of shitty conduct should be severe, and I'm going to assume that is not you. Know this: NEVER LIVE YOUR LIFE IN UNNECESSARY SHAME OR GUILT. If there were ever two words that possess the power to weaken your will, and damage your dignity, those are two of the worst. They will make you question your character. SHAME AND GUILT? IMPLY GUILTY AS CHARGED! Because of that, too many people are made to feel that way, and that's the biggest damn shame of all.

So, whatever guilt or shame you have allowed to build up because of questionable establishment values, or somebody else's input, nobody has the right to say to anybody else, what the hell is right or wrong for them. Remember this always, every day of life, ABSOLUTELY NOBODY IN THIS WORLD KNOWS BETTER THAN YOU WHAT IS BEST FOR YOU. So whatever different ideas and values other people may have, DON'T YOU EVER BE ASHAMED OR UNNECESSARILY APOLOGIZE FOR YOURSELF. At this point in your life using honest evaluation, know absolutely what is right or wrong for you. That's not for anybody else to decide. Don't carry that kind of mind-tiring confusion around. NOBODY BUT YOU, has the full, complete, total right, to question your own thoughts and your own actions. THAT'S EXCLUSIVELY YOUR PRIVATE

PROPERTY. Learn through repetition to develop the habit of forgiving yourself. With all of nature's imperfections affecting all the hundreds and thousands of things we do, God, man, FORGIVE YOURSELF and get on with life! There's not one single person on this planet, who hasn't had to deal with that kind of contrary, contradictory, dilemma. But when you MINIMIZE AND HOPEFULLY ELIMINATE, the kind of heavy mental baggage shame and guilt create, you will think more clearly and confidently. Only then can you most boldly, unashamedly say: "NEVER AGAIN WILL I BE ASHAMED, AND LET THAT KIND OF SELF-DEFEATING MINDSET DOMINATE MY THINKING." I want you to say this to yourself every day of your life for the rest of your life. Always keeping it at the forefront of your thinking: "NEVER WILL I LET SHAME OR GUILT CONTROL MY ABILITY TO EXPRESS MY THOUGHTS IN A MEANINGFUL AND USEFUL WAY. LIVING BY MY OWN VALUES IS THE ONLY WAY, I WILL EVER DISCOVER *WHO I REALLY AM*." Be free-spirited and open minded in expressing yourself! If you haven't already, do it, sir. That's the kind of persona you should want to acquire. Then assured, for the rest of your strong, long life, you will never ever be MEEK, AFRAID, INTIMIDATED, OR FEEL GUILTY OR ASHAMED of what you are THINKING, DOING, and SAYING.

Your Pursuits

39

It's nice to be pursued. And of course it can be even nicer to pursue. And every day, life does give us that advantage. We can and should have thousands of positive pursuits. But know this as unquestionable truth: with any lifelong pursuit, if allowed to be an important part of your existence, know and believe as unshakable, that the older, more experienced you get, the harder you've got to work at your pursuits. So what! IT'S A SMALL PRICE TO PAY FOR THE LARGE REWARD RECEIVED. And, kind sir, that's the only way, during this, the second, MOST IMPORTANT, HALF OF YOUR LIFE, to get the big payoff. You must, with fierce, intense determination pursue those goals and objectives, that are of great value to you.

I want you to know for sure, as these years keep passing by, your efforts must be MORE SHARPLY FOCUSED WITH A STRONGER COMMITMENT. That is not a maybe, kind sir, that is a must! Anything less than your being supremely committed, will lead to a compromised result, putting you on the path to greater compromise AND POTENTIAL LONG-TERM SELF-IMPOSED LIMITATIONS.

This applies to every man in the world past forty. I want you to put less emphasis on your features, size, and shape. As important as all that is to our vanity and pride, that must never become the DETERMINING FACTOR, of who YOU ARE AS A HUMAN BEING. Muscular or meek, short or tall, fat or thin, loud, proud, and super active, or quiet and laid back. With advancing age, our coordination, our reflexes, and our balance are reduced. And after using all those body parts for forty, fifty, sixty years, it should not come as a shock to you, that there's wear and tear that might need and require a little more maintenance. So don't be intimidated by it or ashamed of it, IT'S JUST NATURE TAKING ITS COURSE. Now what I'm about to say is to make a point, not brag or boast, it's very possible I just may be one of the best conditioned men in the world at my age. Well I want you to know, sir, as undeniable fact, what you just read about wear and tear, and hopefully repair, has been happening to me, for forty years, since my fiftieth birthday. So here's the analogy: If you find yourself physically strong, active, and highly energized between forty and sixty, don't expect to have the same reflexes and coordination of a man half your age in half your shape. Don't ever let that kind of negatively false concept of aging, interfere with you positively PURSUING <u>YOUR</u> LIFE TO ITS ABSOLUTE SATISFACTION. Here's what The Old Man is telling you: Your mindset from forty to eighty-plus, should always be to pursue relentlessly every ambitious drive and dream, of getting the ABSOLUTE MOST IN AS MANY WAYS POSSIBLE, MENTALLY, PHYSICALLY, AND SPIRITUALLY, AT THIS TIME IN YOUR LIFE, making the balance of your life live up to, AND ALWAYS BE AT ITS FULLEST.

Real Truth

40

I don't think, of all the qualities we have, all the superlatives that can be said, based on their importance, nothing should be a stronger belief of yours, with more meaning where all your priorities are concerned, than you ALWAYS STRIVING AT BEING MORE <u>TRUTHFUL</u> with yourself. There's an old expression that I believe is an absolute fallacy: "The truth hurts". I believe just the opposite. The truth should never hurt, it should STRENGTHEN YOUR CHARACTER EVEN MORE. The real truth can only hurt, if you let your vanity and false pride or thin skin, get in the way of WHAT IS REALLY RELEVANT TO YOU. So the real truth, the whole truth, and absolutely nothing but the forty year old to infinity truth, is this: You, Y-O-U, are entitled to, and not only can but should, have great expectations, as long as they are NOT FALSE EXPECTATIONS, and they are based on fact and truth. You can take it to the bank, sir, it may be a little uncomfortable now and then, but THE TRUTH WILL ALWAYS SET YOU FREE. In evaluating yourself, only truth, will allow you to know who you are and KEEP YOUR LIFE REAL. Hey young brother, you want to hear some absolute truth? Nobody knows better than me, the clock is quickly tick tocking away! So know how aware I am that every tick of the clock, and every beat of my heart, is ONE LESS TICK AND ONE LESS BEAT I'm going to have in my life. Even if I live to be a hundred, I am well aware I have already lived over ninety percent of my life. Waste the last potential ten years of my life feeling sorry for myself, because I lacked the courage to face and deal with my truth? Are you f-ing kidding?! Never gonna happen to this old boy! And that's MY ONE HUNDRED PERCENT TRUEST OF ALL TRUTHS.

So every day, you must mentally and psychologically from a positive perspective, dance with your hopes and your dreams and your schemes. If you do that this day, and every day of this limited journey of life, that will always lead TO YOUR REAL TRUTH. Now the greatest truth of all, that you may not have been aware of: time started running out from the day you were born! WE JUST DIDN'T GIVE IT MUCH OF A THOUGHT OR PRIORITY, UNTIL WE FACED OUR MORTALITY. Well that's you and that's me and that's OK. Where you are concerned, you may have a guaranteed forty to fifty more years left. BUT DON'T EVER LOSE CONTACT WITH WHAT YOU HONESTLY KNOW TO BE YOUR REAL TRUTH, and remember, those first forty years of yours will have served their full purpose, if you learned and acquired from them the fearless smarts to handle real truth concerning your mortality. I don't believe there is a more efficient and effective way to reduce or DIMINISH THE EFFECTS OF FEAR. So ACCEPT WITH COURAGE AND CONVICTION YOUR REAL TRUTH, AND MAKE THE SECOND HALF OF YOUR LIFE THE BEST OF YOUR LIFE.

Confusion

41

There's not a second that goes by in life that we are not thinking of something. Even when sleeping, our dreams have thoughts. Tens of thousands of thoughts constantly, continually keep running through our brain. Now I know that sounds like a mental overload, and it can be, but only if you encourage it. If you do, it'll be very easy to GET CONFUSED. And the reason those things occur, because all those hundreds and thousands of thoughts, DON'T COINCIDE. They can be conflicting. You've heard that expression "conflicting thoughts", and I'm sure you know what I'm talking about. All those decisions you must make will be based on those thoughts. Should I or shouldn't I? Will I or won't I? And of course, the older we get, the more time lived, the more thoughts we're going to have! Then somehow, somewhere past middle-age, we believe our capacity to handle and RESOLVE THEM, becomes a little MORE LIMITED. Which could lead up to living the balance of your life in a state of expanded confusion.

CONFUSION, MY ASS! THAT IS TOTALLY, COMPLETELY, AND THOROUGHLY UNACCEPTABLE! Neutralize it now, or it could be ONE MORE MENTAL MONSTER OF MISERY. That's exactly what confusion is. So now, Mr. Man In The Middle, you are going to have to work twice as hard, and concentrate twice as much, to keep that mental muscle stronger, more resilient, well ORGANIZED, and well DIRECTED. Absolutely with aging, CONFUSION MUST BE HELD TO A MINIMUM, and hopefully defeated completely.

Now we both know it's impossible to be on-point all the time, with a hundred percent total mental clarity and continuity, every minute of every day. AT ANY AGE IT CAN'T BE DONE! But if you deal with it on a day-to-day basis, you can organize your thoughts, which will greatly reduce the degree of confusion that could exist.

So the first order of business in the first couple of waking hours of every day, is to get your thoughts for that day organized. Get that mind of yours highly focused and poised, only on the priorities that are important to you that day, keeping them as well organized as you can. And IF YOU DON'T GO TOO FAR BACK, AND DON'T THINK TOO FAR AHEAD, CONFUSION WILL AND CAN BE GREATLY REDUCED. If it don't concern the moment you are living in, put it on the back burner. And if your thoughts are current and require immediate attention, then you must concentrate on them a little harder, so they can be resolved. Can you handle that? You know damn well you can! Can you cope with the conflicting nature of those thoughts, and reduce to a minimum whatever state of confusion they might represent? YOU ABSOLUTELY CAN! Once you elevate that process, just the opposite of confusion will occur. You will have created CONTINUITY that, when practiced on a continuing basis, will OVERPOWER CONFUSION AND HOPEFULLY ELIMINATE IT. Achieve that goal, and continuity will set in. And continuity will make you feel strong, confident, AND IN CONTROL OF YOUR LIFE. Sir, that long-term commitment will DEFEAT CONFUSION. This should be a rest-of-your-life commitment to keep the ugly face of conflicting confusion OUT OF YOUR BRAIN AND OUT OF YOUR LIFE.

The Year You Are Living In

42

First, let's go way back before we hit forty-plus. Maybe twenty even thirty years. Well no matter how interesting, exciting, or stimulating your life was during that period, if you don't believe that the age you are right now, SHOULD BE THE BEST YEAR OF YOUR LIFE, sir, you are giving yourself permission to be misdirected and discouraged. The result of which could easily be losing your way. You are obviously not as young as you were then. Things are always changing as you age. But this is the only life you got. YOU MUST ENCOURAGE YOUR MOST OPTIMISTIC VIEW OF THE YEAR YOU ARE LIVING IN.

Now my point, and I want to make it crystal clear. The greatest discovery you will ever make in your life, is finding out EXACTLY AND PRECISELY WHO AND WHAT YOU REALLY ARE. Well my friend, that's going to be hard to know, IF YOU KEEP TRYING TO BE WHAT YOU WERE. How many different ways in this book do I have to say, RIGHT NOW IS ALL THAT COUNTS, because, sir, it's all you got! Which should make you acutely aware of how fortunate and blessed you are. Younger or older should be of NO CONCERN. Of course you should look back at fond memories, and use them as building blocks, to improve and make stronger the foundation of your future. But never forget, the year you are living in, YOU MUST MAKE the most important year of your life. So don't, with a capital "D", ever FALL VICTIM TO THAT MISGUIDED MINDSET, OF CONSTANTLY BEING AFRAID OF GETTING OLDER. Which is the ultimate fate of every baby ever born, if they are lucky enough to have a long life. You must give the year you are living in greater value, than any year you've lived leading up to it. SIR, IT'S THE ONLY ONE YOU'VE GOT!

I gotta say it again: Younger, my ass! Older, my ass! Right now, as you are reading this page, and these words, this is the age of life of the year you are living in, AND THIS IS THE MOMENT YOU ARE LIVING IT. What in the hell on God's good Earth could ever be of greater importance? So it is entirely up to you, to MAKE EVERY DAY OF THIS YEAR THE BEST YOU CAN POSSIBLY MAKE IT. From forty-plus, hopefully all the way up to your century mark, LOVE EVERY PRECIOUS MINUTE, MOMENT-TO-MOMENT, ONE YEAR AT A TIME.

Magnetic Force

43

If your goal is to enhance and remain a strong magnetic human force for the balance of your life, you must definitely take the PURPOSE AND MEANING of that life of yours, to its HIGHEST POSSIBLE LEVEL. That's essential, if you wish to create any chance of realizing your most ambitious and rewarding hopes and dreams. Then however long it takes to reach that level, you must always strive even harder, to elevate it even higher. The message here is, that level that you are aiming for, SHOULD BE INFINITIVE. That's why if you do it right, no matter how many or few of your hopes and dreams come true, YOU MUST ALWAYS KEEP STRIVING. Playing up and emphasizing the magnetic force you know you are, must be a top priority for life, and it must be done in your most emphatic, strong-minded way. This INTANGIBLE ASSET, must always be AT THE FOREFRONT OF YOUR CONSCIOUSNESS. On the other hand, no matter what your preoccupations are, or how long they've been there, if they are more of a liability than an asset, YOU MUST PLAY THEM DOWN. That powerful, positive magnetic force in you will allow you to MINIMIZE your liabilities. Now here's the key, in fact the solution to making all that come to fruition: It's obvious to all of us, we can never eliminate liabilities completely, but what you must do is REDUCE THEIR IMPACT ON YOUR LIFE. Don't you ever think you lack the ability. On the other hand, what can be one of the most restrictive, and ultimately destructive words, in every man's world, because we all, to varying degrees experience it, is that word *failure*. Even though in unique cases it may have some validity, I don't want to hear that crap, about how YOU HAVE TO, FAIL TO SUCCEED. Let me give you my opinion on the context of that statement. Of course we have struggles, and of course we try things that don't work out. That applies to every living body, soul, and brain. BUT FAILING AT LIFE? In that context where failure represents the end result, and nothing constructive comes from it, there is no more of a self-defeating word. So in the course of a full, long life, let as little failure creep in as possible. In other words, even though there might be MOMENTS AND TEMPORARY POCKETS OF FAILURE, that sure as hell does not mean, it has to be a major part of who and what you are, on an extended basis.

So what's our alternative? We must always face up to and be ready to fight it all the way to the finish. Guys, I have found there is no other way to handle and limit, the impact, of whatever you may consider failure in your life. Now once you develop the habit of knowing you are NATURALLY successful, once you build and establish that kind of secure insight into your thought processes, over an extended period, IT WILL REMAIN A CONSTANT IN YOUR LIFE. When you strongly elevate your magnetic positive force, it will automatically become natural, normal, second nature to you. It's a very real life changer when you create such a self-confident mindset. Then the word *failure,* will have little or no effect on your psyche. So you now become an even more resilient magnetic force, from forty to sixty, THAN YOU WERE BY A LONG-SHOT, FROM TWENTY TO FORTY. Lest we forget, as I reiterate so often, it was those years, twenty to forty, when in spite of your sensational discoveries,

147

YOU DEVELOPED ALL THOSE DOUBTS AND FEARS THAT *FEED FAILURE*. Don't you ever forget from this moment on, for the rest of your life, failure has only one opposite: SUCCESS. It's already in you! NOW IS THE TIME IN YOUR LIFE TO EXPAND ON IT, develop it, and bring it out. That should be a top priority, you could even call it JOB ONE, during these very important transitional years. You will be setting yourself up for a lifetime of minimizing failure, gaining confidence, and MAXIMIZING SUCCESS.

Let's focus on that fantastic, fulfilling word *success*. So many useful, effective applications! In this case, I'm not talking about success in business or education, I'm talking about your own personal, individual success as an active, fully functioning, confident, caring, and concerned, DYNAMIC HUMAN BEING. That will be your rock-solid cornerstone, and your failure-proof foundation to build on, TO KEEP MAKING STRONGER YOUR CONFIDENCE AND INTEGRITY DURING THIS CRITICAL TRANSITION. Without those two hard fought for qualities of confidence and integrity, there is no way you will have the courage to step boldly forward, into the rest of your life, as a MAGNETIC FORCE. When I say boldly, I mean with purpose and passion, that allows you to fight and OVERCOME WITH AUTHORITY, any adversity that failure assuredly, and more likely than not, will manufacture in your mind. You must clear the way, for your long-term personal success AS A HIGHLY QUALIFIED, FULLY FUNCTIONING POSITIVE HUMAN BEING. It is essential you totally commit to doing yourself the big favor of opening up new vistas, horizons, and broad kaleidoscopes of expanded life. Sir, ONCE YOU MAKE

148

THAT LONG-TERM COMMITMENT, your new discoveries in life will increase ten-fold and have HIGHLY INCREASED VALUE AND MEANING. I have found this to be the most effective way to become and stay for your entire second half of life, a PERSONALLY *SUCCESSFUL*, DYNAMIC FORCE.

So why would you for any reason even think of giving failure a chance, to get a foothold and show its ugly face? With CONFIDENCE AND INTEGRITY, AND A POSITIVE ATTITUDE, look that lousy loser of a lifestyle – failure - right in the eye, staring it down, let it know in no uncertain terms there is no way in hell it could ever have a major impact on you. FAILURE, MY ASS! You take the destructively debilitating meaning of that ugly, unnecessary word in your life, and as the high-quality human being you know you are, DIMINISH AND DESTROY IT BY BEING A STRONG, POSITIVE MAGNETIC FORCE. Then I want you to say to yourself boldly: "You bet your ass I can do that, all day, any day!" If it's already happening, better than good! Continue being that strong, impressive, and consistent MAGNETIC FORCE, THAT YOU KNOW YOU WERE ALWAYS MEANT TO BE.

Not Ordinary

44

As you speed and race through your youth, more frequently than not in a rudderless, exploratory way, all you are really doing with your new found life, IS LOOKING FOR EXCITEMENT. And, boy, did we all find our share! It seems that almost every discovery you made, in the course of your first forty years, no matter how enticing, is wrought through with CHALLENGES AND STRUGGLES. Those two words you'll find on almost every page of this text. Well, that's the price of exciting new found discovery. At least that's what I found. And the word I thought appropriate to describe such a condition: CARNIVAL. That first forty years of our life was like an ever-changing carnival ride. I remember, I felt like I was on top of the world. Youth gave me a feeling, as I'm sure it gave you, of being a UNIQUE POWERHOUSE. Immature and insecure, but nevertheless, a youth infused powerhouse. Look at all the goals we set, all those mountains we tried to climb to reach those goals. And during all that time, the one constant that was always a top priority, was MAKING A BUCK (hopefully a big buck!). No matter how busy and diversified we were, thinking about any and everything else, and how exciting that was going to be, in the back of our mind we were always preoccupied with the almighty dollar, because of our NEW FOUND INDEPENDENCE, WHICH MEANT RESPONSIBILITIES. I'm sure if you had a family with children, that was of great concern. Whether you know, and you most likely do, you spent a lot of your money, on your raging hormones. I know I sure as hell did. That's what the real purpose of the great chase of those first forty years was suppose to be: EXTRAORDINARY!

But then somewhere just past forty, we slowly with growing consistency become acutely aware of our mortality. Well if we're not careful and level-headed with the way we let that impact our mindset, it can be almost imperceptible, even subconscious how we interpret the variables of that condition. So if you are not even conscious of it, under those conditions, YOUR MORTALITY COULD CAUSE A LITTLE UNKNOWN SLIPPAGE IN YOUR CONFIDENCE. We're almost, I said almost, unaware of it. But, if we don't catch that confidence-killer in time, and reverse the meaning of our mortality, we can go from BEING EXTRAORDINARY to feeling ordinary, never knowing it was from the subconscious effects negativity had on our mortality. Please, sir, don't you ever paint yourself into that kind of confining, CONFIDENCE DESTROYING corner! You must be astutely aware of this insidious mind-altering situation, and face the reality that it does exist. Then you can consciously TURN THE CORNER, and start to take the steps to know that NOT ON YOUR LIFE ARE YOU MEEKLY OR MENTALLY <u>WEAKLY ORDINARY</u>, because that's the effect being negatively aware of your mortality can cause. In fact, no matter what year you are in, right now is the perfect time to expand on your extraordinary potential by putting it in a positive context. This must be something you place a very high priority on, AND COMMIT TO. Say to yourself every day of your life: "Ordinary, my ass! Not me, not for one damn minute of the rest of my life on this planet, should I question in any way MY EXTRAORDINARY ABILITY, to conquer and accomplish any of my ambitions."

Please, kind sir, believe what I say. It's been almost half a century since my fortieth birthday, FIFTY EXTRAORDINARY YEARS. So know with confidence in your heart and soul, if you are not already, you must become an EXTRA-ORDINARY man. And I do mean you being extraordinary in every sense of those words. So as the years pass, with an increasing effort, you should become an even more effective EXTRA-ORDINARY, EXTRAORDINARY, POWERFUL LIFE FORCE IN AN EXPANDING WAY.

So let's recap. Those first forty years, were in almost every way, about the excitement and discoveries of your youth, and the satisfying of your curiosities those youthful drives created. As said several times in this book: YOUR DUES HAVE BEEN PAID IN FULL. YOU ARE NOW A FULL-FLEDGED MEMBER OF CLUB *MATURITY*. Well here's your Old Pops, anywhere from three to five decades older than you, and I want you to know, every single day of every year of all those decades, I have been collecting on the dues I have paid from zero to forty, and I strongly suggest and advise, YOU DO THE SAME. Then, with confidence backed by a strong display of willpower and uncompromising determination, I want you to take these next thirty to fifty years, and not partially, but FULLY COLLECT ON YOUR DUES. Think about the relevance of all those trials by fire, that you went through. God, man, there were thousands of them. Little mishaps and missteps that you and I had to correct, which we did! And this just may be the most important part of going from the first half – ordinary, to making the SECOND HALF OF YOUR LIFE EXTRAORDINARY. Think about all those pros and cons that you learned from, that contributed to the

152

experiences and the expanding of your life. There's one thing I hope you learned from it: first, FORGIVE YOURSELF. Let it go! Then, get over whatever fear of mortality that you might have, if it exists. Don't keep carrying around any unnecessary destructive damage, guilt, blame, and fear that you might have let build up, in your subconscious mind. Again, let it go, get rid of it. Create a new slate. Because when you can do that, you will be setting yourself up to live the rest of your life MENTALLY, PHYSICALLY, PSYCHOLOGICALLY, AND SPIRITUALLY, at the highest level possible. You absolutely DESERVE THAT <u>EXTRAORDINARY FEELING,</u> FOR THE REST OF YOUR LIFE. Just know it's going to take an extra-ordinary, extraordinary effort on your part. But that's the only way to guarantee you will put more real pride, and EXTRAORDINARY PURPOSE into every day you live.

So let's get that word *ordinary*, OUT OF YOUR LIFE. You can bet your sweet, ever lovin' ass, you are an EXTRAORDINARY MAN. AND DON'T YOU NEVER EVER FORGET IT, FOR ONE SECOND OF THE SECOND HALF OF YOUR LIFE.

Guidance And Restriction

45

Every time I use that word *control*, I'm talking to one person at a time, and right now on this page, that particular person is you. So let's talk about you and your self-control. I believe, with all the mental tools you have available, that can provide an even better life past forty, it is all going to depend on your ability to CONTROL THE CONDITIONS AND SITUATIONS, that enter your life. Where your actions are concerned, *control* is of immense importance. It's hard to think of a more meaningful word. Could very well be the key to your psychological word tool kit. So now that we have established our criteria, let's get to the specifics that we're talking about here. Every aspect of every day of your life, is contingent on you keeping THAT DAY UNDER CONTROL. Now that does not mean *restricted* in any of the many negative interpretations of that word. I don't want you to ever feel restricted in any area that is important to your way of life. I repeat: the word *restriction* is loaded with much to many negative interpretations. So let me emphasize: in no way, SHOULD YOU EVER THINK, BE, FEEL, OR EXPRESS YOURSELF IN ANY WAY THAT IS RESTRICTED. Control and restriction have very little if anything in common. CONTROL AND GUIDANCE HAVE EVERYTHING IN COMMON. So in this context, you must GUIDE and DIRECT with almost complete CONTROL, your own DESTINY. That has little or no chance to manifest itself in a PERSONAL, POSITIVE WAY, UNLESS YOU GUIDE, DIRECT, AND CONTROL YOUR OWN THOUGHTS. No one knows better than you, all the essential and relevant needs in life. And if anybody thinks they know better than you how to guide you IN THE LIVING OF YOUR LIFE, it just may be time to guide them, right the hell out of it.

Every last one of us, every day of our lives, are going to have something to worry about. But in almost every situation, *unless somebody has a gun to your back, we have a choice.* That option of making the RIGHT CHOICE is open to every HUMAN BEING on the planet. Every other ANIMAL on Earth lives by instinct. Thousands of species live their entire lives by following their frequently over-emotional instincts. THEY HAVE NO CHOICE. Only us humans have been given the gift of conscious thought to utilize full control. To expand your worries? The wrong choice. The right choice? OBVIOUSLY, MINIMIZE THEM. Guide all those worries and negative thoughts, or as many as you can, out of your brain. We are the only species on Earth possessing that capability. YOU TAKING FULL CONTROL OF YOUR THOUGHT PROCESSES MUST ALWAYS BE YOUR CHOICE. You must always accentuate positives, and as much as you can, reduce the negatives. That's how you eventually eliminate that worthless word *worry*.

I don't think there has been a day in my long life, that I haven't had something to worry about. So know always, you got company. This is part and parcel of day-to-day living. Every thinking human being is going to have something to worry about, and that includes you and me. Now let's take this worry concept and put it into a little NUMERICAL PERSPECTIVE. Numbers don't lie. Literally three to four million people on our little planet, in the last thirty days, who were alive, are now dead. Their life has ended. That alone should serve the purpose of making you realize just how fortunate you are, to be fully alive and in FULL CONTROL OF THIS DAY. So when you take that next breath, appreciate it. THERE IS NO LIFE WITHOUT IT. So are you fortunate, even with all your worries and problems, most of which THROUGH CONSTANT OBJECTIVITY, GUIDED BY A POSITIVE MINDSET, ARE SOLVABLE? Of course you are, sir!

So here we are, back to that word *control*. Even if you're one of those people who maximize your worries, which you now know are correctable through your continually controlled thought, I know you sure as hell don't want to be dead, like the monthly millions I just made reference to. Thank God and nature that you and I are still alive, BEING AFFORDED THE OPPORTUNITY TO CHOOSE AND MAXIMIZE OUR POSITIVITY! So when you pull that next breath that gives you life, suck it in real good, get a lot of oxygen into that brain of yours, and then always do whatever it takes to neutralize and GUIDE, DAY-TO-DAY WORRY-CREATING PROBLEMS OUT OF YOUR LIFE.

I think you'll agree this message is clear. You've got to, in no uncertain terms, take control of your life, and guide it in positive ways. I WANT YOU TO MINIMIZE YOUR WORRIES AND PROBLEMS! Because once they are reduced, space in your brain will open up to MAXIMIZE ALL THE GOOD FORTUNE IN YOUR LIFE. Think of all the positive thoughts you will be able to capitalize on. To have a crystal-clear, optimistic thinking mind, and know you have it IN YOUR POWER, to always be able to love, appreciate, and be grateful for every second of your greatest gift: LIFE. Sir, that's the way it should be for you, as long as you are given your most valuable of all human assets, the PRIVILEGE OF DRAWING YOUR NEXT BREATH.

Like I said in the beginning, problems and worries are always going to be woven throughout our lifetime. But don't be restricted by them, and learn to deal with them through POSITIVE RESTRAINT AND INTELLIGENTLY DIRECTED GUIDANCE AND CONTROL. As you get older and more experienced, it will become lesser of a task. One more time for the memory: Know for sure, we are always going to have something to worry about, IT'S CALLED BEING ALIVE! Dead people will never again have something to worry about. So no matter how big those worries seem or actually are, being alive you still have the PRIVILEGE to deflate and diminish them, replacing them by expanding on all the positive things in your life, none of which will happen, without you being able to take your next breath. Do not take that next breath for granted, IT IS TRULY LIFE'S GREATEST ASSET.

With PROPER GUIDANCE AND CONTROL there will be NO RESTRICTIONS ON YOUR LIFE'S CAPACITY TO COPE. Just continue to give deep profound meaning and purpose, to those two words, *guidance* and *control*. Once that is strongly established, you will have developed the POWER TO LIMIT AND ULTIMATELY REMOVE RESTRICTION-EXPANDED WORRIES, affording you so much more PEACE OF MIND.

Negative Words

46

Every day for just about everyone, in almost every possible category, there is so much more negativity than positivity around us. And you have to be careful not to let it surround and work its way into your reality. So many negative things always seem to be happening. Even when I turn on a half hour newscast, it seems that over twenty minutes have to do with something negative, like robberies and killings. And what could be more negative than polarized politics? With all those negatives entering our conscious mind, it can FEED AND NOURISH negative thinking in the MAJORITY of our thoughts. The sad commentary on that scenario is, we think it's normal, because that's what the world we live in seems to be all about. Then slowly but surely, we're thinking negative thoughts and USING NEGATIVE WORDS to express ourselves. And these are words we use repeatedly every day of our life. And because of their frequency, in what we consider normal everyday discourse and discussion, we don't consciously consider them as particularly negative. Let's take the word *can't*. Now of course you *can't* stand in front of a moving train without it hitting you. But in general terms more often than not, the word *can't* is used in a NEGATIVE CONTEXT. There are not only many things we *can't* do, but we *shouldn't* do. Now once you start along that almost imperceptible, seemingly normal mental path, it can easily become a consistent part of YOUR THOUGHT AND SPOKEN PROCESSES. First it's *can't* do this or *can't* do that. Then another word associated with the word *can't* is *won't*. Now you are on that negative path to *don't* and *shouldn't.* Well instead of *can't, won't, don't,* and *shouldn't,* which the majority of the time emphasize the negative, why don't you jump on that positive thought path, that automatically manufactures words like *would, could, can, will,* and *do* instead. If that hasn't already happened to your satisfaction, there's no better time than now to increase their positive uses. I know that in this more negative than positive world, that presents a major challenge, because through your entire life, the negative incidents and circumstances are going to outweigh the positives at least two to one. So it's going to be a CHALLENGE EVERY DAY OF YOUR LIFE, TO BE MORE POSITIVE THAN NEGATIVE. That's why you must always be acutely aware of the vocabulary you develop and the verbiage you use. WORDS ARE YOUR REAL CURRENCY. In many critical life-changing instances, WORDS ARE OF GREATER VALUE THAN MONEY.

Now let's talk about us older guys. It seems the older we get, as the use of these negative words accumulate, no matter how smart we think we are, the more impact these questionable words seem to have on our thinking. Well every day you gotta fight them off. If you don't, they will become HABITUAL SPOILERS OF YOUR LIFE, AT THIS CRITICAL, TRANSITIONAL STAGE OF THE GAME.

Again, let's go back in time twenty to thirty years and recall our ambitious naive and idealistic time-frame. With all of our youthful life force, and our way-out hopes and dreams, with LITTLE EFFECT we easily fought off, those too-often negative thoughts and words. Now the same mission is going to seem a whole lot harder than it was then. At this stage, as opposed to your youth, it becomes HARDER TO FIGHT OFF NEGATIVE BUILD-UP. And those words like *can't* and *wouldn't* and *shouldn't* and *won't*, and *don't* when you are forty-five to fifty, as opposed to fifteen to twenty, seem to have much more of a PERSONALLY RESTRICTIVE AND OBSTRUCTIVE MEANING. That's Mr. Devil doing his deceiving dirty work. You have only one alternative: stop that negative seed-sowing son of a bitch's entrance into your mind. You must emphasize and give meaning to, and use more often, the words you should fill your vocabulary with. *Would, could, should, will, can* and *do*. Every last one, UPLIFTING, UPBEAT, SELF CONFIDENCE BUILDING WORDS. Whenever you are about to formulate a thought and speak it, you must keep these positive words at the forefront of your consciousness, and use them with frequency and authority. Those are the WORDS THAT WHEN SPOKEN REDUNDANTLY AND PASSIONATELY, ARE ABSOLUTELY GUARANTEED TO PRODUCE GRATIFYING RESULTS. This will have a major affirmative impact on your priorities, so you can optimize, and get much more value out of the next twenty to fifty years of your life. Their repetitious use on a daily basis IS A NECESSITY, to develop and maintain, a PERMANENTLY POSITIVE ATTITUDE.

If I've said this once, I've said it a thousand times, a hundred different ways, and in almost every observation you read, I'm going to keep reminding you: I've been through it, I've done it, and thank God I started doing it forty to fifty years ago right about your age. So don't hesitate, know for sure YOUR TIME NOW, IS MORE VALUABLE AND LIFE-ALTERING THAN

EVER. Again I say, just take a look at the life you have already lived, and many sacrifices you have already made. My greatest hope for you, sir, is that you will step up into the SECOND HALF OF YOUR LIFE, AT THE HIGHEST LEVEL OF QUALITY POSSIBLE, where positive words will definitely make the difference, on the rest of your life, being lived with INCREASED PRIDE, CONFIDENCE, DIGNITY, AND SELF ESTEEM. Qualities that will allow you to express yourself in an exuberant, upbeat, self-deserved way. THAT IS EXACTLY WHAT YOU ARE WORTHY OF, during this most valuable second half of life.

So when you speak with passion and purpose, take that quantum leap from *COULD* OR *SHOULD*, TO *CAN* AND *WILL*. That's how you create your own POSITIVE VOCABULARY! The sole purpose? A LIFETIME OF POSITIVE RESULTS.

History Lesson

47

Now, kind sir, if you have any doubts, any questions or concerns, about how great the gift of getting older is, even with all the increasing aches and pains produced by wear and tear, that sooner or later we all have to live through, here's what I suggest: go back in time, just two to three hundred years. Now I didn't say two to three thousand years in mankind's five-thousand-year DOCUMENTED HISTORY - of which two to three hundred is a drop of time in time's big bucket - I realize, particularly at my advanced age, the older you get, it is so easy to forget things you naturally take for granted. Every so often, we need a little reminder to help us remember, HOW BLESSED AND GIFTED WE ARE, AND HOW EXCEPTIONALLY WELL TIME HAS BEEN TO YOU AND I. So now we're going to take a relatively short trip back in history, that will make you appreciate by comparison, this little history lesson.

In a relatively short three-hundred-year journey back through time, are you aware of how many tens of millions of men and women, who were UNDER THE AGE OF FORTY, NEVER GOT TO SEE, FEEL, TOUCH, TASTE, SMELL, OR EVEN THINK ABOUT THEIR NEXT TOMORROW. Obviously fate and destiny, when it came to their longevity, did not treat them very well. There is no purer truth than mathematical truth, REAL DOCUMENTED NUMBERS DON'T LIE. In just those few hundred years, literally TENS OF MILLIONS of men under forty were KILLED IN WAR ALONE. Then there were millions more, young men and women, lost to natural disasters like earthquakes, volcanic eruptions, tsunamis, and a myriad of other natural disasters. But not you, sir. Think of all the thousands of diseases, many so catastrophic they can and do, snuff out life in the proverbial second. Heart disease, stroke, diabetes, Lou Gehrig's disease, Parkinson's syndrome, DISEASES THAT HAVE TAKEN THE LIVES OF MULTI-MILLIONS OF PEOPLE BETWEEN TWENTY AND FORTY YEARS OF AGE. Thank God that did not happen to you. Let me go a little younger for you, and I mean very, very young. Children between five and fifteen dying by the tens of thousands with child leukemia. THOSE NUMBERS <u>ARE REAL</u>.

That's how fragile life really is. That's why the likes of you and me should take stock, and count all the blessings for the good fortune, our LONGEVITY HAS AFFORDED US. You are already past forty, and hopefully functioning in generally good health. You could have suffered those same kind of misfortunes in your first forty years, but you were spared, WHICH THEY WERE NOT. That's when you should start to think: there but for the grace of God go I. You could have been denied the full human journey, THAT YOU ARE CURRENTLY ON. That's why the only way you should ever look at your aging process, is to know HOW BLESSED AND FORTUNATE YOU ARE to know you have all these extra decades for even further fulfillment. The TOTAL JOY of a well spent COMPLETE LIFE. Sir, never forget what long life affords you: the rare opportunity, of living up to and very possibly OVER ONE HUNDRED YEARS. So remember and be mindful always, of all those tens of millions that were dead before forty, in just three short centuries. YOU, SIR, ARE BEATING THE ODDS AND YOU SURE AS

HELL ARE BEATING THEM *BIG TIME*. Whether you are aware of it or not, that makes you, one of the rare privileged few, to have this opportunity of GETTING OLDER. Anything less than full, positive optimization of time, life's greatest gift would be life's greatest waste. Now when you put your life in perspective, by comparison, you'll agree how fair it has been. BITCH, GRIPE, COMPLAIN PAST FORTY? I don't think so by a long shot! So I got a better idea. How about being immensely GRATEFUL FOR EVERY DAY YOU GET OLDER. GETTING OLDER DOES NOT AND NEVER WILL MEAN, YOU ARE GETTING THE SHORT END OF THE STICK.

In almost every human with a positive mindset, just the opposite is true. Now does life have a beginning and an end for all of us? Of course it does. Without the word *end*, the word *beginning* wouldn't even exist. But right now, BOTH OF US ARE STILL VERY MUCH ALIVE. You at forty to sixty, me a few decades down the road. But one thing's for sure: WE'RE HOPEFULLY BOTH LIVING THIS DAY TO ITS FULLEST. That's why every day that follows, you should create your VERY OWN NEW, POSITIVE BEGINNING. Even though I may only have five years of new beginnings, if I'm lucky enough to live that long, you can bet your ass I'M NOT GOING TO WASTE ONE DAY. You may have fifty to sixty more years of making every day a positive new beginning. JUST DO IT ONE DAY AT A TIME, SIR, AND YOU WILL ALWAYS CONTROL THE KEYS TO YOUR <u>LONG-LIVED</u> KINGDOM. Even as we're living and breathing and aging, so many millions of men and women younger than you right now, WILL NEVER SEE THEIR NEXT SUNRISE. THEIR LIFE WILL BE OVER. That's why you should, with strong conviction, know every tomorrow left in your life, is a new beginning. THERE IS NO GREATER GIFT. Thousands who started this day alive, will have passed on before it ends. But obviously not you and me! You bet your ass, and every other body part you possess, that's a blessing.

Let me tell you something I say a lot, and mean every time I say it. With all the aches and pains aging can produce, I FIND IT HARD TO COMPLAIN AND BITCH. Now do we want them? Of course not. But even if something was life-threatening, at least you and I are still going to have the OPPORTUNITY TO FIGHT IT OFF, and keep ourselves alive as long as we can. So do like The Old Man does, sir: HANDLE IT, DEAL WITH IT, because I think that's a whole lot more preferable to the alternative, and certainly an indicator of your strength of character! So there's your three hundred year history lesson. Don't you ever let getting older DIMINISH THE VALUE of seeing your next sunrise and taking your next breath, which *THOSE TENS OF MILLIONS OF BODIES AND SOULS, WERE NEVER GRANTED*!

Tough Love

48

Let's face it, as we get older, the majority of us probably, more likely than not, have a serious problem, accepting the fact as we age THINGS CHANGE. Guys, things are always changing. They are bound to change thousands and thousands of times, in the course of your hopefully long journey through life. And I seriously believe this is one of the biggest problems we face as men. Now I want you to look at this piece on tough love with a thick skin and an open and fair attitude. I was certainly subjected to it, and a victim of FALSE PRIDE, AND AN EGO THAT WAS BLOWN OUT OF PROPORTION. I learned those two self-centered conditions can alter in a debilitating way, your reality. Well it did me, in a big way. Now I want you to know, if you continue down that negative path, of NOT FACING AND ACCEPTING the facts of nature and what is natural, but compromising your reality, your future world, if built on that flimsy a foundation, will easily become FRAGILE, MISGUIDED, FRUSTRATING, and ultimately UNFULFILLED.

YOU MUST ALWAYS BE <u>OBJECTIVE AND MATURE</u>, WHEN DEALING WITH YOUR REALITY. To over-compromise and allow self-deception can, more often than not, BE SELF DESTRUCTIVE IN NATURE. If you are not subjectively honest, there is a real possibility you will rationalize, even falsely adjust whatever the condition or situation is, THAT COULD BE OF GREAT IMPORTANCE IN YOUR LIFE. What I'm implying here, if you haven't already, and I sure as hell hope you have started down your positive path of change, YOU MUST STOP CHASING YESTERDAY, OR YOUR BETTER TOMORROW WILL NEVER HAVE A CHANCE IN HELL OF HAPPENING. You must never place more value on your past, than you do on the present and future. YOU CAN NEVER AGAIN LIVE IN IT. Pick out great memories from your past, of course. You can search them out all you want with vivid recollection, but those yesterdays CAN NEVER BE LIVED AGAIN. That's why when you UNREALISTICALLY OVER-GLAMORIZE your youth, it becomes even more elusive. I'm telling you, sir, the greater the effort you make to re-live the past, the greater your disappointment and removal from reality. That kind of thinking will set you up for a whole bunch of unfulfilled tomorrows. TALK ABOUT AN EXERCISE IN PROFOUND FUTILITY, AND PROLONGED FRUSTRATION.

So here's what The Old Man thinks ya gotta do: you must take all your valid human experiences, all those experiments of those first forty years, and from a POSITIVE, REALISTIC PERSPECTIVE, use them to not only improve upon, but definitely expand on the value of your second half of life. Now if this tough love hits a nerve, it's for good reason. As sure as rain is wet and hell is hot, if you are totally honest in self-appraisal, your life will become in greater proportion, much more rewarding, fulfilling, fruitful, by NEVER OVER-GLAMORIZING YOUR PAST.

Now that brings us to one of the biggest, in fact maybe *the* biggest frustrating pursuits as you get older. Let's take a little trip down below the belt, and have a man-to-man conversation about our little head! Let's face it, the reality for a lot of guys past forty and fifty? THEY DEVELOP A PENIS COMPLEX. This can be so consuming and intimidating, it has the potential to manifest itself into lower self-esteem, possibly creating A FLAWED MISCONCEPTION OF LESS SELF WORTH. Man's macho explanation? Comes from getting half or less erections than when they were in their twenties, which could easily lead you to falsely believing "I'm only half the man I was". If you think you are losing your manhood because you're only getting half the erections you did twenty or more years ago, without question, that is one of life's GREATEST FALLACIES. In fact, let me be more emphatically direct and politically totally incorrect. That is the biggest bunch of FALSELY MENTALLY MANIFESTED MACHO BULLSHIT EVER IMAGINED BY MAN'S "ME MAN, YOU WOMAN" PRIMITIVE MIND. Now let's add a little levity to that statement. Let's say you were still capable at fifty to seventy years of age, of getting five to ten erections a day like you did when you were twenty, again I say, THERE'S NOT A CHANCE IN HELL YOU'D KNOW WHAT TO DO WITH HALF OF THEM! Don't you ever consider thinking, that just because you may be getting fewer erections, you are less of a man. It is one of man's major crappy misconceptions, where his identity and self-respect are concerned. AND ANY MAN WORTH HIS SALT WOULD NEVER BUY INTO THAT KIND OF DISILLUSIONARY DILEMMA OF SELF DOUBT, AND ALLOW HIS INSECURITIES TO SUCK HIMSELF INTO, THAT KIND OF _TOTAL MISDIRECTION_ OF HIS LIFE. It's a safe bet that most every man reading this right now, weighs a hundred fifty pounds or more. Well I hate to tell you, your prick only weighs a few ounces! Why would any man let such a small part of himself, though important, be such a determining factor where his manhood is concerned? You must always keep your cock in perspective. IT IS NOT, NEVER HAS BEEN, NEVER WILL BE, <u>YOUR TRUE COMPASS IN LIFE</u>. And this is a valid observation, because Yours Truly sure as hell suffered through that kind of misconception of convoluted values. That's the kind of tough love I HAD TO DIRECT TO MYSELF, because I sure as hell was there, in a big way. So we all know, when we were twenty, that little lower head dominated, like a tuning fork ready for f-ing action. But past forty, fifty or sixty, if you keep thinking with your little head that HAS NO BRAINS, instead of the big head, where ALL YOUR BRAINS are suppose to be, you will be headed on a one-way trip, directly to the proverbial shit-house. And that's exactly what brother dick can do to ya, when you give it permission to dictate and dominate your destiny. YOU MUST HAVE YOUR PRIORITIES IN PROPER ORDER, AT THE AGE YOU ARE.

There is no subject in your life, that can produce a more dominant impact, than having a penis complex, and obsessing over it. What you were, and what you've done, is past history. Hopefully you have tons of great memories and exciting, interesting experiences, that went along with that HORMONALLY DRIVEN LEARNING LESSON. Because that's exactly what it was, sir: LEARNING LIFE'S LESSONS. The only purpose it should serve now, when used appropriately and within your capacities, is to make your life better from here on out. And every decade down the timeline of your life, don't worry. Take it from me, everything still works just fine, and it

169

will for you too, less frequently perhaps, but often enough, after all the wear and tear I've given this body, and that insatiably hungry hormonal part of it. It took a long time, but I finally got the message. KEN, DON'T MAKE A F-ING PIG OF YOURSELF! As sexually active as I was all those years ago, I'VE NEVER JUDGED OR EVALUATED MY MANHOOD BASED ON MY SEXUAL APPETITE, *NOR SHOULD YOU,* SIR. It's a battle you just can't win. Let me take it a step further. If I live so long and lose my libido completely, no more erections for Ken Dab-Row, you can bet your sweet ass, that right up to the very last day of my long life, I will still attempt to be any man's match. MY FULL MANHOOD will be TOTALLY INTACT.

So realize at your age, just to have it to use, no matter how frequently or infrequently, is nature's gift. Just think how good taking a piss feels when you really have to. Of course it's fun to look back, remember, and recall. I do it all the time, a part of almost every day. Naturally, the longer you live, the greater your memories become. THAT MEANS, AS YOU AGE, YOU'VE GOT MORE TO LOOK BACK ON. And that's what I hope we're doing right now with this little bit of toughened love: setting you up to make tomorrow's memories even more meaningful and more valuable, WHILE STILL LOOKING STRAIGHT AHEAD WITH PASSION AND PURPOSE. Don't tell me it can't be done, your Old Pops is still doing it! Know for sure, I advise you to use it wisely and discretely, sir. Take all those experiences you have had and apply them all with optimistic emphasis, to the sensational second half of your life. It could and will be hopefully waiting around every exciting corner as you conceive and conquer every coming year. You must use, as a positive, powerful force, all those memories to springboard yourself into your second forty, and know you are entitled to LIVE IT AT A LOFTIER, HIGHER LEVEL. Don't ever think or even entertain the thought, because of your age, YOU ARE HALF THE MAN AND ONLY HALF AS GOOD AS YOU WERE, because just the opposite can, should, and will be YOUR TRUTH. Only half the man? My ass! You are now on your journey of becoming twice the man, twice as good, twice as smart. Which qualifies and affords you TWICE THE REWARDS. JUST KEEP THAT PERKY PENIS OF YOURS IN PERSPECTIVE.

A little afterthought, kind sir: In this one life you have, you not only can look back, you have to look back. But young brother of mine, YOU CAN'T GO BACK. No one knows that better than this old guy. So make sure you use those past memories in a positive way to LOOK BACK ON, and you will assuredly secure GREATER SELF WORTH, and many more GRATIFYING TOMORROWS.

Richer And Stronger

49

Let's make this observation short, sweet, and to the point. Of course you want a RICHER, STRONGER life past forty. The primary ingredient in that requirement: you must be FLAWLESSLY HONEST WITH YOURSELF. As just observed, self-deception will misguide you. Honesty is the only way to make the most of the age you are, and know unequivocally WHO YOU ARE. And sir, I don't mean once in a while or now and then, I mean every day of the rest of your life. Based on honesty, you must reject any and all outside influences, that in any way attempt to alter or directly conflict with your strong mindset. A mindset that will assuredly produce YOUR REAL IDENTITY AND INDIVIDUALITY. If you bend, stretch, or rearrange the truth, so it's to your advantage, that would be considered self-deception.

Getting older means we must more efficiently power up our mental muscle, and make it the builder of your SELF RESPECT AND SELF WORTH. Two priceless personal qualities that must be solidly established during this phase of your life. HONESTY ALWAYS, WHEN CLASSIFYING WHAT YOU CONSIDER HIGHLY RELEVANT, IS FAIL-SAFE AND FOOL-PROOF.

Do this, sir, and the full purpose and meaning of your life's SECOND HALF will be much RICHER AND STRONGER, producing and sustaining GREATER ENDURING POSITIVE RESULTS.

Self-Doubt And Worry

50

We all have self-doubts and worries running around in our brain. DON'T LET THEM DOMINATE, and have a strong influence on your actions and reactions. If that occurs too frequently, you must put a stop to that kind of self-defeating thinking, and ask yourself in all honesty: why would any man treat himself that way, becoming a slave to that kind of conduct, WHICH IS EXACTLY WHAT SELF DOUBT AND WORRY DO TO YOU IF YOU ALLOW. Don't fall victim to them when you know they will feed and foster confusion, which will be a creator of continuing strife, even grief.

What you've got to do with self-doubt and unnecessary worry is, GIVE THEM BOTH A STIFF, FIRM KICK IN THE ASS, RIGHT OUT OF YOUR LIFE! Every human who has ever lived a long life did thousands of things, that they thought were wrong. WE ALL HAVE QUESTIONABLE JUDGMENT FROM TIME TO TIME. God, man, that's as natural and normal as breathing. A permanent human condition. It's impossible for any human on this planet, to do everything right all the time. Let me put it this way: if you are currently doing more things right than wrong, young brother, YOU'RE A WINNER. That will set up the criteria so you know what you've got to do, when your subjective judgment has been less than perfect, creating self-doubt and worry. Just OBJECTIVELY CORRECT IT. And like I've reiterated throughout many observations, always continue to love yourself and forgive yourself. I repeat: FORGIVE YOURSELF. I have justifiably been doing it hundreds of times every year of my life since early manhood, or self-doubt and worry would assuredly, have consumed me and won out, because WORRY IS THE MAIN BREEDER OF SELF DOUBT. Just don't walk around letting a feeling of guilt build up over your remaining years.

I am drop dead damn serious when I say to you, search, find, and validate every positive purpose and reason to LOVE YOURSELF THE BIGGEST PART OF EVERY DAY. In the final analysis, through the entire journey of your life, although thousands will cross your path, when push gets to shove, YOU ARE ULTIMATELY ALL YOU'VE GOT! WE COME INTO THIS WORLD ALONE, AND WE GO OUT ALONE. I don't want you to throw any of it away, worrying and doubting, fretting and stewing, giving guilt, self-doubt, and worry the open door to dominate your life. I want you to use every minute, of every hour, of every day, to JUSTIFIABLY TELL YOURSELF I deserve better, because you sure as hell do. So always power up your B&B, which means your brain and body, and turn better into best. Now I'm not patronizing you or blowing wind up your ass. Don't ever forget, sir, you have to live every minute of your life WITH YOU. Self-confidence, encouraging self-forgiveness? It don't get much better. Or self-doubt, producing worry and guilt? It can't get much worse. Do what this older man did, take the high road and lighten your mental load. Don't ever UNNECESSARILY, get DOWN ON YOURSELF and BEAT YOURSELF UP. Now, if someone is a natural born asshole, they deserve ten-fold the misery they create! But not you, pal, just keep MAXIMIZING THE LOVING OF YOUR LIFE, AND YOURSELF IN IT.

Brainless Head

51

As referred to in so many other observations, this I can guarantee: In my earlier years, like almost all sexually overactive men I ever knew, all of us were victims of being hungrily horny. What we didn't seem to know was if the worlds #1 surgeon did an autopsy on one thousand heads of one thousand penises, there's not A CHANCE IN HELL, HE'D FIND ONE SINGLE BRAIN CELL!

Talk about a brainless monster that every man is mated to for life, brother, your prick takes the prize, especially when you were fifteen to forty. Walk and strut around like it's his Royal Majesty: King Cock! Well be careful with that brainless monster, ESPECIALLY PAST FORTY, TRYING TO BE TWENTY AGAIN, because to be perfectly frank, my friend, that is the kind of King, that can and will make a complete fool out of you.

And if you're going to be honest and objective, you can never point the finger of blame, at any member of the opposite sex. Even if she is the sexiest, most gorgeous, seductive female you have ever laid eyes on, because literally speaking, she can never take your penis away. YOUR COCK IS CONNECTED TO YOU. Only you wear it and use it for life. But if you let it, here's what can happen: you sure as hell can allow her, TO OWN AND MANIPULATE YOUR ACTIONS, and CONTROL YOU THROUGH IT.

So what's the lesson here? I learned, as I got older and wiser, to cultivate the ability to control my sexual urges and appetites.

Which should be the case as you get smarter and use your well-earned mature judgment. As I just mentioned, this magnificent sex organ of yours, with its monstrous sexual appetite, IS ATTACHED TO YOU FOR LIFE. It is without question, on my priority list, one of the most important parts of manhood, as it should be. ABSOLUTELY NOTHING WRONG WITH THAT. But your job now MORE THAN EVER is to keep that MAGIC MAKING MONSTER OF YOURS UNDER *F-ING* CONTROL. I mean never, never ever let MACHO FALSE PRIDE THROUGH YOUR PENIS, take over emotional control, and make you a victim of YOUR UNCONTROLLED THOUGHTS AND ACTIONS.

So as you enter the second forty years of your life, or if you are already several years into it, and knowingly admit you lived largely through the actions of your brainless head more often than not, to a sensibly sensational, eyes wide and wisely open second half, be aware from this day on for the rest of your life, KNOW WHICH HEAD *YOUR BRAINS ARE IN*! You cannot and you must not, during this, the second half of your life, LET BROTHER DICK, BECOME THE TRUE *DIC*TATOR OF YOUR DESTINY.

Stifling Taboos

52

When it comes to working your way through the second half of life, what should be obvious is that you must adjust accordingly and sensibly, to the CONSTANT CHANGES IN YOUR LIFE. Old habits, as we have learned if we are realistic with ourselves, die hard. AND OLD HABITS ARE NOT ALWAYS GOOD HABITS. Of course they were developed during our most fragile formative period between ten and twenty, when we were very young, very impressionable, and NATURALLY INSECURE. Now I have personally labeled that kind of condition as a TABOO, because it can STIFLE the process of maturity. I'm talking about twenty to thirty years ago, when you were a lot more unsure of yourself than you are now. And although you thought your judgment was right-on at that time, you realize twenty to thirty years down the road of life by comparison, IT WAS NOWHERE NEAR AS GOOD AS IT IS NOW. All those things you DID THEN, that you definitely WOULD NOT DO NOW. What seemed so cool then, if you conducted yourself in the same manner today, just might seem dated and foolish. They are boyish values, that we all naturally must pass through to acquire our highly developed MATURE VALUES. So, false judgments and failed experiments, which is what the majority of your youth was, YOU MUST MAKE THEM A PERMANENT PART OF YOUR PAST. If you try to live them now, they will stifle your growth, and interfere and limit the successfully mature living of your life. That's your reality at forty to sixty years of age. MAKE NO MISTAKE, if you try to act like you are twenty again, it will in so many ways restrict, stifle, and frustrate your progress. God knows I sure as hell fell into that dark hole, and, sir, it bit me right in the ass. But I climbed out of that deep, dark, empty, and vain place, after my first forty, FREQUENTLY FAULTY YEARS. Your Old Pops here finally saw the brighter light of reality. So no matter how old you are now, I want you to look back and see CLEARLY AND ACCURATELY, what your life was at fifteen to twenty-five. All those inconsistencies and the self-doubt they created that held you back, that's exactly what I mean when I use the term: YOUR STIFLING TABOOS! If you haven't already, you must GET AHEAD OF THEM AND LEARN TO LEAVE THEM BEHIND, or those youthful STIFLING TABOOS can adversely affect you for the rest of your life.

I'll assume YOU HAVE ACQUIRED A LITTLE MORE WISDOM. That will create the mental power and capability, to fundamentally discard all those old negative taboos. Therein lies the BLESSING, OF GETTING SMARTER AND WISER AS YOU GET OLDER. IN STEPS MATURITY IN THE FORM OF REALITY, SECURITY, AND WELL DIRECTED LONG-TERM VISION. That will provide the light that will guide you and allow you to find and be THAT PROUD AND EVEN MORE ACCOMPLISHED MIDDLE-AGED MAN YOU KNOW YOU SHOULD BE.

One Day At A Time

53

There should never be a doubt in your mind that every day is different, NO TWO DAYS ARE EVER EXACTLY ALIKE. It wouldn't make any difference if you lived two hundred years. No two days will ever be identical. But there is one fundamental you can take into every day: YOU, BEING UPBEAT AND POSITIVE ABOUT YOUR LIFE. If the mood you wake up to contains any negativity, put your stronger, more positive attitude in play and clear that negativity out of your brain, or at the very least neutralize it. You must realize and accept, you have the ability and self-esteem, to make that your reality. Let me tell you why. We are the only species on the planet that has a consciousness. We can determine the mood we want to be in. When you actively exercise your CONSCIOUSNESS, you can CHOOSE ITS DIRECTION, to justify the positive side of any particular situation on that day of your life.

Now the two most needed qualities to affect that kind of mindset, are REALITY AND OBJECTIVITY. As I've mentioned frequently, this world we live in by its very nature, is more contrary and negative than it is positive and inspiring. Just take a look at recent history, no less ancient history. Life being more negative than positive for mankind has been around for centuries, even millenniums. All those thousands of years mankind has lived and survived since time immemorial. Only TEN TO FIFTEEN PERCENT OF THE TIME – PEACE. EIGHTY-FIVE TO NINETY PERCENT OF THE TIME – WAR AND HUMAN DISCORD. So there's no question in my mind, that when surrounded by that kind of pessimistic and stress-inducing environment, it can easily rub off and be debilitating and discouraging. If you allow yourself to become a reaction, instead of CONSCIOUSLY initiating your choice of conduct, you can subconsciously fall victim. Well be careful and be aware, and just DON'T DO IT, DON'T YOU DO IT! Because, kind sir, that is going to be your battle for life, and it's always going to be there, and the odds are going to be overwhelmingly, contrary and negative. And that applies to all people, at any age. But now past forty, it is so much more important to CONTROL THAT CONSCIOUSNESS OF YOURS. It is of the utmost relevance to your survival, that you mentally get light on your feet, and ABSOLUTELY REFUSE, to let anything, any day of your life, drag you down and keep you down. Now are certain things that happen on a day-to-day basis, going to knock you on your ass? Absolutely! But you don't just lay there, sir, you get the hell up! And if you keep getting knocked down again, KEEP GETTING UP. You can't let life's adversities beat and defeat you, badly damaging your spirit and hope. Through your will, discipline, and determination, take on any negative condition, AND REVERSE IT.

There are two words that I use frequently in these many observations: ordinary and extraordinary. The word *ordinary* doesn't really say much. In a negative sense, who the hell wants to be ordinary? Not you, not me! But so many times, because of our NATURAL INBORN INSECURITIES, that's who we think we are. Almost like saying average. Well even though that may sound acceptable, it should never be something you settle for or aspire to. I see it from a different perspective, sir. I don't want you to ever think, you are ordinary, when you have THE ABILITY TO BE EXTRAORDINARY AND ABOVE AVERAGE. And God, man, don't ever forget, of all the seven billion-plus people on this planet, as justifiably CONFIRMED throughout this book, you truly are THAT ONE-OF-A-KIND. You can never be duplicated or replaced. Which means you are an original thinker, whether you know it or not. And that is diametrically opposed and just the opposite of *ORDINARY AND AVERAGE* when you put it in that context. The only potential obstacle to all these observations that I've just made is you. YOU GOTTA BELIEVE DEEPLY AND COMPLETELY, <u>THIS CAN BE YOUR REALITY</u>! You must make it one of your highest consistent priorities. If you don't, in all probability, it will have very little chance of surviving.

So even if you feel extraordinary, above average, KEEP WORKING AT IT, so that it becomes even more of a normal state of mind, of WHO YOU REALLY ARE. Walk like it, talk like it, think like it, and let your body language physically express that kind of self-assuredness. Those boyish imperfections of youth, are always going to be in the back of your mind. Well to the best of your ability, right now is the perfect time to reduce their negative impact. YOU CAN FINALLY THROW OFF ALL THOSE BOYISH, INSECURE, SELF DOUBTING, PSYCHOLOGICAL SHACKLES, that come back every now and then to haunt so many men past forty. What this much older man is attempting to tell you is, after you learn from them, please, sir, put them on the back burner of your life, and seriously pursue your second half of life, YOUR REAL MANHOOD. And if those negative youthful memories keep trying to impose self-

181

doubt and insecurity, KICK THEM THE HELL OUT OF YOUR LIFE. If you don't, they could hold you captive. Keep the fire in your belly burning to its FULLEST IN A MATURE WAY. I have found no more effective way to put purpose and passion, in the pursuit of my desires and ambitions. Keep fueling that flame. Keep it burning big and bright, making all your positive thoughts BRIGHTER AND STRONGER, FROM FORTY TO EIGHTY-PLUS.

Pursue that, and your life will be exceptional past forty, because now you know, you must make this day more fulfilling than the previous, because it's ONE DAY LESS YOU HAVE TO LIVE. So no matter how big the obstacles in life seem to be, you must keep your life going stronger, getting better and bigger. Sir, you are fully mentally equipped, to exceed anything that happened before you were forty, and make the NEXT FIFTY YEARS OF YOUR LIFE MORE MEANINGFUL AND VALUABLE. *Living proof is writing these words*! When you finally arrive where I am, and having expanded your positive perspectives over a full lifetime, YOU WILL LITERALLY ASTOUND YOURSELF, knowing without question that you have discovered the main purpose of a more fulfilling second half. That must always be your first order of business, one day at a time. So open that fine mind of yours, and expand on that FREE-SPIRITED POSITIVE THINKING and put it into full-time action for the rest of your ONE DAY AT A TIME, LIFETIME.

Be Proud

54

When you get a new suit or a new outfit that you really like, you look at that reflection in the mirror, and boy, do you love what you see looking back at you, and a big smile of pride comes across your face. That's you, BEING PROUD OF YOURSELF. Well that's the way you should always think, not just when you are looking in the mirror! Through dogged determination, always elevate your self-worth. You must resolve any obstacle in your life, in your own, POSITIVE, DESERVED, PROUD WAY.

It's rewarding. You know the feeling: you take that deep breath, you expand that chest of yours, and you feel good about yourself all over. It's a momentary state of complete mental and physical gratification. THAT'S WHAT BEING <u>REALISTICALLY</u> PROUD IS ALL ABOUT. And that's a must YOU MUST FIRMLY BELIEVE. You're not just expanding your chest, you're expanding on your overall self-image of PERSONAL WORTH. I know it's not going to be easy, but that's how you must think in every situation and occurrence during this great transition. Remember always, YOU MUST MAKE EVERY EFFORT HUMANLY POSSIBLE, TO BE SUPREMELY PROUD OF WHO AND WHAT YOU ARE. If somebody makes a suggestion that can improve your quality of life, certainly be attentive, open minded. But on this one and only day you are living in, if you want to stay proud and positive, NEVER LET ANYBODY THAT HAS ANY DISPARAGING THOUGHTS OR NEGATIVITY, APPROACH YOU. If that happens and you allow it to happen and become an influence, it could detract from the POSITIVE, POWERFUL, PROUD APPROACH YOU ARE FEELING. Always have your antenna out for that kind of subtly corrosive attitude. The moment you sense any kind of negative reference, to any consequential situation that is in your life at any time, CUT IT OFF. Disengage. Any indication, any outside input that could produce an over-emotional response and get out of control, IMMEDIATELY WALK AWAY. That is the exact kind of person or persons, that will never produce positive results. Know your psychological enemies. Keep them out of your life. ALWAYS BE PROUD OF WHO YOU ARE.

One more time for the memory: For the rest of your life, love exactly who you are AND BE PROUD OF IT. You can make that happen if you live this day and every day that follows with no apologies, no regrets, always finding good reason to justify and feel, REALISTICALLY PROUD of yourself.

Let me leave you with a final thought. In the course of this day, this moment right now, you make a judgment that could have been a little more accurate, or produced a better result, or face a contrary condition that you could have handled maybe a little better, DON'T BEAT YOURSELF UP OVER IT. And most assuredly eliminate any unjustifiable guilt, and replace it with a GIANT PORTION OF PRIDE. If that's your current mindset, sir, terrific! If not, it is of the utmost importance YOU ELEVATE YOUR PERSONAL, PROUD OPINION OF YOURSELF. Do that, and keep deservedly doing it, and you will ALWAYS, be proud of WHO AND WHAT YOU ARE.

Three Major Categories

55

Depending on how specific you want to be, your life can be broken down into hundreds, even thousands of categories and subcategories. But I believe if you keep it simple and easily definable, not only do you create fewer sizable problems and complications, but more important, SMALLER ONES THAT ARE MORE EASILY SOLVED. So although there are thousands of situations, covering hundreds of different conditions, they fundamentally fall under three categories, and you are going to find that all other subcategories come under these three. And, sir, these general categories can and will easily toy with your emotions. *People, things,* and THE *SITUATIONS* those people and things create.

When you think about it, that can represent as much as sixty to eighty percent of every waking hour. So if any part of that percentage is going to be positive, it must be handled with EMOTIONAL MATURITY. What your challenge is now, was my challenge then. All of my life, I expected the people, the things, and the situations created by them, to have a strong emotional impact. So I'm going to give you an honest, self-observation. I haven't always handled my emotions, even in my thirties, WITH THE MATURITY REQUIRED. But being a realist, and not falsely justifying my conduct, I always knew when I was coming up short, and objectively through honest evaluation, figured out accurately what I had to do TO CORRECT AND ALTER IT. So when your emotions get a little frayed and out of control, the most practical thing you can do is

185

take all those people, things, and the situations in your life, and as OBJECTIVELY and CALMLY as possible, understand them for what they ACTUALLY REPRESENT. Don't over-emotionally blow them out of realistic proportion to UNREALISTICALLY defend your position. Because if you do, the majority of people, things, and all the experiences in your life, can and will become burdensome. It is under those conditions that your JUDGMENT CAN CERTAINLY BECOME CONFUSED AND MISGUIDED. The only words that can eliminate that aimless direction is *your practice of self-control.* There is no doubt about it, it is one of the rock-solid foundational facts of life. WHEN YOU KEEP YOUR EMOTIONS UNDER CONTROL the majority of the time - because none of us can do it all the time - only then does the possibility exist, that you can become the TRUE MASTER OF YOUR OWN MIND, and direct your own destiny with accuracy and precision.

Now, is it going to be a struggle and a challenge every day for the rest of your life? You bet your ass it is. You and every single human being on this planet. Even at this late stage of my life, it still is for me. Only one big difference: I know and expect it. It's my responsibility and I would never blame anybody else for it. And I'm going to make sure that's the way it will remain, for the rest of my life. This is everybody's human condition. SO WHAT! HANDLE IT! Expect the battle and the struggle. Know it's never been easy, and know for sure it's going to get a hell of a lot tougher as you get older. Again, so what! What's the big deal? At this late stage of my life, has it been worth the effort? ABSOLUTELY! After almost a century of living, it has produced for me, the highest quality of life I could have ever imagined. So no matter how immense your life-long challenge of PEOPLE, THINGS, AND THE SITUATIONS THEY CREATE may seem, accept it as your own long-term lifetime reality. Then with authority and foresight, handle it with FORCEFUL FEARLESSNESS.

We all know how many dozens of people are involved in our life every day. Well that's not going to change, that's going to be repeated every single day for the rest of your life. So remember, sir, under any conditions, with all these people in your life, when you take emotional control of those three major categories - things, people, and the situations they create – YOU CAN EVALUATE THEM WITH EMOTIONALLY CONTROLLED HONEST PERSPECTIVE. But when you lose emotional control in those three categories, to some degree you always seem to lose and rarely win, in a way that makes you proud of your actions. Even when you think you have won, for all practical purposes, that could be a less than accurate rationalization. So think about what I just told you, because in the long run, there is no more wonderful feeling in the world, than you knowing your life over the long haul, will present literally thousands of opportunities, FOR YOU TO BE AND FEEL LIKE A REAL WINNER IN LIFE. Now that's how I want you to visually in your mind's eye see yourself, even though we all know realistically, nothing goes a hundred percent right ALL THE TIME. So here's the caveat: If you're not quite, but almost completely, in charge of the way you feel, no matter what those people, things, and situations throw at you, you know you're going to be on guard and ready to handle it. AND THAT'S WHERE EMOTIONAL CONTROL MEANS SO MUCH. Every single twenty-four hours, you're going to be challenged to concentrate, focus, and elevate to its highest level, your emotional control. The opportunity for you to make the vast majority of things in your life positive is there. The results you will get, from being in CHARGE OF YOUR EMOTIONS will elevate your quality of life, in every respect. You are setting yourself up for a bunch of better confidence and character-building tomorrows. You must always work at, and watch, the quality of your life, take that quantum leap upwards.

Once you elevate and deepen that belief of greater self-worth, that will be the indicator you are exercising your consciousness, IN SEARCH OF YOUR PERMANENTLY POSITIVE SECURE AND OBJECTIVE IDENTITY. Well, when that's fully developed, you will never let go of that image. THAT WILL BE THE REAL WELL-GROUNDED YOU. So, kind sir, keep it simple, remember always those three categories: *People, things, and the situations they create*. They will be all around you, every day of your life! They must be handled intelligently and wisely, because they are always going to generate more often than not negativity. I want you to JUMP INTO YOUR VERY OWN BUBBLE OF *IMPENETRABLE* POSITIVITY, that is YOURS EXCLUSIVELY. You allow nobody or nothing who doesn't think in a similar way, to have access to your personal, positive bubble. And don't you ever doubt or question the fact that you can be and must be, THE LORD AND MASTER OF YOUR OWN LIFE, FOR THE WHOLE OF YOUR LIFE, UNDER ANY AND ALL CONDITIONS. Savvy? Good!

You May Think: What The Heck, It's Only My Neck

56

Let's examine some body parts that we think are important. The face is one. We'd all love to be handsome, with near perfect features. Some guys are so self-conscious about that, they wind up combing their hair ten or fifteen minutes every morning. Then there's the physique. That's broken down into many body parts that we're proud of, or should be proud of if we're in shape. Every guy likes to have great guns. Big, well developed chest. And what guy wouldn't want that "V" shape created by a small waist, leading up to the wide back. And of course the legs. Now that would be a body any man would be proud of, and justifiably so. But I think we left out, possibly the most useful body part of all: YOUR NECK! If you couldn't move it, or if it was broken or lacked flexibility, you would have no choice but to look straight ahead. That wonderful thing called the neck, that you normally can turn left to right, right to left, almost one hundred eighty degrees, that we use almost every minute of our life, we take for granted, because the neck does that all by itself. If your neck had no flexibility, the only way you could view all your surroundings would be by moving your feet. THANK GOD FOR NECK MOVEMENT! And not only can you look around to a hundred eighty degrees, you can lift that head up, or let it drop down. Personally I prefer lifting your head up, because most times when I see a head hanging down, IT'S USUALLY WEARING A FROWN. Well that just might be the wrong way to go through this day. I want you to use your neck to LIFT THAT HEAD OF

YOURS UP HIGH! It will help square up your shoulders, straighten and stiffen that back, and allow you to display a CONFIDENT, IN-CHARGE, VISUAL PRESENCE. Then turn it left and turn it right, because no matter where you are, there's tons of good stuff to be found, when you look around. AND THAT WON'T HAPPEN WHEN YOUR HEAD IS HANGING DOWN. And we're not just talking about what you see, your neck is involved with a whole lot more than the sense of sight. It enhances all your other senses. SMELL, TASTE, AND HEARING. No other body part can make all those other senses, MULTIPLE TIMES MORE POWERFUL, than your neck. Have that neck keep your head held high, never letting it hang down in dismay.

When you consciously USE YOUR NECK TO HOLD THAT HEAD OF YOURS UP HIGH every day, you will find RESULTS BEYOND STIMULATING. Just keep it turning and moving, searching for something good to look at. Then appreciate it through ALL YOUR OTHER SENSES. Man, what a selection you got. A beautiful woman, a mountaintop, a blue sky, and a thousand more things for you to discover, find, and view, all because of the movement of your neck. Without it, just think of the visual feast you would fail to see, if your head was more often than not hanging down or immobilized. You bet, you can use that fully flexible neck for everything it's worth. It will keep you on the feel-good road of life! All those things I just mentioned? You know they're going to put a smile on your face! Use that hundred eighty-degree movement that neck of yours provides, TO TAKE IN AND TASTE ALL THAT LIFE HAS TO OFFER.

Take Charge

57

Look, I know it's not easy to do, in fact that old expression "it's easier to say than do", really applies here. Every man I've ever known, loves the feeling of TAKING CHARGE. Of expressing authority, and getting a positive, respectful response. How many times have you said to yourself, I'm going to take charge of this or take charge of that. Let's face it, WE DO LOVE THAT FEELING OF AUTHORITY and taking charge, of as many things in our life as we possibly can. But, sir, to make that happen, you gotta say to yourself and truly believe: "NOBODY IS IN CHARGE OF MY LIFE BUT ME!" We both know that is much more easily said than done. Well for all it's worth, believe this: if you haven't already taken complete charge of your life, KNOW IT CAN BE DONE. Power up that mental muscle. Know and show the strength of character and personal dignity necessary. Only then can you realistically make every moment of every day, of your PERSONAL PRIVATE LIFE, obedient to your will. I am talking about being obediently responsive to your PERSONAL, positive sense of insight. And you have those affirmative components in dominant abundance built right in you. Which means any time you want to, you can exercise the power to DEFINITELY TAKE CHARGE, and make anything not harmful in nature, happen, THAT IS AN ADVANTAGE TO YOU PERSONALLY.

But as mentioned frequently, you must be careful of negative words, because they can be troublesome. One main word that can become a barrier to you being in charge is *worry*. Sorry guys, we all got worries to deal with. Man, I've had a million in my lifetime. But I somehow knew they're a part of every human's life experience, at any given time on any given day, and that means your life, for your entire life. THERE WILL ALWAYS BE SOMETHING TO WORRY ABOUT. So here's how I handle it. When I say *worry*, I put a question mark behind it. And the answer to the question, is another word with a question mark: Why? These are two words, when used to separately describe different situations, can be very closely related to weakness. But, when you say *why* after *worry* – as in ME, WORRY? WHY! - you give it an assertive positive connotation. As you probably know by experience, the MORE YOU WORRY, the WEAKER YOUR WILL to minimize and reduce its impact. Well worries are as much a part of life as breathing, they go with the territory, you got a lot of company. But you, sir, gotta do what so many people don't even attempt. You must authoritatively take charge of your worries and RESOLVE THEM from A POSITION OF POSITIVE STRENGTH AND DECISIVENESS. Only then can you deal successfully with them.

When you take charge, you will have given yourself the opportunity to experience, one of life's truest forms of fulfillment called PEACE OF MIND. Don't question yourself unnecessarily, by expanding on whatever that worry is or you believe it to be. All you have to know, IT IS IN YOUR CAPACITY, to alter its effect. Only then will the door open for you to walk through and TAKE CHARGE of the MAJOR PERSONAL MOMENTS of your life.

Negative Environment

58

Maybe the worst word in the world, and one I use so often in almost every observation, when describing a condition or a situation, is the word *NEGATIVE*. What happens in your life consciously and subconsciously, even unknowingly, is that useless word *negative,* used much too often to describe whatever any situation might be. Think about it, unintentionally we repeat that lousy word so often, that if we're not careful, it can and will easily become a PERMANENT PART OF OUR THOUGHT PROCESSES AND OUR VOCABULARY. This can greatly influence our daily environment and penetrate our lifestyle. Now I understand, that when you live through a long eighty-five to a hundred-year life, thousands of negatives are going to show their ugly face. Well again, kind sir, you are not alone. That is definitely a part of the human journey for everybody. But the bigger danger is to get involved long-term and find yourself living in a NEGATIVE ENVIRONMENT, because that will produce a condition where you start to think: THAT'S THE WAY THINGS NORMALLY ARE FOR ME. Well that's just a downright falsehood, and sure as hell not normal. How could anything with a pathway that discouraging and dangerous be worth following. So be very careful. Know that for a good part of any day, the word *negative* is gonna be involved in your thoughts and conversations. That does not mean, IT SHOULD DOMINATE YOUR EVERYDAY WAY OF THINKING. Work your way as rapidly through any kind of negative situation, THEN EXIT OUT OF IT. It's really as simple as that! Your choice: keep something negative permanently on your mind, or capitalize on your positive attitude, to minimize its impact. Then take it a step further and dispose of it as rapidly as possible, TO INCREASE YOUR POSITIVITY ON LIFE, which will automatically DECREASE NEGATIVE CONTENT. Work at it until that negative content is reduced to a minimum or ELIMINATED. In most every situation you are confronted with, in almost every aspect of your life, this is so almighty important: Unless you are threatened in a harmful way, you always have a choice. Many times we find ourselves surrounded by uncomfortable and awkward conditions. But we cannot, and in this case you must not, let them dominate. ALWAYS YOUR CHOICE.

Now how do we do that? As previously mentioned, we have our major senses of sight, sound, touch, taste, and smell. You gotta use those senses to take POSITIVE POSSESSION OF NEGATIVE MOMENTS. Get that powerful mind of yours in high gear, because that's the only instrument you have, to confront any form of negativity in your life. So know you are equipped to combat it. You have all those weapons in your MENTAL ARSENAL. You can change from negative to positive, in that moment you are living in. Those five senses you possess WILL STRENGTHEN YOUR PHYSICAL, MENTAL, AND PSYCHOLOGICAL POWERS. Focus on all of them concurrently in a positive way, when something you don't want to see, hear, or feel is about to be initiated.

So many things to see and smile about. So many ways to appreciate every single second of your life. How fortunate you are to have the gift of good vision. All those elements, all those things that you could easily take for granted, outside of your next breath, ARE BY FAR THE GREATEST GIFTS IN THE LIVING OF YOUR LIFE. Use those five senses of yours as often as possible in a positive way. What a powerful, psychological weapon to MINIMIZE YOUR PREOCCUPATIONS OF A NEGATIVE ENVIRONMENT.

That's how you, with YOUR POWER-PACKED THINKING, take complete control personally, and reduce the importance of any negative situation or condition. In the final analysis, through that kind of long-term ultra-strong mind control, YOU CAN NOT ONLY REDUCE, BUT EVEN DISPOSE OF, WHATEVER NEGATIVES YOU THINK MIGHT EXIST IN YOUR LIFE. That's how you ultimately, completely, make substantially and proportionately more dominant, YOUR PERMANENTLY POSITIVE MINDSET.

Physical Condition

59

Like the hour hand on a clock, you can have your nose five inches away from it, focus on it completely, even through a strong magnifying glass, and chances are, you will never see the hour hand is moving. But, sir, make no mistake, that hour hand of that clock never stops for ONE FRACTION OF A SECOND OF YOUR LIFE. My point? That's not only how life can be, that is exactly how life is. So obviously, like that deceptive hour hand on a clock, you are not going to see physical change one day at a time, no less a week, a month, or sometimes even a year or two. But make no mistake, every second, minute, day, week, month, or year, WE ARE EXPERIENCING OUR OWN PHYSICAL CHANGE. And as we get older, particularly between forty and sixty, we start to, in a very insidiously slow way, lose some of our physical strength and stamina. So know beforehand, YOUR PHYSICAL CHANGE IS DEFINITELY ALWAYS TAKING PLACE. And during this transitional period in your life, there is going to be a hell of a lot of it. So you gotta psychologically prepare yourself for it. That is the only way to set yourself up for, and be ready to fearlessly accept the challenge. KNOW IT'S COMING! Accept the challenge you are facing for what it is, A BASIC FUNDAMENTAL ACT AND FACT OF NATURE. That's why you should at least optimize your physical potential, minimizing its reduction in strength and stamina, that getting older is bound to have. What you cannot or should not do, and hopefully what you will never do for as long as you live, is QUIT ON YOURSELF PHYSICALLY OR, FOR THAT MATTER,

MENTALLY. Even though this observation is focusing on the physical, never underestimate the power of the mind, to have great influence on your healthier body. Because my friend, that's where it all starts, in your brain. Which takes us to the next step in this progression.

Let's discuss slowing down. Slowing down? Now although those are not dirty words, and in fact, they are not specifically negative words, like it or not, over the course of the rest of your life from here on out, you and everybody approximately your age is in the process, no matter how subtle, of slowing down. Unless you suffer a physical condition that limits and restricts you, the rate at which that progresses IS ENTIRELY IN YOUR POWER TO CONTROL. And kind sir, don't forget who is talking to you. I'm still physically strong thank God with tons of energy. And fortunately have been blessed with clarity of thought, which would lead many to believe: "In year 90? He still hasn't slowed down? *Wow*!" Well my friend, that would be a misevaluation, and total self-deception on my part! You bet I have slowed down! And I don't mean maybe or I think so. I POSITIVELY HAVE SLOWED DOWN PHYSICALLY. So even though the muscle mass is still there, I do not have the same strength, flexibility, and stamina, that I had thirty to fifty years ago. After extended living and use, human body parts, like part of any machine, tend to show wear and tear. SO NO MATTER WHO YOU ARE, TIME AND TIDE ARE GOING TO TAKE THEIR TOLL. They have on me, but that's OK, I accept it, I know it's IN THE MASTER PLAN. But the key to optimizing that master plan is to lengthen and strengthen the time it takes. All I want you to do, is make the most of your mental and physical potential. Now let me tell you what I haven't done, what I will never do, IS QUIT, or even think of quitting physically, or mentally. I will maintain to its max, til my last day of life, my strong, fearless ways. Now if you have already started, great. If not, at forty-plus, IT'S TIME TO START. You must never, ever quit, for one second, the living of your life to its absolute highest physical potential. When you RESTRICT AND LIMIT YOURSELF PHYSICALLY, what you are subconsciously doing, YOU ARE LETTING THE WALLS THAT WIDEN AND BROADEN YOUR LIVING EXPERIENCE, *CLOSE IN ON YOU*. Please, young brother, with fifty or more years to live, WHY IN THE HELL WOULD ANY MAN ALLOW HIMSELF TO FALL VICTIM, TO THAT KIND OF DESTRUCTIVE SELF-INFLICTED BEHAVIOR.

Whatever condition that body of yours is in, as long as you are not physically infirmed or restricted, YOU ABSOLUTELY CAN SLOW DOWN THE AGING PROCESS. It's never going to be reversed, that is pure myth. Don't you ever buy into that kind of quackery! But also know that you are endowed with the strength, mentally to enhance physically, THE SLOWING DOWN DRAMATICALLY, OF YOUR RATE OF DECLINE.

So no matter how tough it seems, and whatever your limitations are past forty, always do the best you possibly can, to activate and affect your best results physically. Now after all that's been said in this observation, THINK HOW SIMPLE, SENSIBLE, UNCOMPLICATED AND DOABLE THIS ENTIRE PROCESS REALLY IS. Knowing, even at seventy-plus, the possibilities ARE STILL THERE, if you make the effort to produce positive results. And I don't just mean physically, but in every other area of your collective mentality. So develop and get into that habit, because the reality is, for the umpteenth time, as you get older, it is not going to get any easier. Just accept it with positive, dogged determination. I repeat, IT'S GOING TO GET TOUGHER, AND YOU GOTTA GET TOUGHER WITH IT, AND TOUGH IT OUT. Come on, my better than good man-in-the-middle, who would know better than your Old Pops, it's never too late. And when you fearlessly do, always keep pursuing the physical, it will PEAK YOU MENTALLY, and strengthen your psyche. When you get your yin and yang accurately balanced, your mental and physical will operate more harmoniously. And that will support and sustain you, when you firmly commit to that positive mindset.

Hard to overemphasize how relevant this is. WITHOUT that kind of strong mental and physical connection, life can, as years pass, UNNECESSARILY lose, little by little, meaning and purpose. I see it all around me in my contemporaries, no less men ten to twenty years younger than me. THAT'S HOW IMPORTANT AND VITALLY RELEVANT YOUR PHYSICAL CONDITION IS, to the greatly increased quality of your remaining long human journey. No matter how smart and respected you are, when you think your life may start to lose positive purpose, that will be one sad moment. IT IS DEFINITELY ONE HUNDRED PERCENT AVOIDABLE, AND NEVER HAS TO HAPPEN TO YOU for as long as God and nature afford you, the gift of life.

Waste Not

60

Not only what crosses your mind, but what do you actually think when I say the word *strength*? I would imagine the first thought would be muscles, power, being physically strong. But in reality, that's your OUTER STRENGTH. You could be built like a two hundred fifty-pound rock. Possess tremendous power. And of course that's an asset, your OUTER STRENGTH IS OBVIOUSLY IMPORTANT. God knows that after over seventy years in the gym, it has certainly been a great blessing and one of the most important components of my life. I honestly believe, under a variety of very difficult and adverse conditions, my strength has served me well. But, even after all that time, effort, and energy expended to build my body, I must admit, so many other strengths are just as, and in many cases MORE IMPORTANT, THAN MUSCULAR STRENGTH. Of course I'm talking about the development and sustaining power, of what I describe and label YOUR MANY INNER STRENGTHS.

You know, there are certain words we throw around and use loosely, too often failing to live up to their OPTIMUM INTERPRETATION. Well, it's these very same words, that we should concentrate, focus, and expand on, so we can extract their full and accurate meaning, and THOROUGHLY UNDERSTAND, the relevance and importance they have elevating the quality of our life. Powerful, positive words like *discipline*, *willpower*, *character*, *ethics*, *principles*, and that overall encompassing word, INTEGRITY. Because without them, no matter how successful you may be in business, or other areas of your life, and regardless of how much outer strength you've developed and built, if you are LACKING IN ANY OF THESE INNER STRENGTHS, you will also lack proportionately, the self-respect and self-worth so essential to YOUR FULL SUCCESS as a human being.

That's why these valuable and absolutely necessary human qualities of inner strength, no matter how much of them you are putting into play right now, it's of vital importance, THAT YOU FURTHER DEVELOP THEM so they can be used with increased activity, productively optimizing your life, during this mid-life merry-go-round, of MIXED EMOTIONS AND ADJUSTED PRIORITIES. You heard The Old Muscle Man right, sir. Without all these INNER QUALITIES playing a highly valuable part in your life, all your outer muscles, will have VERY LITTLE LONG-LIVED MEANING. And to prove that point, let's compare the human species, with some of the two and four legged creatures we share this planet with. However strong a man can become physically, a bear or a bull or a Silverback gorilla, are all so superior in strength, that any one of these magnificent creatures are ten to fifty times stronger, than the strongest man who ever lived. But in their case, as opposed to ours, all that animal physical strength, is TOTALLY CONTROLLED ONE HUNDRED PERCENT BY INSTINCT. And instinct in most any emotional form, has a tendency to be extreme, initiating and accentuating greater uncontrolled anger, that can easily take on a destructive form.

Now let's get back to the human species. I want you to think about all the times in the course of your life to this point, where you put your OUTER STRENGTH IN PLAY, because you were overreacting emotionally. How many of those times when you were out of control, would it have been much more important, to monitor and BE IN CONTROL OF YOUR OUTER STRENGTH? In spite of my strong beliefs of nourishing and strengthening the body, and how essential that has been to me, the point I'm making in this observation, is for you to give an even HIGHER PRIORITY, TO YOUR INNER STRENGTHS. And these inner strengths are, a very rare quality that only humans have. Out of over ten thousand species of mammals, no other two or four-legged creature on this planet, has the one quality only humans have. WE have been endowed with a much higher level of CONSCIOUSNESS. WE have the ability to conscientiously differentiate. WE can choose, evaluate, disseminate, and rationally THINK THINGS THROUGH. What a great and VALUABLE TOOL that is, when used to CONTROL OUR EMOTIONS. I know how hard it is to fight those animal urges and base instincts, because I'm loaded with them. So whatever adversity arises in my life, that I know could anger me to the brink of being emotionally out of control, if I didn't objectively think them through, and reacted only on my instincts to those conditions and situations, I would have lived a life completely out of control. I would have created for myself insurmountable, unsolvable problems. THAT'S WHY YOU MUST NOT LET YOUR INSTINCTS DOMINATE YOUR EMOTIONAL REACTIONS. I don't want you to rationalize, where honesty and truth in their purest form come into play. Ask yourself: "Have I developed to their potential, all my inner strengths and qualities? Can I exercise more understanding? Can

202

I be more patient and increase my tolerance?" Of course you can, IF YOU DON'T OVERREACT AND ARE LESS JUDGMENTAL and think more rationally. That's how you optimize emotional control of your instincts. All these inner strengths, know you possess them in abundance: *discipline*, *willpower*, *character*, *ethics*, *principles*, and of course the father of them all, *integrity*. All those strengths, like all the muscles in your body, will not grow overnight! Your muscles took months and years of your commitment to grow. Well that is exactly how your INNER STRENGTHS RESPOND. By using and developing them over the course of your life, so they can be used with more CONFIDENCE effectively and efficiently. And with the passage of time, they will get easier and more natural to access, HAVING A STRONGER, MORE LASTING INFLUENCE.

One of the GREATEST LOSSES IN LIFE, is to not utilize our human potential to its fullest capacity, where all your inner strengths are concerned. PLEASE, SIR, DON'T WASTE THE VALUE OF THOSE SIX PRICELESS WORDS. They truly represent the essence of a full and completely higher quality of life. THEY <u>MUST</u> BE DEVELOPED TO THEIR <u>ABSOLUTE</u> POTENTIAL, during this transitional period of the second half of your life. You must accept with crystal clarity, all your inner strengths with NO COMPROMISE. You want a more rewarding life, DEMAND IT OF YOURSELF. Activate those immensely critical and essential inner strengths of *discipline*, *willpower*, *character*, *ethics*, *principles*, and of course, *integrity*. Then with total conviction, WASTE NOT, THESE MOST VALUABLE OF ALL HUMAN QUALITIES!

Constipation

61

Whatever is relevant in your life that you consider positive, when it passes through your thought processes, make sure you mentally GRAB IT, FOCUS ON IT, AND EXPAND UPON IT. Keep it as strongly at the forefront of your consciousness, as you possibly can. Then take and transfer it from thoughts to words. Say it out loud or softly to yourself, but say it again and again and again. Then once you are confident in its continuity, use and apply it in a constructive, creative way to improve your lifestyle. Then, after a given period of time, it will ultimately sink in deeply enough, to become a recurring and useful asset, increasing your power to relate and communicate. That's how you make sure that any PARTICULAR POSITIVE, BECOMES A FULL ACTIVE PART OF WHO YOU ARE. Let me give you an example: I don't want you to ever think, from forty to sixty and even beyond, that the aging game has caused you to lose the smallest fraction of the POWER OF YOUR WILL, or the raw human desire, to make your life more meaningful. You must set up your own priorities in exact accordance with your values, BASED ON YOUR REALITY. If you don't take those positive thoughts and words and utilize and activate them progressively and geometrically, if you let them stagnate, they become useless. That's what your Old Pops calls: CONSTIPATION OF THE BRAIN!

I may have to repeat myself in the course of this read, because it's something I say to myself hundreds, even thousands of times due to its immense power. Now here's what I want you to say, and I want you to damn well mean it: "AFTER LIVING AND LEARNING FOR THE FIRST FORTY-PLUS YEARS OF MY LIFE, I DESERVE BETTER THAN TO MERELY EXIST AND SURVIVE, DURING MY SECOND FORTY-PLUS. *I must make my life have more meaning than to merely sleep, put food in one hole and watch it come out the other. This I will do, as absolute necessity to my fulfillment as a human being. I WILL MAKE THE REST OF MY LIFE, MUCH MORE VALUABLE AND MEANINGFUL. I WILL DO THAT, KNOWING THIS WORLD IS SO MUCH MORE NEGATIVE THAN POSITIVE.*"

So here's my suggestion to you, sir: you must create, get into, and surround yourself with, your own strong, invisible but absolutely IMPENETRABLE BUBBLE OF POSITIVITY. And know in no uncertain terms, that's where you intend to spend the rest of your life – IN THAT INDESTRUCTIBLE, INVISIBLE BUT POWERFULLY POSITIVE BUBBLE YOU BUILT. That does not mean isolating yourself from the outside world. But don't you ever forget, it means you staying in, and playing the game of life, when dealing with people on a daily basis. YOU MUST MAKE IT YOUR PLAYING FIELD. As long as you are drawing a breath, and thinking positive thoughts, the odds are with you. So let's have no self-imposed CONSTIPATION OR BLOCKAGE OF THE BRAIN FOR YOU!

As you get older, you must never let constipation of the brain take hold. Even at this late stage, I want you to know that with people THREE GENERATIONS REMOVED FROM ME, in their twenties and thirties, no generation gap, you know why? On that given day with that particular twenty to thirty-year-old, I'm still as alive and passionate and as energized and INVOLVED as they are, with the *living and sharing of life*. At that moment, we're both living in the same world at the same time, even though I'm sixty to seventy years older than they are. That's why you must, with passion and purpose, get yourself involved in and with the game of life, REGARDLESS OF GENERATIONAL DIFFERENCE. It can be done if you play this game called life with confidence. That's how you AVOID constipation of the brain.

I still take that full approach at my age, so there is absolutely no valid excuse at your age for anything less, and hopefully a whole lot more. Don't you ever let your age become A *MINIMIZER* OF YOUR NATURAL, TIME-TESTED ABILITIES. That confidence, which I'm sure you are achieving, can still be taken to a higher level. You should always be prepared and on guard to STRONGLY ASSERT YOURSELF, and do it with a genuine self-pride, because of your genuine belief in who you are. You must remove, if there are any, all those self-imposed limitations we all thought went along with aging. They D-O-N-T, don't! I want you to get and keep yourself on the right track, always headed and moving in the right direction. I repeat: no constipation or blockage of the brain for you. No matter the obstacles or discouraging situations, you must sustain and maintain a strong-minded ALWAYS ASSERTIVELY ACTIVE ATTITUDE. Then on a continuing basis for one hundred percent of the second half of your life, you will keep expanding on it, and that will be YOUR TICKET TO MAKING FATHER TIME YOUR TIGHTEST ALLY. Constipation of the brain? No way! Just keep your mental bowels moving the negatives out.

It's No Accident

62

It's no accident, that this old boy, as previously indicated, is still loving every facet of his life. Notice I said "no accident", because nothing comes easy at this age. With all the years of use and limitations they have imposed on my life, I know every day it will always take that extra effort. So WHAT'S THE BIG TRAUMATIC DEAL? In what more of a productive way, could I possibly spend my life at this age? What greater value or usefulness could I give life, than BEING AN ASSET TO MYSELF AND HOPEFULLY TO OTHERS. It's important you know, no matter how many aches and pains I have, and believe me pal, they are numerous, but what I do know is, they pale in comparison to the many other catastrophic conditions, so many millions of other people are victims of. People ten to twenty years younger than me. Life will always, and can only be, measured accurately BY COMPARISON. So there is no way in this world, with all the CRITICAL SUFFERING so many other decent human beings go through with aging, that could ever justify me letting a few little physical inconveniences, I can still handle and with a bit of grit, get myself through, get me down, no less keep me down. Feel sorry for myself? Whine, complain, cry in my beer? Are you f-ing kidding me?! GOD FORBID I SHOULD FALL INTO THAT DEEP, DARK SELF-PITYING SELF-CENTERED HOLE. Not on your life! I hope you see where I'm going with this. You at forty-plus or me at ninety, know it's never too late, at whatever age you are, to CHANGE YOUR FRAME OF MIND AND UPGRADE YOUR WAY OF

LIFE. I truly hope this analogy, will allow you to realize, how fortunate you are by comparison and know, you are still capable of SPREADING YOUR WINGS A LITTLE WIDER, AND FLYING A LITTLE HIGHER AND FARTHER. So whatever ailments you may have, and activities they might reduce, if you are still capable and have the capacity to live every piece and parcel of this day, and hopefully the balance of your breathing journey, on this one in one-hundred million oxygen covered planets, in a grateful, thankful, upbeat way, HOW RARE OF A BLESSING. I'm really into it now so let's get specific. Even if you are in a wheel chair, or suffering from any other kind of incapacitation, as long as that mind of yours is still fertile, and your thoughts are still coordinated, even under those adverse physical shortcomings, you can still live your life with grateful and graceful pride, NEVER BEING AFRAID TO EXPRESS YOUR POSITIVE SELF, ASSERTIVELY AND FEARLESSLY.

I gotta keep coming at you hard with this kind of sometimes tough to take truth, because I know how valuable time is, not having that much of it left! So throughout the body of this work, that is the main message you are going to get again and again, to keep reminding you as many times as I can, TIL IT SINKS IN DEEPLY AND SATURATES COMPLETELY, to make damn well sure that you are one-hundred percent aware, that you should never accept anything that is LESS THAN THE BEST YOU CAN BE. Always know unequivocally, that you possess those positive qualities and abilities. They are available and ready for you to express yourself completely. Sir, that is built right in your DNA! So please highly utilize it. Don't you ever leave anything to chance, when you know YOU HAVE A CHOICE. This is the day we are living in (assuming I'm still around!). Easy choice. Take this day and make it, to its optimum, WORTH YOUR INCREASINGLY VALUABLE TIME. That will be your fool-proof valid guarantee, that you are THINKING, SAYING, FEELING, AND EXPRESSING your true identity, through your ONE-OF-A-KIND POSITIVE INDIVIDUALITY. Do that, and this message will be irrefutable and unmistakably clear: IT'S NO ACCIDENT! IT'S THE REAL YOU. If your Old Pops here can still do it every day at this late but great stage of the game, WHAT THE HELL COULD POSSIBLY BE HOLDING YOU BACK, KIND SIR?

Stop Groping

63

Everybody seems to think, because they use the word *groping* so much, they believe they know its correct interpretation. But what every man in this category has to figure out, is what the hell does that word accurately mean when personally applied, and right now, that's you. THE DICTIONARY SAYS: "FEEL ABOUT, SEARCH BLINDLY, BE UNCERTAIN, OR LOOK FOR SOMETHING THAT'S UNKNOWN." Well let's apply that to what is the most important thing all of us are trying to find. Even after forty-plus years, of establishing an identity, we are still always searching TO DISCOVER MORE of who we really are, and how much more we can possibly be. There is no other way, to make your life more authentic, than to uncover and expand on the whole of your identity. That's real AFFIRMATION, real CONFIRMATION. It can take a lifetime to fully achieve, in many cases many men never do. It's through your continuing realizations, and accurate evaluations, that you will finally find what you are looking for – THE REAL YOU, IN EVERY SENSE OF THE WORD, AND IN EVERY PHASE OF YOUR LIFE.

It really is sad when you see so many people, who for almost their entire lives are groping, and rarely find what they're looking for. They keep blindly guessing. And by the way, guessing? That's groping's twin brother. So if you are never COMPLETELY SURE of what your objective is, you will more likely than not be GROPING AND GUESSING. And if you do that more frequently than not, then those are the words that will eventually define and describe you. Because there is still one word we haven't mentioned: *rudderless*. THAT'S WHAT GUESSING AND GROPING CAN LEAD TO. Being rudderless, or having little or no direction in your life. Only by discovering who you are, can you live by your real values and priorities, DEVELOPING A STRONG, TRUE, DIRECTION IN LIFE. I realize as well as anyone, we can all be indecisive now and then, but we can't allow ourselves to become rudderless on any protracted basis. That would be a foolish WASTE OF YOUR TIME AND TALENT. The only way to find your personal positive path, is to put aside, if it exists, FALSE PRIDE as a defense mechanism. False pride is an obstacle and barrier to knowing your valid identity. That's why it's called FALSE pride. YOU MUST AT ALL TIMES BE HONEST WITH YOURSELF, or you will always be in that state of guessing and groping, and could wind up living the majority of the rest of your life, without a strong sense of identity, and lack an accurate steering mechanism, to point you in the right direction.

Now let's get to the heart of the matter of why I established this groping and guessing premise. Assuming you are a man of sound mind and balanced common sense, no way in the world would you willingly accept those confusing conditions. I know how easy it is to overreact, even overcompensate and allow an existing positive circumstance, to become a negative. We are both aware of our strong, natural urges, which you and I have used with great anticipation time and again, all our life. They are not NATURALLY NEGATIVE. We all have those drives and desires that seem insatiable and can EASILY BECOME EXCESSIVE. And as previously mentioned, I unashamedly admit I love indulging all my basic instincts, that fire up and excite my five senses and my inner desires and feelings. Do I love them and do I want them, are you kidding? The urges are so strong, you can bet I'm gonna have them. I can't imagine life without them. But – *and a big but here* - when I'm involved in any one of my potentially overpowering base instincts, the one absolute that I have firmly established: I AM NEVER GROPING OR GUESSING OR CONDUCTING MYSELF IN A RUDDERLESS WAY. Therein lies the KEYS TO YOUR KINGDOM OF TOTAL GRATIFICATION! Of course you must be strong of will, of course you must know and establish, what your CONTROLLED LEVEL OF SENSIBLE INDULGENCE is. That's exactly what I do, because when I've had just a little bit more than my share, I KNOW WHEN TO STOP. If you do too, sir, good. You are gonna take and love life and live it to its POSITIVE LIMIT.

So if you want to enjoy and be rewarded by all your base instincts, that provide such pleasures all your life, you must get rid of that unnecessarily distracting guessing and groping and being rudderless, leading to uncontrolled indulgences. IF YOU DON'T, setting yourself up for ALWAYS BEING OUT OF CONTROL, and COURTING PERSONAL DISASTER will be more than possible. So remember, all those positive, most super rewarding human experiences, can only remain that way *WHEN YOU EXERCISE THE WILLPOWER AND DISCIPLINE TO GOVERN AND CONTROL THEM.* DON'T EVER ALLOW YOURSELF TO BECOME A VICTIM OF THEM. When it comes to our base instincts, which we all know are going to be exercised thousands of times in life, we must emphatically know to keep them from TAKING OVER OUR LIVES. And, kind sir, that means they must never ever, exercise control over you, NEVER. And you must always establish full control over them, ALWAYS. And that will come to be your reality when YOU SUMMON UP THAT EXTRA STRENGTH AND EXTRA POWER, OF YOUR SENSE OF CHARACTER, WILL, AND DISCIPLINE. Weakly groping and guessing, my ass! Not for you, sir! Now I know there's lots of confident men out there, and I also know how well intended they are and what their potential is. But I want you to know, you definitely can exercise your confidence and character, that can and will dramatically reduce and eventually eliminate completely, whatever pockets of guessing and groping, may still exist in your life. ONLY THEN CAN YOUR DESIRES, URGES, AND APPETITES BE TOTALLY SATISFIED, and provide you even more than your fair share, of all the pleasures they were designed to produce FOR A LIFETIME. Because now, young brother, you will be in control out of PERSONAL DIGNITY and SELF RESPECT. To consider anything less, IS BENEATH YOU.

That's how I want you to think and act. You bet your ass you are entitled to keep getting your fair share of life, every single day FOR AS LONG AS YOU ARE BREATHING LIFE INTO THAT MIND AND BODY OF YOURS.

Master Of Your Mind

64

Only with your consciousness being very sharp and precisely focused, will you ever know who the REAL YOU IS. That is so fundamental. By far, of the most relevant importance in every man's life past forty. Once achieved, you will have earned the official designation of being MASTER OF YOUR OWN MIND, which rarely happens until you've lived and learned through those first four decades. But there's always two sides to the coin and two sides to every story, and sadly, a lot of men instead of being master of their own mind, BECOME A SLAVE, AND SUBSERVIENT TO THEIR OBSESSIONS AND DESIRES, as strongly suggested in my previous observation. So what you have to ask yourself is: Am I a master of my thought processes, or have I become a slave to them." Boy, what a total dichotomy those two words – master or slave – represent, extreme opposites. Once again I say, you always have a choice, BUT, you must have the strength of character to back up the right choice, which is becoming the MASTER OF YOUR MIND AND LIFE, which will allow you to dictate the conditions you live by, or becoming A SLAVE TO LIFE, having others impose conditions, that control your will. *Please, sir,* GIVE THAT SOME VERY SERIOUS SELF HONEST THOUGHT. Because the facts are, those two words, *master* or *slave,* with their diametrically opposed values, are absolutes. When you become your own master, you take total charge of THE WAY YOU FEEL, THE WAY YOU THINK, AND THE WAY YOU ACT. At all times, concentrating and focusing on the valid and best view of you.

And that should always be, and I mean ALWAYS be, YOUR TOP PRIORITY. Obviously in business or relationships of any kind, all parties must compromise relevant to a mutual interest. That in no way interferes with you being one hundred percent your own person, BEING IN CHARGE OF THE WAY YOU FEEL, THE WAY YOU THINK, AND THE WAY YOU ACT.

Come on young brother, you are just now becoming, out of necessity, a positive-thinking warrior! Your Old Pops here knows all about self-doubt and insecurities in life. Over the years, more than a few of them have popped up and slipped into my thinking once in a while. Make sure in YOUR LIFE THEY SLIP IN THERE ONLY ONCE IN A VERY, VERY LONG WHILE! Make those times as few and as short as possible. So know, they are always going to be a part of the ebb and flow of your life, as they have mine. So make no mistake, in this difficult and hard-fought challenge, you are definitely not alone. In fact, just the opposite is true, WE ARE ALL IN IT TOGETHER, THERE ARE NO EXCEPTIONS. This master or slave thing is a lifetime struggle, for everybody. So if you put it in play positively, you can spend the majority of your life, BEING THE MASTER OF YOUR OWN MIND. But don't bullshit yourself into thinking, you are WHAT YOU ARE NOT. Those things that would enslave you, all those self-doubts and insecurities, always work at GIVING THEM A MINIMUM OF IMPORTANCE. Then with the passage of time, having become more the master of your own mind, you can eliminate them so they represent little, if any, priority at all. And there is only one way to achieve that: keep all the most positively important things in the active living of your life, at the top of your list of priorities. Now the way to do that is

215

to keep THINKING THEM, SPEAKING THEM, DOING THEM. My friend, don't kid yourself for one minute, they are as much a part of your life as they are mine, and every human being alive.

You can be the master of your mind if you never forget, that little DEMON CALLED SELF-SLAVERY, who is always trying to sneak his way into any little brain cell he can find. Don't ever underestimate your ability to activate mastery over it, knowing it could possibly victimize you.

Easy choice: take that mastery of your mentality to its limit. I'm going to say it again so you don't have any excuses: IT'S YOUR CHOICE! IT'S *YOUR* CHOICE! You must let your positive self-dominate, so that the PROCESS GETS STRONGER WITH EVERY PROCEEDING YEAR. I'm telling you, failure is highly improbable, if you focus strongly on it, and build your life around it. If you do that now, this I guarantee: you will, with unshakable mental strength, wind up being the MASTER OF YOUR OWN MIND, FOR ALL OF YOUR MANY THOUSANDS OF POSITIVE, INDULGENT, AND REWARDING TOMORROWS.

Turning Life On

65

As referred to in several observations, those first forty years were an automatic turn-on. Our physical powers were so highly energized and peaked, stoking our curiosity, not to mention our mental excitement. During our youth, THERE WAS NO EXTRA EFFORT NEEDED. IT ALL CAME IN ABUNDANCE SO NATURALLY. From fifteen to forty, hell, man, you had twenty-five years of every single day, finding a NEW MENTAL AND PHYSICAL PART OF YOURSELF. I think you'll agree, that's a more than fair evaluation. Growing from a young boy to a young man. What expanding appetites you and I had, because there were still SO MANY UNKNOWNS TO BE UNCOVERED AND DISCOVERED. More fantasies and desires than your imagination could create. All there at the same damn time. Wow, what a wonderful twenty-five years of wonderment and amazement. You were on that never-ending road. THAT WAS SUPER EXCITING STUFF. And all those things were happening almost every minute of every day of your life, during that time period from fifteen all the way up to forty. Twenty-five bombastic, fantastic years. Could you keep up? You bet your ass you more than kept up! That YOUTHFUL PUMP OF YOURS COULDN'T STOP PUMPING, NEVER RAN DRY. Talk about being primed for action on a moment's notice. Seemed like almost every step you took, there was something to excite and arouse you. Well as many years as I have on ya, I remember it like it was yesterday. It was GREAT STUFF, and like you, I loved the living hell out of every minute of it.

Now without fear of contradiction let's get real. Let's talk about assuredly this being the biggest, most important time frame of our entire life. When entering that second half of life, you are given a tremendous amount of time, twenty years, to establish and complete successfully, your transition. The big battle? Instead of YOUTHFUL NATURE TURNING YOU ON, with each year after forty, you must make an even GREATER EFFORT TO KEEP NATURE TURNED ON. And that, kind sir, is not a maybe. It's your realistic *must*! It's a different ball game now. You and I had our fifteen to forty-year shot, hopefully we both capitalized on it, and got the most out of it. WHAT CAME SO NATURAL THEN, IS NOW GOING TO REQUIRE A LITTLE MORE INCENTIVE. Now you must have even greater motivation, because at forty-plus, if you don't, you could wind up slowly quitting. You could get to the point over this forty to sixty twenty-year period, where you would allow life to turn you off, because of FALSE EXPECTATIONS you associate with youthful memories. More often than not this transitional condition, if you are not aware of it, can happen so INSIDIOUSLY SLOWLY, it's almost imperceptible on a day-to-day basis. I sure as hell know, because that's exactly where I was at my midway point. But I either got lucky or smart. More than likely, lucky. I caught it midstream. I SOMEHOW KNEW WHAT A WASTE OF MY VALUABLE TIME FALSE EXPECTATIONS WOULD BE. All they would create, was continuing frustration.

So know this: IF YOU ALLOW YOURSELF TO BECOME A VICTIM OF NATURE TAKING ITS COURSE, REGARDLESS OF HOW LONG YOUR LIFE EXPECTANCY IS, YOU WILL

218

BE LIMITING THE FULL MEANING AND PURPOSE OF THE SECOND HALF OF YOUR LIFE. Sir, why in the hell would you do that, when you know full well you still have the power to ENHANCE AND EMBELLISH THE LIVING AND LOVING EVEN MORE, THIS SECOND HALF OF YOUR LIFE. I want you to thicken that skin of yours, sir. Toughen it up. Because in real life, in all honesty, that's how it works.

Let's recap: during the first half, those first forty, especially between fifteen and forty, all that good stuff comes naturally. But during the second half of your life, YOU GOTTA SEARCH IT OUT AND MAKE IT HAPPEN. That requires you having the willpower, backbone, and tenacity to tough it out. It will mean you developing even more character, self-respect, and a greater appreciation of PERSONAL PEACE OF MIND. During the second half of my life I have found this to be the most effective way to PRIME MY OWN PUMP WITH PASSION AND PURPOSE, knowing that I no longer can *naturally jump out of my skin*.

So I'm telling you, little brother, if you slowly QUIT ON LIFE, you are short-changing yourself big time. WHY THE HELL WOULD ANY CLEAR THINKING, POSITIVE MAN IN HIS RIGHT MIND DO THAT TO HIMSELF? Please, kind sir, dedicate yourself during your remaining years to fill them up with deservedly EXCEPTIONAL QUALITY, infusing them with all the passion, purpose, and positivity, your now more valuable life has to offer.

Hate Or Happy

66

If there were ever two words that had totally opposite meanings, they are *hate* and *happy*. You should NEVER DEFINE HAPPINESS, when it is based on any object, person, or premise YOU THINK YOU HATE. Now that's a fight you and I and everybody else has to make. Whenever you find that ugly emotion welling up in you, never be happy or find any gratification IF IT PROVOKES HATE. God, man, think how habitually destructive this could be. Just one minute of hate, no less an hour, generated by vengeance or vindictiveness, will assuredly mean you have wasted valuable, happy, joyful time, in SELF DESTRUCTIVE BEHAVIOR.

I hope you know how dangerously serious this observation is, particularly at this time of your life. Because if you don't control it, it will absolutely INFECT LIKE A DISEASE the overall quality of your entire mode of life. We're talking about absolutes here. When the intent of hate is there, and you feed it with more hateful thoughts, you will find IT'S CONTAGIOUS, AND YOUR STATE OF MIND COULD BE CONSUMED BY IT, during this critical time frame when our psyches are so sensitive. If you make hate a consistent part of your thinking, it will dominate, where your collective thought processes are concerned.

Now if you ask me: "Ken, what's your justifiable source of authority and expertise on hate?" Well, kind sir, I have been there, almost to the point OF FULL CONSUMPTION. I know from years of personal experience! Hate became so prevalent, I knew subconsciously, there was nothing in my life, that could be more debilitating, and eventually lead to A LIFE OF FRUSTRATION AND FAILURE. But again, somehow I saw the light. So know this as one of life's surest facts: if you don't neutralize and ultimately DISPOSE OF THIS MENTAL MONSTER OF MISERY CALLED *HATE,* it will dominate, and I do mean completely. Now I know, over a lifetime, it's almost impossible to completely eliminate. But I'm telling you, if you don't minimize the DEMONIC INFLUENCE OF HATE, over the course of your life, the consequences will be OVERWHELMINGLY DESTRUCTIVE. DO NOT SET YOURSELF UP FOR YOUR OWN PERSONAL DOWNFALL. Make no mistake, sir, when strongly encouraged, hate, more than likely will lead to a failed life, when happy and hopeful are waiting for you, around every OPPOSITE corner.

I know those are strong and potentially crippling words, but this wizened old man is talking to you and sharing with you HIS OVERPOWERING EXPERIENCE WITH HATE. How strong was it? It was on the verge of obsession with me. Your Old Pops here can remember as clear as crystal water, his earlier formative years, so vivid, like they were yesterday, fighting with an anger and a hate in the streets of Philly. I ALLOWED MYSELF TO FALL VICTIM IN A BIG WAY TO HATE, to the point where it was so overwhelming, IT TOOK CONTROL OF MY CONDUCT AND ACTIONS. I was caught up in it so completely at that time that my anger more often than not, became uncontrollable hate. Then, thank God, a light went off in my brain. Maybe it was just simple common sense. But it told me that if I didn't do something about it damn quick, I WAS GOING TO DIE A VERY YOUNG MAN. I can look back and see that

221

angry, uncontrolled, young hateful man that I was, and this near destructive experience more than qualifies me to make this observation. Make no mistake my young friend, know what you are honestly dealing with: HATE IS AN AUTHENTIC DEMON AND A MASTER OF MISERY, and hopefully you won't fall victim to it.

Not hard to figure that bad is the opposite of good. Well know as a matter of full truth, and personal psychological fact, being HURTFUL AND HATEFUL will always be the direct opposite of HAPPY AND HELPFUL. So know for sure, kind sir, in no uncertain terms, in every phase of your long life, almost every thought you generate, the LESS HATEFUL YOU ARE, THE MORE HAPPY YOU WILL BE. Don't you ever for a second bullshit yourself into ever believing different. THERE IS NO JUSTIFYING HATE. Always be on guard against this demonic, dark cloud of impending disaster – thank God I did, or I would have been stone-cold dead over sixty years ago! I repeat, BE ALERT, AWARE, ALWAYS ON GUARD. It's always going to be coming at you from all angles and every direction, and how it would love to consume you. But before it can do that, it has to grow in you. CUT IT OFF AT THE QUICK AND CRUSH THE POISONOUS CRAP RIGHT THE HELL OUT OF IT. That's how you handle hate. If there's one thing worth killing, IT'S THAT UGLY DESTRUCTIVE BASTARD, HATE. Do it and you will automatically quantify your happiness and establish an ELEVATED PERMANENT PERSONAL QUALITY OF LIFE.

Every Possible Effort

67

One of the most obvious and redundant facts of life, you know it as well as I, consists mainly of questions and answers. We're always asking questions, trying to get the right answers. It's a part of almost all your thought processes, questioning yourself in SEARCH OF A <u>VALID</u> ANSWER. Well, there's one question that not anybody should ever be asking you, because no one but you has the answer. Ask yourself: "HAVE I REALLY, OBJECTIVELY, MADE EVERY POSSIBLE HONEST EFFORT, EVERY DAY OF MY LIFE, TO DO EVERYTHING I COULD IN MY POWER, TO OPTIMIZE MY LIFE TO ITS POTENTIAL <u>SELF WORTH</u>?" I want you to ask yourself that question on a daily basis. I'm talking about you honestly evaluating and defining, every phase and condition of your ever-changing life. I mean all those little and big personal situations, that you have to deal with on a day-in and day-out basis. Always ask yourself: "HOW CAN I MAKE <u>EVERY POSSIBLE EFFORT</u> IN RESOLVING THEM TO ADD INCREASED VALUE TO MY LIFE?" And your answer to yourself should always be: "Of course I can, every day in every way!"

You must understand how essential, critical, and of great personal importance making that extra, HONEST effort is, in SEARCH of your CORRECT answer, to the eternal long-term quality of your life. How you follow through on ACCURATELY OPTIMIZING your answers, will determine how HIGH A LEVEL you can take the quality of your life. So if I were to ask you, is it worth making EVERY POSSIBLE EFFORT to achieve that? I don't believe anybody who is practical would answer "no". Of course it is worth it! It's an absolute, common sense must, and deserves the most ambitious, constant commitment you can give it! You have the built-in potential to make that a reality, WITHOUT ANYBODY ELSE'S INPUT OR ASSISTANCE. Make no mistake, in order to reach that highly elevated quality of life, it's going to require EVERY POSSIBLE HUMAN EFFORT on your part. Then when you get to that elevated place, where you are doing exactly and precisely what you want to do, then, kind sir, I want you to think again, because for you, THAT SHOULD ONLY BE THE BEGINNING. When you reach that high level, fortify it, sustain it, and make it your norm. That being achieved, look to improve upon it for your life's complete journey. Imagine, my friend, having that euphoric feeling, at least a part of every day for life. YOU, ELEVATING TO ITS HIGHEST LEVEL YOUR PURPOSES FOR LIVING ON A DAILY BASIS. Worth repeating: After you reach that potential, continually sustain and maintain it, for as long as your faith and nature allows.

Now I know you don't need me to tell you, where you could be coming up short, if in fact you are. I do know, even at this late stage of my life, CONSTANT VIGILANCE in making every possible effort is A MUST. Every man past forty including Yours Truly, if he's completely objective and honest in evaluating himself, will know precisely HIS OWN STRENGTHS, AND WEAKNESSES. And we all know as men, the willpower and commitment needed to make ourselves mentally, physically, spiritually, and psychologically stronger. NOW THAT IS REAL SELF TRUTH.

224

So when we talk or even think about this coming up short concept, WHICH WE ALL DO, for God's and your sake, man, don't throw an unwarranted guilt trip on yourself. Don't do that. We all have those little missteps through life. I've had thousands! FIRST, FORGIVE YOURSELF FOR THEM, THEN LEARN THROUGH THEM. Because what I have found in nine decades of living is, coming up short can be as normal and natural as breathing. So know, like any and everybody else on this planet, you and I are not only gonna come up short, sir, hundreds, maybe even thousands of times in our life, it's almost a guarantee! Each and every last living man and woman on planet Earth is, at one time or another, in the willpower and discipline departments, gonna come up a little short of making every possible effort. JUST DON'T KICK THE HELL OUT OF YOURSELF, EVERY DAMN TIME IT HAPPENS. Common sense should tell all of us this: If you admit to yourself HONESTLY, that coming up short can create situations that could become a liability, what's of utmost importance, KNOW IT'S NO ONE ELSE'S RESPONSIBILITY BUT YOURS. You must take full and complete ownership of it. But that does not mean FEELING GUILTY AND LESS WORTHY. What it means is you have found the correct way to improve yourself in whatever area it is, WHERE YOU JUST MIGHT BE COMING UP SHORT.

There is no better way, to REDUCE AND MINIMIZE YOUR LIABILITIES, AND INCREASE AND MAXIMIZE YOUR ASSETS. In my estimation, many things in life are infinite, so even after you've made every possible effort, and have succeeded in elevating yourself to new, higher levels that almost feel stratospheric, I want you to ask yourself: "HAVE I DONE

225

ENOUGH? Have I really done everything in my potential capacity, to optimize my life?" And hopefully your answer will be: "THERE WILL ALWAYS BE ROOM FOR IMPROVEMENT no matter how good I've made it." Say to yourself, sir: "I KNOW I CAN AND I WILL DO MORE TO MAKE ALL MY ASSETS IN LIFE, INFINITELY BETTER." That's how I want you to think, because that is the only positive choice all of us will ever have. Of course you should always keep at the forefront of your consciousness and never forget, TIME WAITS FOR NO MAN, and you have already used up close to half of yours! So no matter how long a period you have left to live - three, four, five decades or more - why the hell would you or any man in his right mind WASTE A SINGLE DAY OF YOUR LIMITED TIME. And the only guarantee any one of us has, is making EVERY POSSIBLE PERSONAL EFFORT every single moment, for as long as we are breathing life into our body. That is the only way to ensure, that every aspect of your life, will be LIVED TO ITS LIMIT. Your reward? *TRUE PEACE OF MIND*.

Ally Or Enemy

68

When it comes to people, and generational changes - case in point, like political correctness and all the facades it creates - life can be awkwardly challenging, and very confusing. Much more often than not, the FULL TRUTH never seems to be spoken CONCISELY when attempting to be POLITICALLY CORRECT. So that sets up a condition where the line between ally and enemy can be so blurred, where it's hard to figure out and intelligently define, your allies as opposed to your enemies. Now I'd like to think I'm a pretty savvy guy, who has a real feel for human nature. Well even after all these years, I'm still learning. I cannot tell you how many times in my life, after considerable insight and evaluation, people who I knew quite well, I ULTIMATELY CAME TO THE REALIZATION, THEY WERE A WHOLE LOT LESS THAN MY ALLIES. It's more than possible, sir, someone you may have been very close to in your life, and for an extended period of time, you considered a TRUSTED ally, but as the years wore on, that relationship could have changed noticeably. Well that damned-if-I-do, damned-if-I-don't situation happened to me often enough. And what a confusing dilemma it caused. CHANGE IS INEVITABLE, WHERE UNDERSTANDING HUMAN NATURE IS CONCERNED. Well give yourself at least the benefit of the doubt. Look, you have lived forty years or more, and hopefully have developed an instinct where all those unknowns about who is or is not your ally or enemy are concerned. You have to be totally HONEST AND REALISTIC, when you evaluate and separate them. Your most important ingredient in drawing an accurate conclusion is ZERO RATIONALIZATION and one hundred percent HONEST REALIZATION. And during this twenty-year transition into life's second half, you should be able to fine-tune that natural instinct, with greater accuracy.

Maybe the best part of the second forty, is you having developed greater clarity through your powers of perception. So now at this age YOU SHOULD KNOW with improved insight, YOUR ALLIES FROM YOUR ENEMIES. But don't think that has one chance in hell of happening, UNLESS YOU FILTER OUT ALL THE DISTORTIONS AND BULLSHIT, connected with the COMPROMISED TRUTH OF POLITICAL CORRECTNESS. Make that a reality, and you will have HIGHLY DEVELOPED ONE OF YOUR GREATEST ASSETS. That's why this one generation out of your potential five, IS OF UTMOST IMPORTANCE. At this stage of your life, friend or foe should be a lot easier to figure out! But please, sir, get it done so you can fill that last thirty to fifty years of your life, with people you have developed great long-term trust and respect for, YOUR REAL TRIED-AND-TRUE ALLIES. That's what spending the better part of half a century past forty, is all about. You being able to EVALUATE MORE ACCURATELY, those people that are going to have a long-term positive influence and effect on you, and in the process eliminate the negatives, that enemies bring to your existence. So let me ask ya, WHY IN THE HELL IN THE NAME OF EVERYTHING THAT'S SMART AND SENSIBLE, WOULD YOU LET ANYONE WHO COULD BECOME AN ENEMY EVER PREVAIL, no less even enter your life, when through your strength of character, and personal integrity, you can develop and secure for the balance of your life, STRONG, CONFIDENT, TRUSTED ALLIES.

Your mind now contains that capability, to turn those people you NOW EVALUATE MORE ACCURATELY, into your most beneficial allies. Then you will have effectively accomplished making your second half of life at the very least, much more fulfilling and secure than the restless, unknown, unsettling first forty. You are now maturely and finally qualified, to make every minute of life a building block - AN ALLY - TO FORTIFY, SOLIDIFY, AND STRENGTHEN, your future purposes in life. This will make your remaining years, all the more valuable.

Now a little change of pace and interpretation. Everyone knows, TIME ONLY MOVES IN ONE DIRECTION. That should be everybody's Holy Grail. I remind you, sir, being a WISE MAN IS MORE IMPORTANT THAN BEING A SMART MAN. Where a very smart man can be overwhelmed by fear, a wise man has the mental tools to conquer fear. A wise man, when it comes to the REALITY OF TIME and its ABSOLUTE LIMITATIONS, never has his blinders on. In his fearless way, he has developed the wisdom to ALWAYS BE, WITH HUMILITY, APPRECIATIVE AND GRATEFUL. He accepts with gratitude his time limitations AS HIS MOST RELEVANT TRUTH AND ALLY, and places greater value *ON THE TIME HE HAS LEFT.* No matter how smart you think you are, when you FIGHT THE MOVEMENT OF TIME, that's a battle you will lose every time, MAKING TIME YOUR ENEMY instead of your ally. Be wise and realistic, sir, you must make time your MOST TRUSTED, VALUABLE ALLY.

Now if you march along that timeline, all that's needed of you is to keep moving at your pace, in the right direction to fulfill your needs. Then watch the adversity of all those conflicting conditions and seemingly insurmountable situations, fade into time-consumed less importance. Then with conviction and total belief, you will be able to say: "I HAVE MADE TIME MY MOST <u>RELIABLE</u> ALLY." That has been and always will be for me, the best way to optimize with great success, my human journey. I pray you are so blessed, kind sir. With four to six decades of life yet to be lived, the biggest mistake could be: DO NOT MAKE TIME YOUR ENEMY, OUT OF FEAR. It will weaken and ultimately damage your body, mind, and spirit. DON'T EVER MESS WITH FATHER TIME. Cooperate with the Old Timer, and the precious gift he provides will surely optimize and justify your living experiences. SO COOPERATE WITH FATHER TIME, OR THAT DUDE WILL SURELY, DAY TO DAY, LEAVE YOU IN THE DUST. So please make time your top priority, for the rest of YOUR TIME on Earth, and you will have forged your tightest, most VALUABLE AND DEPENDABLE ALLY.

Sincere Belief

69

What a great word, *sincerity*. A word capable of elevating so many prospects and concepts of our belief system in positive ways. Sometimes we're only mildly sincere, because we may not consider a particular situation that relevant, concerning specific circumstances of our life. But, we can easily and rapidly work our way up to being VERY SINCERE, about things that are VERY IMPORTANT TO US, like our religious or political beliefs. So quite obviously, the word *sincere* is a variable. So let's measure it on our one to ten scale. One being the lowest amount of sincerity, and ten being the highest. You can be mildly sincere at a three or a four, or up to a ten, where you are totally immovably unshakable, in your SINCERE COMMITMENT to whatever that might be. WELL, SIR, IT IS MY SINCERE BELIEF YOU MUST BE OBJECTIVE AND REALISTIC, in taking stock of yourself and the current world's technology and its effect. Hopefully an eight to ten on your sincerity meter.

When most people my age were born, there was only radio. And even then, radio was in its infancy. So I'm talking about being born decades before TV and of course, generations before the internet. Now we all know the national and international influence, of both these gigantic and immensely powerful means of communication. All this new technology, has created a vastly DIFFERENT SET OF PRIORITIES, VALUES, MORALS AND STANDARDS, that would have you VERY SINCERELY BELIEVE as your years accumulate, this world is mainly for the young. Not so, where you are concerned, not on your life. Your sincere belief, on younger BEING MORE MEANINGFUL, than being older, on a one through ten sincerity scale, SHOULD BE A BIG FAT ZERO. Totally false! Anybody half your age, no matter how advanced their technology is, has only half your experiences and has developed only half your instincts, insights, and clarity of well-directed thoughts. Why would anybody believe that somebody with LESS in all those categories, is MORE qualified than you, to SET YOUR ONGOING HIGHER STANDARD OF LIVING. That is not only a contradiction in terms, to be more pointed and honestly blunt, it is a full crock of unadulterated crap. PURE NONSENSE! Your self-confidence should always be based on your ideas, values, and the application of, YOUR MANY PROBLEM-SOLVING ACHIEVEMENTS. Don't you know you are living proof, that no matter how much more knowledge somebody half your age has acquired, REALISTICALLY, THEY ONLY HAVE HALF OR LESS OF YOUR LIVING EXPERIENCES AND WISDOM. Well, sir, I can tell you this. That is one of MY SINCEREST BELIEFS, AND MOST PERSONALLY HELD TRUTHS, or who I am would have been UNATTAINABLE. So where YOUR WORTH AND VALUE on your sincerity meter should be rated, is an eight to ten. Don't you ever let anybody that much younger than you, IMPOSE their value system on you. Now, they can suggest and recommend respectfully, if you care to share or take an interest. But to have YOUR WILL IMPOSED UPON, where there is any degree of intimidation, demand, or disrespect, absolutely not! It is SINCERELY BENEATH YOU.

I believe what you gotta do as you age, is be more self-assured. Of course you are smarter, but as just mentioned, more importantly, you are wiser. So there is absolutely nothing wrong with you becoming a little more JUSTIFIABLY DEFIANT, in defense of your expanding CONFIDENCE and INDIVIDUALITY and the values they truly represent to you. You don't under any conditions, ever let any other human being of any age, compromise the <u>POSITIVE VALUES</u> OF YOUR NATURAL AGING EXPERIENCE. You must make your aging experience your most relevant asset, and believe as SINCERELY as you can in the VALUES AND IDEALS you have built your life on. Please, sir, you must, I mean you MUST DEEPLY BELIEVE, without arrogance, but with OBJECTIVE SINCERITY, how FAR SUPERIOR those VALUES and IDEALS are, and the GREAT PRICE you have paid in TIME-TESTED TURMOIL to acquire them. And now during this great transition, THEY <u>MUST</u> BECOME YOUR INDESTRUCTIBLE ARMOR, as a time-tested asset to make your life EVER MORE VALUABLE AND MEANINGFUL.

Be intimated by younger or stronger? Not a chance in hell where you are concerned. Don't you ever forget, it was <u>your</u> value system that created <u>YOUR</u> SUPERIOR WAY OF LIFE, and you should be sincerely, damn proud of that. Now that's the kind of assertive, aggressive, ultra-strong thought structure you must keep at the forefront of your belief system, FROM THIS POINT ON FOR AS LONG AS YOU LIVE. Of course, adjust and upgrade, but don't ever abandon your fundamental priorities and values. WEAR THEM PROUDLY! Keep them sincerely UNSHAKABLE AND IRON-CLAD.

Older Bolder

70

Don't you ever believe, as you get older, you can't become bolder. Being bold was one of your most positive assets between twenty and forty. Well now that you are forty-plus, instead of losing it little by little as you get older, don't only retain it, INCREASE AND EXPAND UPON IT, and not out of resentment or frustration. Think as clearly and honestly as you can, about what you considered one of your most positive qualities of those first forty years. I know I was idealistic, loaded with passion and strongly expressing my views, BOLDLY AND PROUDLY, as I'm sure you were. But in reality, you know what both of us were doing? SEARCHING, trying to figure things out. Looking to find that certain special something that could make life better. Well sir, let me ask you this: why in the hell would YOU GIVE UP THAT APPROACH NOW, when you're gonna need it the most, because of the negative way our psyche can react to getting older. Look at all the practice you've had, to increase and improve your abilities. BEING BOLDER was a big part of effectively figuring things out. You must never let the aging experience, OUT OF FEAR, INTIMIDATE AND TAKE YOUR BOLDNESS AWAY.

With aging, the human body, over extended periods of time, gets weaker. We all know that. Now, can you slow that process down? Yes you can, dramatically. But, YOU CANNOT REVERSE IT! That is a complete contradiction to nature. But THE RATE OF YOUR DECLINE, will always be in accordance with HOW WELL YOU TAKE CARE OF YOURSELF. We,

234

like any professional athlete, hit our peak physically between twenty and thirty-five. Your mental clarity does not necessarily, have to decline at the same rate as your body. Just because the body, with its exceptional ability to constantly function over long periods of time, will naturally get a little weaker with age, while your mind can remain strong, because it is not subject to that kind of extensive physical use and abuse. And that, my friend, just may be your great saving grace, IF YOU USE IT WISELY, like being EVEN BOLDER THROUGH YOUR SECOND FORTY, THAN YOUR FIRST FORTY.

Now I understand completely, even though my physical prowess has been reduced, I have never let that impact me mentally, AND NEITHER SHOULD YOU. I knew what was happening! I knew I had to stop it in its tracks! It was only the power of my presence of mind, and strength of will, that told me in no uncertain terms that my mental potential was still strongly intact. So if you play it smart and work diligently at being bolder, it will definitely COMPENSATE FOR WHATEVER THE PHYSICAL LOSS. You must work on improving your brain. And I personally know from experience, BEING PERSONALLY BOLDER is fundamental to that process. And that, kind sir, is how you balance the scales. If we are going to lose some of our physical prowess with age, we should make it our main mission in later life, to get AS MENTALLY SHARP, strong, and EXPRESSIVELY BOLD as we can, with the passage of our ever INCREASINGLY VALUABLE TIME.

So whatever your current age is, or even your current condition physiologically, as long as you're not mentally impaired, you can not only become more lucid and alert with improved clarity, but also more physically able than you currently are because of it. Your positive mind, WILL BOLSTER THE EFFECT ON THE PHYSICAL BODY. So please do your priceless body a big favor, by making every effort to maintain it, at its highest possible level. It will encourage you, to optimize your mental and psychological assets. Then mutual support will result in inspired performance. That's why you must never let your priority to maintain physical strength DIMINISH WITH AGE. Anything you can do physically to effectively feel stronger will be a CONFIDENCE BUILDER IN THE YEARS AHEAD. How well I know that feeling. When you see and feel that turnaround from forty to sixty and beyond, THE FEELING IS AMAZING. Just when you thought the surge of energy and strength, was in a natural, normal state of decline, soon enough to be done and gone, you experience by far one of the MOST EFFECTIVE AND EUPHORIC MENTAL STIMULANTS, YOU WILL EVER BE WITNESS TO IN YOUR ENTIRE LIFE. No, you are not getting younger. But why the hell should that stop you. As you get older, your attitude really can become BOLDER AND BETTER. It's amazing how high it will take your self-respect. If you haven't already, wait til you come to that realization. You are going to find yourself, as I have, RIDING A LIFELONG UNMATCHED NATURAL HIGH.

You know what my hope is? FOR YOU BEING HELL-BENT on believing you are the *best of what you can possibly be,* keeping that bolder part of you constantly regenerated, and actively alive and energized. ALL THOSE DEEPER INNER STRENGTHS, you thought you might have been slowly losing, well this older man is telling you, it's just WAITING AND BEGGING FOR YOU TO IGNITE IT. Like I have said and you have read many times on these pages, and this is not me being humble, this is one of my most valued, rock-solid beliefs: I am you and you are me. And you know why? WE COMPREHEND EQUALLY. EQUALS WE ARE. Please, sir, let that penetrate your believability. DON'T YOU EVER, under any conditions, no matter how adverse and uncomfortable it makes you, don't ever UNDERESTIMATE YOURSELF. You make damn sure in the living of this second half of your life, and I do mean DAMN SURE, to become a MORE MEANINGFUL, PURPOSEFUL, CONFIDENT, AND SECURE HUMAN BEING.

Know always that if you exercise your powers of commitment, purpose, and self-respect by BEING OLDER AND BOLDER, only then can you keep that PASSIONATE WAY OF LIVING intact and healthy, from eighty to a hundred. Why the hell should I be the exception. My young friend, the stuff I'm made of, from toes to nose and all those trillions of cells in between, is the EXACT SAME STUFF YOU ARE MADE OF. Only one big difference: I'm a hell of a lot farther down the road of life. I got one more "damn" left in me, it's damn important. The only *damn* ability it is going to take as you get older, just get and be naturally, A HELL OF A LOT BOLDER. Make that your MUST-DO LONG-TERM COMMITMENT. You MUST exercise a little more mental, self-confident muscle. That WILL fully prepare you to capitalize on getting older BY BEING *JUSTIFIABLY* BOLDER, and make your second half of life, an ongoing KICK-IN-THE-ASS BLAST.

Right – Smart - Real

71

You know, in life, when it comes to playing games, you have a choice. You can play golf, you can play tennis. Those are great games at this stage of life. Maybe in your youth you chose one of the big three: baseball, football or basketball, or any combination of them, maybe all of them, maybe none of them, maybe soccer! But make no mistake, there's one game, whether you like it or not, that you are not only in it, but you must play it for all its worth for your entire human journey: THAT IS THE GAME OF LIFE. And, sir, that is exactly what it is, and you are in it up to your eyeballs for as long as you live. And the main purpose of course is, TO MAKE IT A WINNING GAME. That will certainly depend on the decisions you make, and the actions you take, from here on out. But know this: If you play the game of life and keep it authentically in balance and believable, you just may be fortunate enough, to have another forty to sixty more years of RIGHT, SMART, AND REAL, to support and underscore your KNOWABLE, GO, GO, GO-ABLE, WINNING WAYS. That kind of positive thinking, will create situations that outnumber and overpower what you might justifiably consider, certain little negative losses along the way. Well let me assure you, sir, it will be the most effective way to navigate your long human journey, giving you a feeling of having lived a marvelous and complete second half of life.

But it ain't no cinch! It's essential you understand, you must establish this constant standard of RIGHT, SMART, AND REAL. Without it, there will never be A SENSE OF

PROGRESS, PURPOSE, AND ACCOMPLISHMENT. Sir, they go hand in glove, it's up to you to make it a perfect fit. But make no mistake, the hill is going to get a little steeper as time passes. Because now the winning of this long game of life, is not part time or some of the time, IT IS FULL TIME. You must work at it endlessly, and willingly welcome as a character builder, every minute of the challenges it presents. You know, when you work diligently at something, and finally ACCOMPLISH FULLY AND COMPLETELY YOUR OBJECTIVE, it will always guarantee the purest essence of joy and fulfillment. IT WILL ALWAYS RESULT IN YOUR LIVING A BOUNTIFUL AND GRATIFYING LIFE.

So if you want an exhilarating, play it right, play it smart, keep it real, fulfilled life, one thing you should never look for, as mentioned, is that proverbial but highly misguided concept called: THE SHORT CUT. Because in the reality of living a complete and successful life, THERE IS NO SHORT CUT, NEVER HAS BEEN, NEVER WILL BE. If you want to see that kind of positive environment waiting when you are seventy-five to a hundred, you must face up to the fact it is going to be a ROUGHER, TOUGHER JOURNEY, FROM HERE ON OUT. Short cut, easy way, my ass! Let me tell you what I do know: In spite of all those age-related obstacles, we all want to live a long and fruitful life – one hundred years if possible. Well know that during that century of living, no one is going to escape what you just read. Know for sure what really MAKES ALL OF LIFE'S STRUGGLES WORTHWHILE, WILL ALWAYS BE THE OVERCOMING OF THEM. That is the only proven way you will ever know you have justifiably earned, all of life's joys and

239

rewards. And if wisdom, maturity, and fulfillment are going to be found in this, your second half, BEING REALISTIC IS A MUST. There will be moments you can kick back and relax, sort of get a second wind, take a second look. Evaluate and re-evaluate. But long term, there is no easy way, never has been, never will be. THERE ARE NO <u>SHORT</u> CUTS TO A <u>LONG</u>, FULL, COMPLETE, TOTALLY PRODUCTIVE, AND REWARDING LIFE.

You all know my theme throughout this entire dissertation: Never run away from what you think is a worthwhile challenge. LOOK FOR IT, FIND IT, TAKE IT ON, AND OVERCOME IT. That's how you handle and make more rewarding, the struggles that life presents. And God, man, don't be impatient and put a time limit on something this valuable. Don't ever run from even one mission or activity, that you place great importance on, and consider WORTH PURSUING. If by chance you don't think you asserted yourself with sufficient authority, face up to it if you feel you didn't make the necessary effort. That's how you build strong underpinnings, and develop the feeling of confidence necessary, for taking every worthwhile cause in your life HEAD-ON. That's how you keep it RIGHT, SMART, AND REAL. Now, are you gonna get knocked on your ass once in a while? Of course you are, we all do! But what the hell are you gonna do, just lay there? Of course not! You are gonna get your ass right back up off the floor, get your attitude in positive gear, and AGGRESSIVELY take all the challenges of your life, every last one, all head-on again. THAT'S EXACTLY WHAT THE HELL YOU DO, AND YOU MUST DO IT WITH YOUR MOST ASSERTIVE AUTHORITY, FEARLESSLY AND BOLDLY. That kind of action is the only way you will ever, establish the rock-solid cornerstone you need, to BUILD THE PURPOSE AND THE MEANING OF YOUR LIFE ON. When you do that every minute of the rest of your life, never fearing the challenges or struggles it presents, you absolutely, definitely will find yourself living THE NEXT FORTY TO SIXTY YEARS, IN AN UPBEAT, UPLIFTED, SELF ASSURED, ON-TOP-OF-THE-WORLD WAY. Now that is what I call being damn right, damn smart, and damn real. Because what you will have done, to such a highly elevated level, you will have validated YOUR SELF WORTH, and you will have earned a greater degree of self-pride and self-respect, WHICH WILL PROVE TO BE SELF CONFIRMATION. Impossible during life's first half, but much more than possible in this, your life's second half.

One last thought: This is an every day deal. The moment you take that first breath when you wake up, and your feet hit the floor, that very second, get your butt and your gut and your mind in gear. Not only will you be ready for, but you will take on willingly, whatever struggles that day has to offer. JUST LOVE THE FACT THAT YOU HAVE THIS DAILY OPPORTUNITY, TO ACCEPT WHATEVER THAT DAY IN LIFE AFFORDS YOU! Only then will you have guaranteed the EXPANDED LOVING OF YOURSELF, and the life you will be living. And, kind sir, that is about as RIGHT, SMART, AND REAL as it will ever get!

Keep Your Spirits Up

72

As I've discussed so consistently, there are limitations physically past forty, and as you'll see sprinkled throughout these pages, that's all a part of the aging process. But what you definitely should not do, is let whatever kind of limitations they are, eat away at the heart and soul of your HOPES, DREAMS, AND AMBITIONS for living a full, more rewarding life. If you allow the natural process of aging, to have any kind of preoccupied debilitating effect, it will not just weaken, but you will have created a condition, that has the potential to KILL YOUR SPIRITS. My God, man, the optimum strength and increasing value of your spirit is stratospheric in importance, BECAUSE THE WHOLE OF YOUR LIFE IS NOT ONLY BUILT AROUND IT, BUT IS SOLELY DEPENDENT UPON IT. That spirit you carry around with you twenty-four hours a day for your entire life, will affect EVERY ASPECT OF EVERY SECOND OF EVERY LIVING EXPERIENCE YOU HAVE. Make no mistake, that is absolute truth. To accomplish anything or feel any form of gratification, which should of course be your whole purpose for living, it is an essential necessity to KEEP YOUR SPIRIT STRONGLY NOURISHED, AND ENDLESSLY HEALTHY. That's how you keep it resilient and intact. It's very possibly IMPOSSIBLE, to achieve any worthwhile goals in your life without it.

When your life is loaded to the limit, with the struggles of constant problem solving, you must at all costs, no matter how adverse existing conditions may appear to be or actually are,

PLEASE, SIR, YOU MUST KEEP YOUR SPIRITS UP. Make no mistake, that spirit you're carrying around in you, that is the motivating force that powers and inspires, all other positive elements of your entire persona. It is in my estimation, the only word that has the power to ELEVATE EVERY TANGIBLE AND INTANGIBLE ASPECT AND ELEMENT OF YOUR LOVE FOR LIFE. In no uncertain terms, and there is not a doubt in my mind, without a strong, resilient, well-nourished spirit, your purposes in life would not only eventually weaken, but ULTIMATELY FALTER AND CRUMBLE. Let me give you an accurate analogy: let's compare your spirit to the power of a motor. Well, I don't want the motor that drives your spirit, to be some little lawnmower motor. I want your spirit to be driven by a six hundred horse power, zero to sixty in three seconds V-12! And make sure your personal fuel, which feeds your mental muscle, is the highest octane you can produce. If you never let that mental tank of yours run dry, it will be only then, that you will have assured yourself a LIFETIME OF SUPERIOR AND POSITIVE RESULTS.

We all know, there are so many negatives in life, that can weaken or even break your spirit. They live in every nook and cranny of your conscious and subconscious mind, and seem to be around every unknown corner of your life. THAT'S THE CONTRARY NATURE OF NEGATIVITY! So it's not hard for somebody who is high-spirited to have that spirit reduced, or even weakened by an overwhelmingly negative environment. Well, the effects of a weakened spirit for any extended length of time, can not only badly damage, but break your spirit, adversely affecting and turning optimism into pessimism, negatively impacting and

243

rejecting your many positive purposes in life.

So in every psychological way, you must feed and nourish your spirit. You keep that high-powered motor of your spirit running strong and long, because when that spirit of yours is healthy and active, the <u>LOVING</u>, <u>LIVING</u>, AND <u>EXPANDED GRATIFICATION OF LIFE</u>, WILL CHANGE DRAMATICALLY FOR YOU IN EVERY POSITIVE POSSIBLE TANGIBLE AND INTANGIBLE WAY.

That spirit of yours if you keep it elevated, will take you on a natural high so exhilarating, so euphorically exciting, that no artificial stimulant could ever possibly equal. But know for sure, kind sir, you and only you, where your spirit is involved, must be that POWERFUL LIFE FORCE FOR THE SECOND AND MOST IMPORTANT HALF OF YOUR LIFE. Come on my man, what a sin it would be to waste and chance losing the full meaning and high value, of that most magnificent word: SPIRIT.

Twice As Much

73

A lot of people find it unique that a man just ten years shy of the century mark, can be strong minded, and determined as he was at forty to fifty. Guilty as charged! One-hundred percent true! And here I am, talking to you with passion through the positive written word. Now you might ask, after reading all these observations, how in the hell did The Old Man make that happen? I justified what was the most important thing past forty: BEING HAPPY AND FULFILLED. Now let's take it a step further. The effort necessary to protect and preserve my body and my mind, which would hopefully produce greater self-respect and self-worth, and what we just talked about on the previous pages - MY PRICELESS, PRECIOUS SPIRIT. Let's get razor sharp and more precise about these three IMMENSELY VALUABLE WORDS: MIND, BODY, AND SPIRIT. If you neglect any one of them, the other two will function less efficiently, and reduce your overall quality of life. Which means, all three must be functioning at their highest possible level. If they are not, therein lies the main reason so many men past forty, FIND THEMSELVES ON THAT SLOW DOWNHILL SLIDE. When the BODY, with the passage of time starts to function a little less effectively, it's a given the quality of life in those other two categories of MIND AND SPIRIT, will also be ever so slowly reduced, making you feel a bit more LIMITED AND INHIBITED. The obvious result, subconsciously and psychologically, can cause your SPIRITS TO DROP, and the quality of life can suffer and be adversely affected. Again, I say the obvious: why in the hell would any clear-thinking, level-headed man past forty ever permit that kind of negative condition to exist knowing full well IT IS TOTALLY AVOIDABLE.

Well sir, let me reassure you, that definitely does not have to be you. Just stay as strong as possible, and hopefully get even stronger during this great transition. But you must, as your top priority, respect, nourish, and protect those THREE HIGHLY IMPORTANT HUMAN COMPONENTS, THAT ARE THE CORE ESSENTIALS OF YOUR ENTIRE LIFE. But make no mistake, it all starts with your body. Simple conclusion here: You neglect and disrespect your body, YOUR BODY SURE AS HELL WILL RETURN THE FAVOR! Any man at any age can and should wear their body proudly. Then that brain will build more confidence, and you will have a soaring spirit.

As we get older we should finally wake up to the fact, it's not a level playing field anymore. You want that uphill ride? Don't get lazy with the body. Keep that body of yours as active and busy as you possibly can. That's how you elevate and keep producing a more powerful, resourceful mindset, resulting in and assuring your spirit for living WILL NEVER WEAKEN. The end result of that kind of PRECISELY DIRECTED STRATEGIC THINKING, will make all the good stuff in your life INCREASE IN VALUE, making life more exciting and exhilarating with each passing year. That can absolutely be every man's reward past forty, who cultivates the willpower and determination to follow through, on that TOUGHER-AS-WE-GET-OLDER, COMMITMENT.

I will constantly repeat in this book what you already know but

246

on occasion possibly compromise: The physical change that is associated with your aging process, is something we all must learn to live with, BECAUSE THERE IS NO ALTERNATIVE. From the day every human being is born, up to a hundred years of life, we are always in a state of constant change. You and I are no exception. So not only accept, but welcome the challenge. Remember, the process of change is so damn slow, it's easy to take a particular time segment of your life for granted, and trick the mind into believing, it's never going to change. Then when you finally recognize over an extended period of time, what is so obvious and natural – YOU DO CHANGE - many men are inclined to get frustrated and allow getting older to become a liability in the form of fear and frustration. Well my friend, only one way to handle that. Definitely say to yourself: "Liability, my ass! Of course I know I'm going to get older, so f-ing what!" YOU CANNOT LET IT INTIMIDATE, DOMINATE, THEN OVERCOME AND CONSUME YOU. You dig those psychological heels in. Your JOB, your TASK, your MISSION as things get tough, you damn well sure as hell GET EVEN TOUGHER! This older man is breathing, living proof, that this observation is one hundred percent doable. SO MAKE IT YOUR REALITY.

Beware Of The Wall

74

As old as this older man is, you should all know and understand, that during the time you are living in now - this Great Transition – even though it was fifty years ago, I can recall clearly that time period of my life. I unmistakably know, almost totally recall, what you are going through starting the second half of your life. So if I'm shooting for a hundred, that should also be your target. And why not? Why the hell not! Now make no mistake, NO SUPER MAN HERE, JUST A MAN LIKE YOU. When I was your age, the aging process did become a major concern for me also. Through all the adversity, and all my questionable judgment, I made it! I knew all the negative trappings that can come into play during that first twenty-year period of life's second half. But I actually made it through, pretty successfully. What I'm saying to you is this: I emphatically and sincerely believe, that if I could make it through in the often adverse transitional environment of my time when I was your age, SO CAN YOU.

So the big challenge now is how do you handle it? How do you work your way through this thing called getting older? Well there's one thing for sure: in this instance you have no choice. YOU HAVE TO DEAL WITH GETTING OLDER, LIKE IT OR NOT. That's an absolute. What you don't want – tough love time - is to bitch, moan, whine, complain, and cry in your f-ing beer, feeling sorry for yourself, about a NATURAL PROCESS YOU CAN EFFECTIVELY ALTER, BUT THERE IS NOT A CHANCE IN HELL YOU CAN CHANGE. That's like banging your head against a concrete wall, thinking your head is going to win. That's the kind of unrealistic negative thought process that can only lead to a restricted and frustrating rest of your life. Make no mistake, THAT'S THE LOW ROAD DURING YOUR MID-LIFE. Now the common-sense question: Why in the hell would you take that low road, that can only produce disappointing results, when you know THERE IS AN EASILY ACCESSIBLE HIGH ROAD IN YOUR LIFE PAST FORTY! Now don't expect to find it around every corner, in fact, it may be hard as hell to locate. You may have to search long and hard, but when you find your upward, open road, it will be entirely up to YOUR STRENGTH OF CHARACTER, to keep it wide open, for clear and smooth sailing for your life's long second half. But you better know right now, there are going to be a whole lot more psychological low roads than there are high roads, STAY OFF THEM. I repeat, you must search a little harder to find your high road, because as long as this old dude is breathing a breath, I'm going to keep reminding you: what you were, that's history. BUILD ON IT, know what you still can become when you take that high road. There's going to be marvelous mysteries just wanting and waiting to be discovered, and the only way that will become your reality, is for you to use the AGE YOU ARE RIGHT NOW, to make more rewarding, your twenty-year great transition to secure and ensure the forty years to follow.

So let me repeat for your edification: You must take the experiences of what you were doing, saying, and thinking during those earlier years, TO A HIGHER LEVEL. I have found this to be, after a vast variety of approaches, the most effective and efficient way, to elevate the quality of my life. You must develop

249

the habit so that it becomes a NORMAL, NATURAL, EVERY DAY LIFESTYLE. That will allow you to continue to program in your mind, those thoughts that make you feel good about who you are at the age you are! OTHERWISE YOU WILL HIT THAT MENTAL WALL. You have to understand and recognize, that is the primary and major purpose, of the long life you've already lived, and hopefully will continue to add on to. Now this is worth repeating: Of course look back on it, reminisce, think about all the POSITIVE THINGS that were part of your lust for life, during those first forty years, and use them in a CONSTRUCTIVE WAY. It will expand and reward your present state of mind. I can't say it strong enough, beware of that wall that creates a mental block. When you think in any way you are approaching it, you must find a way around it, over it, or under it. Better yet, BREAK THAT SON OF A BITCH DOWN TIL IT CRUMBLES TO THE GROUND! Now that's how tough I want you to be mentally, at this critically transitional time of your life. If you are already there, wonderful, great. For God's sake and your sake, keep it going! You do that with emphatic force, and this older man is telling you, there is no way in hell the REAL YOU, will ever let aging decay and diminish away THE POWERFUL FORCE OF NATURE YOU REPRESENT. You must for the sake of your own successful survival, take life and your second half of it to even greatest heights, and without question you will solidly and strongly become that FULL COMPLETE PACKAGE OF MATURE MANHOOD.

Love How You Look Or Change It

75

If you have a picture album stuck away in the archives, I want you to pull it out, and look at yourself throughout your life. You got kid pictures when you were five or six years old. Then in your teens. Young man pictures at twenty to thirty. More than likely, you had that big full head of hair, possibly a tight gut. But now here you are at forty to sixty-plus, AND ONE THING IS OBVIOUS. Of course visual change happens so slowly, you can't measure it from day to day. Sometimes even a year or two or three passes, and you still are not aware of that visual change. And then comes what could happen, if you let it become an ongoing, growing, psychological liability: WE WAKE UP TO OUR MORTALITY. Something many men past forty prefer to ignore. CONSTANT CHANGE. As we get older, that once thick head of hair could be getting a LITTLE THINNER, and that once thin waist might have gotten a LITTLE THICKER! Now to most men's way of thinking at your age, that could sound like, if you let it, a cruel fact of life, and in your own subjective mind, because of established values and our built-in natural vanity, you just may start to think, it's a change for the worse. Well, it sure as hell has not been for me, and never will be, and hopefully these many pages will inspire you to believe, IT WON'T BE FOR YOU. After all these decades, I really am proud of the fact, that I am still in control, of getting the most out of my physical condition every day at the age I am. And therein lies the secret. Not trying to be what you were, but getting the most out of WHERE YOU ARE AND WHAT YOU ARE NOW. So as things change from year to year and decade to decade, there will always be noticeable physical and visual change.

Let's face it, there are certain things you just ain't gonna change, and, sir, your age is obviously one of them. YOU CAN'T GO BACKWARDS. Every year, you know you are going to be a year older. As you become that year older, please sir, LOVE YOURSELF A LITTLE MORE, not a little less! And do your utmost to be in the best shape you can.

So let me assume if I may, that you put in your first forty or more years, and maybe over the last five or ten of those years, your hair did get a little thinner, maybe not. And you could possibly have put on a little extra weight around the middle, maybe not. And you are probably not as fast on your feet, as you were fifteen to thirty years ago. Maybe so! But here's the key, and this is the crux of the matter: whatever you think is changing for the worse will turn out exactly that way, IF YOU KEEP THINKING THAT'S THE WAY IT'S SUPPOSE TO BE. Don't do that! Don't ever do that! You will be heading in the wrong direction. You will be developing the wrong frame of mind. Please, kind sir, living proof is talking to ya! NO WAY SHOULD THAT BE YOUR SELF-IMPOSED, FLAWED FATE. Time again for one more of my "why the hells". Why the hell would any man worry about losing a little bit of hair in this day and age, when some of the most virile, masculine men in the world who aren't even bald, SHAVE THEIR HEADS! Any man with an ounce of common sense and real self-pride, would not live by those FALSE VALUES AND STUPID STANDARDS. Do yourself one of life's biggest favors: FIND YOUR OWN REALISTIC PATH,

AND IMBUE IT WITH STRONG WILLED POSITIVE PURPOSE. Always see and be the best of who you are, by creating your own vision of self-perfection. That is the only valid way, you are going to MAKE THINGS BETTER FOR YOURSELF AS YOU GET OLDER. All these assets can easily be found. Open your eyes, search them out and FIND THEM. Then fixate on them and make them fundamentally fit your belief system. It's time to get OBJECTIVELY ACCURATE, AND MATURELY LIVE IN YOUR REAL WORLD.

Now let's go on to what can be a touchy subject, and in this case we gotta forget political correctness, because this is about how you look. Without question, man's biggest problem is not just getting older, even with young people, it's WEIGHT, being out of SHAPE and in QUESTIONABLE HEALTH. But as you get older, this condition can have a much more debilitating effect on the state of your health. If you don't like how you look, it will produce a diminished overall, more negative than positive frame of mind. Now if you are a little overweight, maybe ten to fifteen pounds, what you gotta make sure of is, that ten to fifteen doesn't become twenty or thirty. Then all of a sudden it's fifty. OUT OF CONTROL in just a matter of months. You could become morbidly obese, VERY UNHEALTHY AND UNHAPPY. Well the answer to solving that problem is simple. Stop eating SO MUCH <u>MORE</u> FOOD than you need, FOR PROPER NOURISHMENT. Guys, I gotta be very blunt here because I feel so strongly about this. If that's your story, you are eating too damn much. Simple solution: SLOW DOWN, EAT LESS! Now notice, I didn't say GIVE UP all the foods you like. You don't have to do that. Eating is something we do three and four times a

253

day, that brings us such great gratification and satisfaction in so many different rewarding ways. So why would I or should I deny myself, and why should you deny yourself? Example: I love baby back ribs. Those greasy things are fifty percent fat. I love crisp bacon too. Also fifty percent fat. But my secret is: These are NOT daily or weekly habits. I've been eating foods like that all my life, and will do it for the rest of my life, BUT INFREQUENTLY. What you gotta do is start paying very strict attention, to how much of what you put in your body. When you were younger, with your pituitary releasing all that growth hormone, which encouraged muscular growth and reduced fat, it was easier to keep weight off. But somewhere between thirty and forty, the pituitary stops releasing growth hormone. So now you have to make that extra concerted effort, to eat the sugary and fat foods that satisfy you, IN MODERATION. Now if you do that consistently out of respect for your body, it will become a life style and hopefully a lifelong habit. Over-eating can easily turn into a life threatening, life shortening lifestyle. YOU START EATING SENSIBLY and you can eliminate that potential problem in just a couple or three months. And, kind sir, I am talking results that will definitely amaze you, but more important, make you very proud. IT'S ALMOST UNBELIEVABLE HOW THE BODY WANTS TO COOPERATE, WHEN YOU TREAT IT WITH RESPECT. So of course eat what you want. Again, I have been doing it all my life. Why not you? But do it with the exercise of DISCIPLINED AND CONTROLLED CONSUMPTION, so that you can eliminate whatever and wherever that bulge might be, and the health threatening conditions it could represent. Just take charge, sir. You know

254

when you are stuffing UNNEEDED food in your face.

Now the next necessity of course, heavy exercise has been an important part of my life, and I don't expect to be duplicated after almost seventy-five years of working out four to five days a week. But let me recommend this: whatever your age past forty, as late as sixty-five, let's assume you've hardly done any consistent exercise in your life. And lets further consider that even though you don't exercise, YOU HAVE THAT EIGHTY TO NINETY YEAR LONGEVITY IN YOUR FAMILY GENES. And no matter what you eat, you could easily live that long or longer. Now you might say to yourself: "Boy, ain't that great – I've got longevity, what an asset! I can eat as much of anything I want and still live to be 80, even 90 years old - WOW!" But with bad eating habits and a lack of physical activity, you could make your extra-long life a GREAT LIABILITY. Sound confusing? It's not. If you don't treat that body of yours with the RESPECT IT DESERVES, it sure as hell is going to DISRESPECT you in kind, and potentially make the last thirty years of your life, instead of being lived at the highest level of activity, your health those last twenty to thirty years will be GREATLY COMPROMISED and REDUCED CONSIDERABLY. Please, kind sir, why would you allow or permit that to exist, when it takes such little effort, in a relatively short period of time to accomplish just the opposite. Choose whatever form of exertion you want to, but you most definitely should, if you do not already, from here on out, EXERCISE AND EAT AS SMART AS YOU CAN. This kind of conduct is so much more important during the second half of your life, than it was during the first half. Let me emphasize, if you live to be a hundred, and you don't get it together from forty to sixty, and get your thinking straight and EXERCISE THE CHARACTER it takes to control your food intake, and get that body of yours as healthy and strong as it can possibly be, even if you make it to a hundred or more, common sense tells you, those last thirty years ARE NOT GOING TO BE VERY DAMN PLEASANT. Why would you settle past sixty, for all those years, even decades, of a LOWER QUALITY OF LIFE, when with what I just described, which requires very little of your valuable time, with a few good health habits, can make the end game what it should be: beneficial and rewarding, producing authentic peace of mind.

If you are doing what I just described, fine. If not, now is a good time to start. Gotta say it one more time: Why in the hell would any man, after overcoming all those forty-plus years of challenge and struggle to reach this elevated level, LIMIT HIS POTENTIAL, when these should be the ABSOLUTE BEST, most PERSONALLY SATISFYING years of your life. Hey guys, if this flawed, but older bolder man is still doing it, you gotta know, it just ain't gonna be THAT DAMN TOUGH. ASK YOURSELF: "Do I deserve, and can I be better, as I get older?" I'm as serious as an avalanche: YOU BET YOUR SWEET, ROUND, FIRM, AND MUSCLE PACKED, EVER-LOVIN' ASS *YOU ONE HUNDRED PERCENT CAN*! And don't you know, now more than ever, YOU'VE EARNED IT!

Half A Life

76

Being that I am writing all these observations, I guess I gotta keep interjecting myself, using my own experiences, as a comparison. I hope this is not interpreted as arrogance because, sir, it is anything but. At this advanced age, it is out of concern for you, who still has so many more hopefully gifted years to live. So here's the premise I'm setting up using myself as that example: KEN DAB-ROW IS NOT GOING TO SETTLE FOR *HALF A LIFE*. Not a chance in hell that's ever going to happen. And as far down that human road as I have already traveled, not for one minute of the rest of whatever time I have left, will I ever settle for less than ONE HUNDRED PERCENT OF A FULLY SATISFYING AND COMPLETE LIFE. It will be lived at the highest level I can possibly achieve, until my very last breath, AS SHOULD YOURS! No matter how difficult and strictly limited my conditions become, this older man is going to be up to it, and so must you if we both are to retain deservedly, OUR SELF RESPECT AND PERSONAL DIGNITY. Now make that your mindset. Take this mid-life time-frame, and SET YOURSELF UP for the best thirty to fifty years of life. And without question or doubt, if you, sir, make your SUPREME EFFORT, you will definitely make this YOUR BEST HALF OF LIFE.

Young brother, as you work your way through these pages, know you can take it to the bank, I will do everything in my power to consciously appreciate my life at this stage of the game. NOW THAT'S HOW I WANT YOU TO PROGRESSIVELY THINK, FOR YOUR NEXT THIRTY TO FIFTY YEARS. Although my

257

life has been rewarded with thousands of gratifying, satisfying experiences, I am never going to stop searching out and investigating, from every human perspective possible, the rewards to be found that are going to fulfill my life, THAT I KNOW ARE THERE. Now no one knows better than me after all my trails and error, I may not find them all, but I sure as hell will be making every effort, to find a lot more than expected. Now that's the mode I want you to sharply focus on at this stage of your life. And I want and expect you to do it all the way up to where I am, and HOPEFULLY BEYOND. Because it is unquestionably there for you. Please capitalize on it, so when you get to my age and look back, there will be a thousand good memories and very few regrets. THAT'S MY WISH FOR YOU. In my mind, because of that kind of locked-in mindset, I WILL SUCCEED TO EXCEED, what happened yesterday, no less thirty to sixty years ago, where you are now. That's the way to think consistently, and it will become SOLIDLY SUSTAINABLE. I certainty had a very interesting first forty years. In fact, considering the strict puritanical world they were lived in, they were nothing short of sensational! I did my very best not to miss a beat, no matter the risk or the heat, of most anything that was in front of me. For me personally, I not only enjoyed those first forty, I truly tried to make them as purposeful and productive as possible, so they could strengthen, fortify and prepare me, FOR MY ENTRANCE INTO THE SECOND HALF OF MY LIFE. Well it worked! I did use that acquired knowledge, it did embellish, expand, and elevate the quality of the second, then unknown half of my life. Now having said all that, how many times do I have to tell you, that WE ARE CUT FROM

THE SAME CLOTH. There's no unique superior individual exceptionalism here. What this man did, you too can ABSOLUTELY DO. So do it with confidence and full SELF BELIEF. Don't ever settle for less, THAN YOU JUSTIFIABLY DESERVE. And that's a hell of a LOT MORE than you just might be giving yourself CREDIT FOR.

There is only one question left to ask yourself: "WHAT IN HEAVEN OR HELL COULD OR WOULD BE HOLDING ME BACK?" And I want you to say to yourself: "If something is unnecessarily adversely affecting the quality of my life, I'M GONNA GIVE IT A STIFF, FIRM KICK IN THE ASS, *RIGHT OUT OF MY LIFE,* so I can personally find the abundant rewards THAT I AM MORE THAN ENTITLED TO." Younger brother of mine, THOSE LEARNED AND EARNED SELF-DESERVING REWARDS, ARE STRATOSPHERIC. So no negative self-deception please. YOU AND I ONLY HAVE ONE SHOT AT THIS GAME OF LIFE. I've taken most of mine, IT'S YOUR TURN NOW. Please, sir, with unquestionable deep and lasting self-belief, live the rest of your valuable life with ever increasing self-esteem, self-confidence, and let PERSONAL INTEGRITY, DIGNITY, AND PRIDE ALWAYS BE YOUR DESERVED DESTINY.

More Important Now

77

Boy, as a figure of speech, how often have we heard: time marches on? Well it just may literally be the truest of truths you'll ever hear or see written. But those people that are saying that to us figuratively, they LITERALLY mean TIME WAITS FOR NO ONE. And I'd like to believe its essence and true meaning, is expressed on every page of this book. That's why no matter how long that life of yours may be, you must recognize that nothing is more important, than the present time you are living in. KEEP THAT ALWAYS AT THE FOREFRONT OF YOUR THINKING. That's how precious your time is, so your correct evaluation should be: THE LESS TIME I HAVE, THE MORE VALUABLE IT SHOULD BECOME.

Every once in a while, go back in time, reminisce when you were a young teenager. I think about it a part of almost every week, and I'm talking seventy-five years ago. And because I focus on it so frequently, I can recall and visualize it clearly. All those people we listened to that we were so dependent on, telling us what were supposedly the rights and wrongs, the dos and don'ts, could only express, WHAT THEY KNEW AND BELIEVED. So it's important you keep in mind, that they also had their own limitations, and SLANTED IDEAS AND VALUES. So they could only convey to you what was taught to them by others. Well it was, during those FORMATIVE YEARS when we were so dependent on their directions. We normally did what we were told. Their sincere concern for you growing up? NOT TO WASTE YOUR LIFE. But I honestly believe what they were trying to say was: DON'T WASTE WHAT SHOULD BE YOUR VALUABLE TIME.

Now common sense tells you as a man past forty, if your time was that important as a teenager, when you still had potentially seventy to eighty more years to live, think how much more important YOUR TIME IS NOW. Please, sir, let the gravity and IMMENSE REALITY of this statement, sink deeply and permanently into your vividly CONSCIOUS MIND. Let me repeat how important your time is now, all these years later, even though you still may have a half a century or more to live. My point? YOUR TIME NOW, IS MORE THAN TWICE AS VALUABLE THAN IT WAS DURING THE FIRST FORTY, BECAUSE YOU HAVE USED UP APPROXIMATELY HALF OF IT. Well it is your personal responsibility, to elevate and get all you can out of the time you have left.

This is simple mathematics, it's so obvious. The less time you have left, becomes a hell of a lot more important with each passing day, no less week, month, or year. Well sir, there is only one person who has been endowed by nature with the ability and responsibility, to give that remaining time greater value. THAT'S YOU, ONLY YOU, NOBODY BUT YOU! The only variable is, the cooperation of others. Any kind of encouragement and assistance that's available, is an asset. But take it from The Old Man, don't OVERLY depend on outside help, because when push gets to shove, THE USE OF YOUR TIME, under almost every condition, IS SOLELY AND ENTIRELY UP TO YOU.

Just maybe the world's most worn out phrase, that has been used millions of times is *time is money*. It is supposedly one of the world's best-known expressions. Well Mr. Man In The Middle at forty-plus, it's no contest, not even close. YOUR TIME NOW WILL ALWAYS BE, MANY TIMES MORE VALUABLE THAN MONEY. You must be realistic, they don't even live in the same world. You must realize one irrefutable fact: the longer you live, the less time you have left, which absolutely means THE MORE VALUABLE YOUR TIME BECOMES. You can make more money up to your last breath, but you can't MAKE MORE TIME! Now if you spend your time in a positive, passionate, productive, and useful way, your life will be enriched regardless of how little or how much money you have. The moral: You can always make more money, but you CAN'T MAKE MORE TIME. WHEN YOUR TIME IS UP, ALL THAT MONEY AND POWER WILL NOT BUY YOU ONE EXTRA MINUTE. That's why YOUR TIME in the living of YOUR LIFE is not only priceless, but GROWING IN VALUE! That's why you must make every proceeding day more valuable. The MOST IMPORTANT ELEMENT OF _YOUR_ LIFE, WILL ALWAYS BE _YOUR_ TIME. Why in the hell, kind sir, would you waste even ONE PRECIOUS MINUTE, OF YOUR ONE _TIME_ ONLY LIFE.

The Basics

78

I'll never understand why in the course of living an entire lifetime, anybody would deny themselves, any of their many appetites and desires. Think of all the indulgences that are there to be savored and enjoyed. I mean gratifying in almost every exceptional tangible and intangible way. Well The Old Man has indulged almost all of them (but no drugs!) all his life. I'd like to hope, that when my journey through life is over, that I haven't missed very much of anything. But know this, even at my advanced age, that POSITIVE PASSION for the living of my life to ITS FULLEST, young sir, your Old Pops, still got it. Why? I never threw an unnecessary guilt trip on myself, because of my indulgences. When it comes to you indulging all of life's appetites, desires, and fantasies, and I'm excluding none, one hundred percent of all of life's potential pleasures, AS LONG AS YOU ARE IN CONTROL OF THE ACTIVITY, and fair and honest in its application, causing no harm to another, you will never have a reason to throw a GUILT TRIP ON YOURSELF. You and I both know, and it should be obvious to almost every man, that when you satisfy those feelings, that gratify your appetites, you know you have just created, some of the most REWARDING AND MEANINGFUL MOMENTS you can or will ever experience. But know as indisputable truth, even if you are super successful and wealthy, and could afford any and all kinds of extreme gratification, as often as you wanted, there's a damn good chance, IF YOU OVERDO IT, YOU COULD - AND MOST LIKELY WILL - COME-UP-EMPTY.

The key word in this discussion of indulgence is *basics* - your five basic senses of touch, taste, sight, sound, and smell. It is through any one, or all of those five senses, that our appetites and desires are STIMULATED, ANTICIPATED, AND SATISFIED. And my good man, they are with you in your mind and body almost every minute you are alive. TEASING AND TEMPTING YOU ALL THE TIME. You are so busy using all of them, almost all the time, every day of your life. So it's natural not to give them a second thought, and take them for granted, because you assume they are always going to be there, right? NOT ON YOUR LIFE, MY FRIEND.

If you still have all five of your basic senses, DON'T *EVER,* TAKE THEM FOR GRANTED. Cherish and count your blessings for each and every one, and be constantly conscious, every day of your life, how gifted and blessed you are to still HAVE THEM ALL. Let me offer a few illustrations of how valid and serious this observation is. Every waking moment from the first second you open your eyes, is a VISUAL FEAST. Your eyes, rolling around, taking in all the action. The gift of sight, if you still have yours (which you obviously do if you are reading this book!), it's a blessing beyond compare. What a kaleidoscope there is to visualize: mountains, valleys, oceans, big cities with their sky-high buildings. Then there's the pastoral beauty of rolling hills. The movement and actions of people. Your ability to see beauty in all forms, plus a thousand MORE THAN MAGNIFICENT visual treats. Now close those eyes of yours for just a few seconds, blinding yourself to all those beautiful sights and visions, you were just viewing. You can rest assured, YOUR EYES WILL NOT STAY CLOSED VERY LONG. They will be open in a second or two searching for something else to view, because the APPETITE OF YOUR EYES NEVER ENDS. You keep them open to see all you can see. Well, sir, a blind man does not have the blessing of that magical, magnificent gift. If you ask that BLIND FOR LIFE MAN if he had a million dollars, I guarantee you down to his last dime, he would give it all, just to see one single sunset. NEVER TAKE YOUR SIGHT FOR GRANTED.

Now the sensation of sound. The cheer of a crowd, right down to the soft whisper of a meaningful phrase, or being moved emotionally by music, plus all the other second-to-second sounds of life. The rare, wondrous experience of being surrounded by the excitement of sound in all its forms ALL THE TIME, during ALL YOUR WAKING HOURS, of ALL YOUR LIFE. As with sight, it would be easy to take that for granted, because it is such a constant. Now if you could communicate in sign language, and ask a deaf person, WHO LIVES IN TOTAL SILENCE, never for one moment of their entire life, to know the sound of a soul-searching song, or a word spoken with passion and purpose, how big a sacrifice would he or she make, just to HEAR ANOTHER VOICE SPEAKING A SENTENCE OR SINGING A SONG. No way that can ever be MEASURED IN MONEY.

Then there's taste and smell. Imagine: you are sitting in one of the finest steak houses in the world, about to eat the most delicious, fragrant, two-inch thick, perfectly aged filet mignon. You got that knife and fork poised in your hands, your mouth is literally WATERING WITH ANTICIPATION of the flavor, then all of a sudden you have no sense of smell, that steak is odorless.

And when you go to take your first bite, IT'S TASTELESS. How would you like to lose those basic senses of taste and fragrance? You know how to put that in perspective? DON'T EVEN TAKE YOUR NEXT MEAL FOR GRANTED. Appreciate, savor, and be grateful for every taste-full mouthful of food you eat.

If you are fortune enough to have all five basic senses fully functioning at this stage of your life, realize how blessed you are every second of your life. CHERISH AND APPRECIATE EVERY ONE OF THOSE FIVE BASIC SENSES. All these things that seem normal and come naturally to us, that we often don't give a second thought to. With all your Old Pops got going, and as good as life has been to me, kind sir, I don't just give them a second thought, I GIVE THEM A THIRD, FORTH, AND FIFTH THOUGHT, every single day that I am afforded THEIR GREAT GIFTS to the living of my life, that SO MANY MILLIONS LESS FORTUNATE THAN ME, HAVE BEEN DENIED. So I want you to be always appreciatively aware of your basics. Always being conscious of how valuable they are, to the FULFILLMENT OF YOUR LIFE. NOT FOR ONE EXTRA MINUTE, FROM THIS MOMENT ON, FOR YOUR ENTIRE LIFE, SHOULD YOU EVER AGAIN TAKE ANY SINGLE ONE OF YOUR FIVE GOLDEN SENSES OF TOUCH, TASTE, SIGHT, SOUND, AND SMELL FOR GRANTED, KEEPING IN VIVIDLY CLEAR PERSPECTIVE, *WHAT THE LIVING OF YOUR LIFE WOULD BE WITHOUT THEM.*

Dim And Grim

79

No matter how dim and grim things in your life may seem to be, or even are, in the course of these your first four to six decades, keep in mind you are only half way there. Well the time has come for you, to make your REMAINING TIME EVEN MORE VALUABLE! Of course you are going to be surrounded on a consistent basis, with many negative situations and adverse conditions, but you must never get DOWN ON YOURSELF, because right now, you have the available capacity to control, neutralize, and eventually conquer, ALL THOSE DIM AND GRIM MOMENTS. They are right inside you. Now, let's discuss your ABILITY TO DIMINISH their meaning, and overpower them with a POSITIVE FOCUS during this second half of life. You must believe that capability is in every fiber of your being. Mine has been a very long and diversified life. It's been lived through a myriad of various relationships, situations, and circumstances, that were present every day of my life. And so many of them could have easily been interpreted in a dim and grim way, and of course, like any other human being, many were. I can honestly and objectively say, there were literally thousands of times in my life that condition was very real. But, I NEVER GOT DOWN ON MYSELF. I knew the challenges to overcome those many circumstances were immense. IT'S EASY TO BE POSITIVE WHEN EVERYTHING IS GOING YOUR WAY. But when life may be going south on you, that's when you must take the bull by the horns, and like I say, dig those heels in, and let dim and grim know, by the very presence of your powerful persona, they are NOT GONNA WIN. Well, kind sir, FIND THAT FEELING. Then when you do, give it the full power of your motorized and fueled mental muscle. When you do, you should and will conquer, whatever is causing dim and grim in your life. And I'm talking about any moment in your life. I don't mean tomorrow, I mean right now as you are reading and we are sharing these words and thoughts. You must make this an every moment lifetime project, when you are dealing with this MENTAL MONSTER OF MISERY, THIS SON OF A BITCH WITH ITS UGLY, DEPRESSING NATURE, CALLED DIM AND GRIM. As I've suggested with many negative situations that could arise in your life, GIVE DIM AND GRIM, ONE OF THE BIGGEST, STIFFEST KICKS IN THE ASS, RIGHT THE HELL OUT OF YOUR LIFE. Because, kind sir, if you don't, it could become a lifetime loser of a habit. THAT'S EXACTLY WHAT THE HELL YOU DON'T WANT DIM AND GRIM TO EVER BECOME. And it won't when you forcefully diminish and discard it from your life. Then and only then will you be able to wear every square inch and ounce of who and what you are, with OPTIMISM AND GREAT PRIDE.

Straight In The Eye

It is so convenient to alter the facts of life, in order to make a situation more comfortable to live with. That's what happens when you adjust reality, which would mean being self-deceptive. DON'T YOU EVER RUN FROM REALITY OUT OF *FEAR*! Know the stuff you are made of! It's damn good stuff, sir. So reach as deep as you can for it. Search it out. Find it. Put it in organized positive perspective, then you can TAKE POSSESSION OF YOUR REALITY, and be totally secure and comfortable with it. You should know by now, having lived almost half your life, how to cope in a confident way, then conquer, any difficulties that come your way. Always look every adversity, no matter how troubling it may seem to be, or actually is, look that son of a bitch straight in the eye, psychologically stare it down fearlessly, and guaranteed you will assertively win BIG TIME in a BIG WAY. That's how you optimize to your full potential, your STRENGTH OF MIND, BODY, AND SPIRIT. That means, at any given moment in your life, you will be able to look at and face up to, the HARSHEST, MOST SHOCKING, AND DEPRESSING CONDITIONS POSSIBLE, and take them all on, every last one. Always let that be your mindset, always being on guard and prepared, to do that EVERY SINGLE DAY OF YOUR LIFE. That's how you give yourself a big advantage, in dealing with adversity from a position of FULL MENTAL POWER PREPAREDNESS. You bet, you should stare down and take on willingly, forcefully, and fearlessly ALL ADVERSITY THAT ENTERS YOUR LIFE.

Healthy Body

It is indeed time, to inject a little bit more of what and who Ken Dab-Row is into this observation. During my great transitional generation, I experienced the contrast and personal psychological contradictions many men in your age group do, that after having lived their first forty-plus years believed for whatever reason, that an extra strong and healthy body was mainly, for that fifteen to thirty age group. Even though aging is a natural process, they somehow SOLD THEMSELVES ON THE IDEA, AND SINCERELY THOUGHT, what they saw in the aging of men sixty to eighty, to be normal - BEING FEEBLE, FRAIL AND FAIRLY WELL WORN. Well the facts are, although that situation is prevalent and appears to be the normal condition, that assumption is flawed. Don't you ever believe it for a second. OF COURSE YOU NATURALLY HIT YOUR PHYSICAL PEAK BETWEEN TWENTY AND THIRTY FIVE, BUT, THAT DOES NOT MEAN A _DEEP STATE OF DECLINE_ IS NOW YOUR AUTOMATIC FATE AND DESTINY. Because living proof is here to tell ya, just the opposite can be your truth. It's every man's natural gift! White, black, brown, yellow, or red, tall, short, heavy set, or thin. Any man can absolutely have a healthy, active, highly energized, and strong body, WELL INTO THEIR EIGHTIES, as long as they are willing to REORIENT THEIR THINKING AND REARRANGE THEIR PRIORITIES. You must find the discipline to fully accomplish that, and make it a REST-OF-YOUR-LIFE commitment. Now look, know this and know it as actual fact, and, sir, I mean it, again I say, I am not blowing wind up your ass: whatever I did to accomplish what I accomplished, know unequivocally, YOU CAN DO IT AS WELL OR BETTER, but make no mistake, you gotta bust your balls and commit a bit more effort, if you want that stronger, more active body.

Now in that previous paragraph, I said *they,* and I said *me* a lot. But *you* know who I'm talking to! You! Y-O-U. Now with me it's been weights. That's my choice. I love that feeling of resistance, so that's what I've been doing for over seventy-five years. But when you are talking healthier, stronger, greater energy and stamina, YOU DON'T HAVE TO LIFT WEIGHTS. That is not the only way to a healthier, fit, and energized way to maintain an active, stronger body, all the way up to and well over eighty years of your life. Big muscles are nice, but there are so many other ways TO ACCOMPLISH YOUR LIFE-LONG HEALTHIER AND STRONG GOALS. You can be just as healthy, active, and hopefully as strong as Yours Truly, when you are beyond sixty-five to seventy, approaching and well into your eighties.

So let's establish this premise: You D-O-N-T, *DON'T* have to lift weights to accomplish your live-longer, be stronger life. But what you must do with that body of yours IS SOMETHING PHYSICAL TO *FIGHT OFF FEEBLE*. And the older you get, the more essential it becomes. Just put in the time, and your HIGHER QUALITY OF TIME, will last for a hell of a lot LONGER TIME. I'm talking any kind of exertion, that creates any kind of resistance, that challenges the body, in whatever form you find personally rewarding. Tennis, swimming, walking at a

271

fast pace, or even walking around a golf course. Let me play up this word a*nything*. ABSOLUTELY *ANYTHING* PHYSICAL IS A GOOD START, because whatever that activity, you will eventually, within the course of only A COUPLE OR THREE MONTHS, begin to feel that increased energy and strength building and expanding, SEEING VISUALLY HOW MUCH BETTER YOU LOOK. And I'm dead serious, all you gotta do is just give it ninety to a hundred twenty days, three to four months, and you will be more than pleased, you will be amazed with the improvement you see and feel. Just when you think you should be getting, feeling, and looking older, surprise, surprise, just the total opposite will be your deserved fate. You will in just over a few months, be FEELING AND LOOKING BETTER, WITH A SURGING ENERGY INCREASE. With just a half an hour to an hour a day, of any kind of resistance exercise, just three to five days a week, will afford you the most gratifying results you could have ever imagined. YOU WILL HAVE A GREATER BELIEF IN YOURSELF AND YOUR PURPOSES IN LIFE. *It happened to me, and it can and will happen for you.* YOUR SELF ESTEEM AND SELF RESPECT, WILL GO RIGHT THROUGH THE ROOF! Your presence will demand great respect and admiration of others. It is absolutely the most exhilarating feeling, YOU WILL EVER EXPERIENCE, BAR NONE.

Tough love time. If you are overweight by twenty to thirty pounds, or frail and meek and underweight, (here I go again) why in the hell would any man in his right mind, with an ounce of common sense, accept those less than totally fulfilling conditions, at this, his most vital transitional age, and cheat himself out of

272

being the best he can possibly be. WHY WOULD ANY MIDDLE-AGED MAN SETTLE FOR ANYTHING LESS THAN HIS PHYSICAL BEST? The normal excuse is "I don't have time." Well, there are one hundred sixty eight hours in a week, and all you need is four to five of those hours, less than two and a half percent of your total weekly time, to make yourself feel ten, a hundred times better, knowing that you have elevated in great proportion, almost EVERY OTHER ASPECT OF YOUR LIFE, FOR THE REST OF YOUR LIFE. That's how you avoid ever becoming a victim, of frail and feeble and mentally lazy.

YOU DO NOT <u>HAVE TO</u> GET WEAKER AS YOU GET OLDER and impose self-restriction on yourself. Forty-four or eighty-four, if all your faculties and extremities are in working order, it's never too late to take control, and make FAR MORE EFFICIENT AND EXCITING YOUR ENTIRE LIFESTYLE. When you walk, walk a little faster, and swing those arms as you walk, and don't be afraid to put a five-pound weight in each hand to further flex your muscles. I kid you not, just those simple little movements, are going to wake up and activate all the muscles in your body, and you will find, kind sir, your world will be taking a QUANTUM LEAP IN THE DIRECTION OF A GREATER LOVE FOR LIFE. So jump on board and make that conscientious decision. As sure as hell is hot, that's the key past sixty, to still being THE POWERHOUSE OF A PERSON, <u>YOU WERE ABSOLUTELY BORN AND MEANT TO BE</u>. This is not a maybe, it's me and you and any man who chooses to. Then you will be able to say, as I am still saying, with a little more emphasis: *Age, My F-ing Ass!*

Big Battle

82

Everyone should be aware that there is one absolute through the living of your entire human journey - LIFE IS A <u>BIG</u> BATTLE. Now there is no doubt in my mind, that with the thousands of experiences you have had, up to this time in your life, one thing you must be cognizant of, and recognize as your purest truth is: THE OLDER YOU GET, THE TOUGHER AND BIGGER THE BATTLE BECOMES. A battle every man past forty will have, and must be ready to face up to and willingly confront with advancing age, AND BEAT if you are fortunate enough to be blessed with long life. As the years pass the hills are going to get a little steeper, and the climb up those hills will definitely be a little harder. Again, so what! You know you saw it coming! In the final analysis, this big second half of life battle we are all fighting, is not only worth winning, it is absolutely by a country mile, THE GREATEST BATTLE YOU WILL EVER WIN. This is the only way to overcome, ALL THOSE INSECURITIES A LOSING BATTLE WITH AGE CAN PRODUCE. Then you can knowingly, confidently, and fearlessly embark on and start winning, the natural, normal, BUT DEFINITELY CONTROLLABLE, negative aspects of aging.

Make no mistake, sir, THIS *"AGING THING"* WILL BE BY FAR THE BIGGEST, LONG-TERM BATTLE OF YOUR LIFE'S ENTIRE SECOND HALF. It's a forty to fifty-year encounter, that gets tougher every year. So for God's sake and your sake, PREPARE YOURSELF FOR IT. What a challenge to overcome, conquer, and win. Keep searching, finding, and developing more of your inner strengths. That is how you reduce, eventually dispel, and hopefully eliminate the impact of aging. Because, sir, if you don't, AGING HAS THE ABILITY TO CREATE SELF DOUBTS IN LATER LIFE, THAT CAN LEAD TO QUITTING ON LIFE.

There's a term we all use: *Old man.* In my case, it's been said in a loving, admiring way, thankfully. But if you interpret it from a pessimistic perspective, it will have negative connotations. So The Old Man is giving it a new twist, a new slant, when it comes to this old/old-man negative theory. Literally speaking, I think of myself as an inspired, motivated, *older man.* My greatest hope, just ten years shy of the hundred mark, is to make a big difference, in the life of every forty to sixty-year-old man in America. Please be open, and let my positive attitude be ENCOURAGINGLY CONTAGIOUS. Please do it, sir, and you will be building all the remaining years of your long life, on a ROCK-SOLID SENSE AND BELIEF, OF EXPANDING CHARACTER, PRINCIPAL, AND SELF ESTEEM.

A big part of this big battle is, that there is going to come a time in the future, between sixty and seventy-five years of age, where you just might retire from your job. Well your frame of mind should be, as you approach that period in time, having ANTICIPATED IT, means you will have prepared your mindset for that transition. Never let that word *retire*, morph in any way to have negative meanings. Just make sure you NEVER RETIRE FROM ACTIVITIES, that takes the loving and living of your life, to a higher level. I repeat, NEVER LET THE WORD *RETIRE* <u>IN YOUR LIFE</u>, RHYME WITH *EXPIRE*. Here's how I believe you can keep that from happening: Go just the opposite direction from *retire* to *inspire*! If you stay productive, active and motivated in all of your endeavors and encounters, you will work your way in a positive mode, successfully through this transition. That is the biggest part of YOUR BIG BATTLE.

So for as long as you possibly can, recognize, acknowledge, that there are parts of life, all through life, that are going to REQUIRE YOU TO BE A FIGHTER, knowing you are always in a battle as life progresses, and that battle will be never ending, AND THAT'S OK, BECAUSE IT IS A TRUE ACCOMPLISHMENT AND DISPLAY OF YOUR STRENGTH OF CHARACTER. The one thing this *older man* has learned was, I knew all those years were going to accumulate, producing mental and physical changes. And knowing that, I prepared my mindset for that eventuality. So with the passage of my time in getting older, I accepted that reality! I knew bigger battles were yet to be fought. And, kind sir, that is a must, you have to KNOW AND ACCEPT, EVERY WAKING MOMENT OF THE REST OF YOUR ANTICIPATED LONG LIFE. Build that mental fortress, because that big battle is undoubtedly worth fighting, to achieve the highest possible quality of your second half of life. YOU MUST NOT ONLY WIN THIS BIG BATTLE, YOU MUST WIN IT IN A BIG, BIG WAY!

Loud And Proud

Now if you feel you've lost, to any degree, some self-esteem, through this very slow process of aging, you should know, after reading the 82 previous observations, just the opposite is true. Kicking off the second half of your life the right way, CAN BE SO DAMN EXTRA SPECIAL. You have been afforded thousands of opportunities, to develop the wisdom and common sense, throughout your long, interesting human journey up to this time. That should serve but one positive purpose: you taking your second half of life and making it even more meaningful. A VERY VALID, SOLID, AND STRONG REASON TO SOPHISTICATE AND ELEVATE EVEN MORE, ALL YOUR PERSONAL POWERS.

Well here you are, friend, smack dab in the middle of your long journey. You have finally arrived at the time with the experience needed, to be in control of your FUTURE SELF ESTEEM AND PERSONAL DIGNITY. You must keep pushing those two great qualities of self-esteem and personal dignity, to their highest possible levels. Now you do that, and the SECOND HALF OF YOUR LIFE WILL CERTAINLY HAVE GREATER MEANING. As important as those two qualities were during your first forty formative years to battle self-doubt, they are much more important as you get older. Back then, it was all about vanity, and too frequently, false pride. TRUE INDICATORS OF YOUTHFUL INSECURITY. Something we all go through in our formative years. Well the time to diminish them has finally come, AS YOU CULTIVATE AND SOLIDLY REINFORCE YOUR

SELF ESTEEM AND PERSONAL DIGNITY. That's precisely where you are now. Well there is no time like the present to FEED AND NOURISH THEM WITH POSITIVE BRAIN POWER, AND WATCH THEM GROW STRONGER. That will certainly equate to and produce more confidence. YOU MUST NOT PERMIT THE PASSAGE OF TIME TO WEAKEN YOUR DIGNITY AND SELF ESTEEM, AND PUT LIMITATIONS ON THE BALANCE OF YOUR LIFE.

So that establishes your personal reality that getting older, must never mean crawling weakly into a corner of your mind, and let the experience of aging intimidate you. JUST THE OPPOSITE MUST BE YOUR TRUTH. You are now more than ever before qualified, to express yourself in a LOUD, PROUD, MORE CONFIDENT WAY! Then psychologically and philosophically, the positive advantage is yours, to powerfully make every tomorrow more meaningful. Please sir, recognize and accept that loud and proud ARE IN YOU FOR THE TAKING. Just think and evaluate: *There is no more important reason, for you to have lived your life up to this point than to know, you are talking and acting louder and prouder with greater self-reliance and elevated purpose.* Over the course of your long four to five decades of life yet to be lived, that's the ATTITUDE YOU MUST ACQUIRE, if you are going to get bolder as you get older. And once that mindset is in place, you will realistically become, A PERSONAL, POSITIVE MENTAL POWERHOUSE, with a mind so strong that any negative force will not have a chance in hell, to create doubt in any way possible. Let me put it in clearer, unquestioned context: No way any libelous thought regarding your age will be able to DENT, NO LESS PENETRATE THE

278

MENTAL ARMOR YOU HAVE BUILT. And one thing's for damn sure, sir, ABSOLUTELY NOBODY, regardless of how strong a natural life force they think they might be, will they EVER BE ABLE TO INTIMIDATE OR BULLY YOU. WHAT A POWERFULLY CONFIDENT, CONTROLLED FEELING THAT IS.

Know for sure, the more pressure society tries to put on you, IF YOU ALLOW IT, the more personal control you sacrifice! Sir, stay away because that kind of thinking can drain your meter down from bold to MEEK. Take that lousy, loser of a word, and all that it implies and represents, out of your vocabulary. DON'T EVER THINK OF IT. MEEK, MY ASS! So from here on out, young brother of mine, you make sure that you, getting older, means being LOUD, PROUD, CONFIDENT, WITH A WILL UNBREAKABLY STRONG. You do that, sir. You use those tools you positively possess, and the rest of your life will be lived, WITH INCREASED PRIDE AND PURPOSE. Don't you ever be afraid to express your thoughts and views, in an assertive and authoritative way. You have earned LOUD AND PROUD! Whatever the surrounding environment consists of, make sure the WHOLE WORLD AROUND YOU KNOWS, that through these forties and fifties, and for the rest of your natural life, you are and will always be A FORCE TO BE RECKONED WITH!!!

The "F" Word

84

God knows I've used the "F" word frequently, but most of the time in a constructive or humorous way. Well in this case, not to worry. It's not the one you hear being so blatantly thrown around these days. With me, these "F" words have a completely different meaning. They fall into what I consider a negative context if not utilized in a positive way. Those three words are: *flawed, failing,* and *frustrated*. They seem to be used much more frequently, as we start that so-called BIG MALE MENOPAUSE STAGE OF OUR LIFE, this great twenty-year transition, to our greater second half. But then diametrically opposed to those negative three words, are three more "F" words at the opposite, POSITIVE END OF THE SPECTRUM. And they are: *fruitful, fulfilling*, and *fortunate*. Like anything else in your life, the words you choose to express your thoughts, ideas, and values, when used repetitiously on a daily basis, will not only have a major impact, but they will REPRESENT AND ENCOMPASS YOUR OVERALL STATE OF MIND. So here we go again, your choice. Which group of words do you want to DOMINATE, AND CONSTITUTE YOUR WAY OF THINKING? No middle ground, no gray areas here. It's like flipping a coin - heads or tails.

So in the living of your life, your choice literally will be based on one of two things psychologically and philosophically: DO I WIN OR DO I LOSE in my life's long journey. You must understand, everything you say on a consistent basis, WILL BECOME YOUR STATE OF MIND, which will surely determine how elevated your quality of life. Every aspect of it will be the results of the thoughts you function by, and the WORDS YOU CHOOSE TO USE TO EXPRESS THOSE THOUGHTS. That's why you must be careful, thought structure and word content will become HABIT FORMING. If you constantly let words like *flawed*, *failed*, or *frustrated* dominate your thinking, then your life has the potential of being lived in a FLAWED, FAILED, OR FRUSTRATED WAY. It will affect every aspect of your life - marriage, work, friendships, associations. So here's what I suggest: Take those negative "F" words out of your mind, BEFORE THEY REACH YOUR MOUTH. And if you can't do that, at least minimize their use and effect, so there will be more room for those more naturally positive words like *fruitful*, *fulfilling* and *fortunate*. Let them dominate your thought processes, and contribute to your positive lifestyle.

I think you have to develop a belief system that allows you, to have that kind of ability. Throughout this entire text I'm going to keep reminding you, this belief system of POSITIVITY IS BUILT RIGHT IN YOU. Please, sir, develop it, encourage it, DON'T LET THE WINNER IN YOU WITHER AWAY, and ultimately die. God, man, please don't do that! If you allow that, no matter how many years you have to live, and you may have it in your genes to live way beyond ninety years, PLEASE DO NOT PLANT AND CULTIVATE THOSE NEGATIVE "F" WORDS DURING THESE TRANSITIONAL YEARS. If you do, you will have sowed the seeds of psychological, subconscious failure and self-restriction, through pessimistic auditory. Not a very smart move, when you know YOU CAN JUST AS

281

READILY, TAKE A POSITIVE COURSE OF ACTION. Really something to think about. Why in the world would you do anything in your life, that has even the slightest potential of being self-defeating, when being a lover of life, is JUST A THOUGHT AWAY. So focus on those positive "F" words. With one single thought, you will be able to change the course of the whole of your life, in a PERMANENTLY POSITIVE DIRECTION.

We know that throughout history, be it a century or a millennium, in fact, almost all of modern western civilization, we know this world has been negative, uncertain, and generally a dangerous place. Well knowing that, you should know you must consciously RESIST LETTING THAT RUB OFF ON YOU, where you could become a reaction, or worse yet, a victim, of those negatively influenced habits and conditions. SIR, THAT SHOULD BE TOTALLY UNACCEPTABLE TO YOU. You are always going to be surrounded by negativity, it is always going to be around every corner and every unknown twist and turn of life you take. Those three negative "F" words have thousands of cousins, that suggest and imply trauma, trepidation, and more likely than not, ULTIMATE FAILURE TO FUNCTION EFFECTIVELY. You want that better, more rewarding life? Well it's entirely up to you to know, every minute of your life is lived above the neck in your brain, in your psyche! You must on a persistent basis, exercise all the brain power you can, to make and keep your twenty-four-seven world positive and productive. Now I've said this more than once: THIS IS NOT A NOW-AND-THEN OR ONCE IN A WHILE PROPOSITION. Every day of life you are given, you gotta work on developing and keeping in play, your positive, productive, and passionate attitude. Do it, and it WILL DEFINITELY BECOME YOUR REALITY. So use as repetitiously as you possibly can those fundamental upbeat, uplifting words: *fruitful*, *fulfilling* and *fortunate*, plus the dozens more that make your life, a big, winning experience.

ANYBODY CAN SAY THE WORD *WIN*. But just as sure as rain is wet, saying it is not enough. You gotta think it, believe, and feel it in every cell of YOUR BODY, YOUR MIND, AND YOUR SPIRIT. Then you gotta live it out every minute of your life. THAT'S HOW YOU FEEL LIKE AND BECOME, A LIFELONG WINNER. And now more than ever during this twenty-year man-in-the-middle period, IT IS OF THE UTMOST IMPORTANCE. So from this moment on, one more time for the memory. Reduce the use of those negative little "F" words: *flawed*, *failed*, and *frustrated*, and all their cursed cousins, that can contribute to MAKING YOU FEEL LESS THAN YOU ARE. Nip them in the bud. In that way, they can never DOMINATE YOUR THINKING AND AFFECT YOUR ACTIONS. That's how you eliminate ever relating in any way to that lousy, luckless word, *loser*. Let's say it together, kind sir: LOSER, MY ASS! JUST KEEP THINKING LIKE THE WINNER YOU KNOW YOU ARE. Make no mistake, this is not QUESTIONABLE THEORY, this is A LONG-LIVED, PROVEN FACT OF LIFE telling you unequivocally: the more meaning you put behind those three productive "F" words and their carefully chosen cousins, THE BIGGER OF A WINNER YOU WILL DEFINITELY BE!

Disagree and Dislike

85

I would like to believe in most all respects, I am fundamentally similar to any other man. Let me tell you why: When you find yourself being too different, too removed, then you are going to find it will be very hard, even difficult, to RELATE TO AND IDENTIFY WITH OTHER PEOPLE. And in life, there is nothing more important than people relating to each other. Now this is where we all must take stock of ourselves. I personally knew how it affected me as a younger man. I was very opinionated. I knew precisely the things I agreed or disagreed with. Like any other man who is secure enough to admit it, I KNEW THE MISTAKES I MADE DURING MY FIRST FORTY, AND DURING MY SECOND FORTY, I TRIED TO DO EVERYTHING IN MY POWER TO CORRECT THEM. So in general terms, there is very little difference between me or you or most any other man in that regard. Now here's what's really of great relevance to me, and I hope to you also: Why would I be argumentatively or disrespectfully different, and wind up UNNECESSARILY KICKING PEOPLE OUT OF MY LIFE for no good reason, when I could have, by intelligent choice, the option TO RELATE AND COMMUNICATE IN A LESS JUDGMENTAL AND MORE REASONABLE WAY.

Right up to this late stage in my life, there are still a ton of things that I fervently disagree with. Well not for a minute would I let anything I disagree with, have such a negatively reactionary effect on me, that I would ever let it get in the way of MY LOVE FOR LIFE AND LIVING IT TO THE HILT. Trust me, sir, that would not have had a chance in hell of happening. How STUPIDLY SELF-SERVING that would have been, when all I had to do was be mature enough to realize, THE TRAP I WAS SETTING FOR MYSELF, if I pursued THAT KIND OF SELF-DESTRUCTIVE BEHAVIOR. It would dominate and take control of my emotions, having a restrictive negative input, ON ALL MY ASSOCIATIONS AND RELATIONSHIPS. Think how dumb that would have been on my part, to create and allow those conditions to exist, and have them DICTATE the course of most of MY LIFE'S ACTIONS. When those daily demons tried to do their disruptive deeds, I muscled up my mental powers and said to myself: THERE IS NOT ONE GOD DAMNED CHANCE IN HELL, THAT IS GOING TO BE MY ULTIMATE DESTINY! And I still say that every day of my life, out loud, because I knew that was MY DAILY FIGHT. Now, did I win every battle? HELL NO! Did I win a whole lot more than I lost? HELL YES! So not on your life should you let the things you disagree with and dislike, DOMINATE TO THE POINT OF KICKING GOOD PEOPLE, WITH DIFFERENT OPINIONS, OUT OF YOUR LIFE.

Afterthought: The more interesting people in your life, AGREE OR DISAGREE, the more exciting and rewarding will be the living of your life! It is definitely to your long-term interest and advantage.

The Big Double "M"

86

You know what is of great value and importance, in fact the top priority of the aging process? MEMORIES! As you continue your long climb up the ladder of getting older, it's only natural that you will accumulate a MULTITUDE OF MEMORIES. Now we all know, all memories are not necessarily good ones. In the course of your life, all actions you may take and the decisions you make, do not always represent your best judgment. But it's of vital importance the assets outweigh the liabilities, making damn sure YOUR GOOD MEMORIES OUTNUMBER THE BAD. What I'm asking is not easy. So much depends on your day to day judgment. But no matter that judgment or how questionably accurate it might be, you must always work at making your memories, WORTH LOOKING BACK ON. Now, with your naturally active mind, and your innate ability to recall and magnify those memories, just make sure the majority of them are more often than not WELL WORTH REMEMBERING. Of course they can't all be good memories, but if the good outnumber the bad at least two-to-one, you are going to win big in life. EMPHASIZE AND FOCUS ON YOUR POSITIVE MEMORIES, they always constitute and represent, the largest part of the successful living of your life.

In fact, here's how important memories really are: All you have right now is the moment you are living in. Well that moment has just passed, it's now a memory! But here's what I also suggest: All those memories of yours that make YOU FEEL GOOD, JOYFUL, HAPPY, AND EVEN HELPFUL, DON'T JUST

RECALL THEM, EXPAND ON AND EMBELLISH THEM. When you do that, they will constantly fortify your self-worth, and stimulate your self-confidence. Now of course there are the ones that may have been bad or sad. They are always going to be there for everyone alive. But why, sir, would you or any man of sound mind MAGNIFY AND EXPAND MISERABLE MEMORIES? Just the reverse should be your course of action. REDUCE AND DIMINISH THEM. In that way, every memory has more room in your mind to become a POSITIVE MENTAL BUILDING BLOCK. Then this memory making moment will assuredly fortify and strengthen who you are. You will definitely REDUCE THE IMPACT OF THE BAD ONES.

So, if you want to guarantee yourself a mountain of HAPPY, CONFIDENCE BUILDING MEMORIES that improve every remaining moment of your life, that's how to do it. That's why it is so damn important, that your mind SHOULD START CREATING NEW, MORE VALUABLE, MORE MEANINGFUL MEMORIES. Now that's what I call GREAT ANTICIPATION. You looking forward to building FORTY TO SIXTY MORE YEARS OF MARVELOUS MEMORIES. Now remember what I said: If they need a little bit of positive adjusting, adjust them, WITHIN THE BOUNDARIES OF REASONED REALITY. You will find out just how much more rewarding life can be.

So remember always, all but the moment you are living in, ARE MEMORIES. Shine your positive light on MEMORIES PAST, that will with certainty make your remaining human journey, MUCH MORE MEMORABLE.

Positive Passion

87

It's so easy to be victimized by the world we're living in. So it is of utmost importance you know and understand, this is more often than not a VIOLENT, HOSTILE, UNSTABLE WORLD. More likely than not, as mentioned earlier, there are going to be thousands of things that you may disagree with, even find distasteful. Well, kind sir, if you lived a thousand years, our accurately documented past history is a strong indicator, it's not going to get very much better, considering how FLAWED WE ARE AS A SPECIES. Advanced technology has very little chance of changing fundamental and basic nature. That's why your big challenge will always be to give yourself, AS MUCH POSITIVE PASSION AS POSSIBLE, for your living and loving of life in general. Because no matter what you agree or disagree with, if you don't LOVE YOUR LIFE, and the way you are LIVING IT, there's a damn good chance you could literally turn yourself into, one miserable, misguided maladjusted, middle aged man. I know those are strong words, but my own personal experience over almost a century of living, has led me to believe they are accurate. Why would any man want to remain or feel unfulfilled, particularly your age, when WITH AN EXPANDED PURPOSE, AND INCREASING PASSION, YOUR LIFE CAN EASILY BECOME SO MUCH MORE GRATIFYING. But know, it's all on you. Only you can produce that more satisfying alternative. Now, be acutely aware of all the negatives that exist in this overwhelmingly pessimistic environment. So to effectively exercise your positive passion, it is going to require a daunting determination. So what! Do it! You and I both know that's the smart move. Always reduce the FALSELY PERCEIVED IMPORTANCE of environmental negatives. That's what common sense should tell you. And that's exactly what will occur by you creating your own PERSONALIZED POSITIVE PASSION, for the loving, respecting, and BELIEVING in every aspect and action of your life.

I don't care how challenging the conditions seem to be, YOUR POSITIVE NATURE AND STRENGTH OF WILL, can vastly upgrade your respect for the person you are. Now you might ask: Is it hard to do? Are you f-ing kidding me? It just may be the hardest thing you'll ever do! Diminishing half a lifetime of memories, that could easily have affected your psyche in a negative way? It's as tough as a turtle's shell! But I'm here to tell ya, AFTER EXERCISING MY POSITIVE PASSION every day for over seventy years of my adult life, I can guarantee, it will represent the BIGGEST PAYOFF you will ever know in your life.

It's so easy to be narrow minded in this contrary world. BUT YOU MUST NEVER, EVER, LET THE THINGS IN LIFE YOU DON'T LIKE, CONTROL AND DOMINATE YOUR EMOTIONS, AND IN THE PROCESS, DICTATE YOUR COURSE OF ACTION, AND *DIMINISH YOUR QUALITY OF LIFE*. If you have started down that dark, dangerous road, please, sir, get the hell off it, and get off it post haste! Because if you don't during this pivotal, critical, first twenty years of this great transition into the second half of life, your miseries and disappointments, will continue to manifest and multiply. Pause for a minute. Scratch that head of yours and think, how UNNECESSARY AND SELF DEFEATING that kind of self-imposed conduct would make you feel. Sir, I traveled that dark, dangerous road to near oblivion. But finally, I PULLED MY HEAD OUT OF MY ASS. Make no mistake, young brother, like you, I'm a man. Just as potentially susceptible and vulnerable to life's realities as most any guy. I DID NOT LET THAT HAPPEN TO ME, AND IF YOU ARE STRONG MINDED AND STRONG WILLED, YOU CAN PREVENT IT FROM EVER HAPPENING TO YOU.

So thinking objectively, practically, and fair, without any false pride or ego getting in your way, and being brutally honest, ask yourself: "HAVE I WITH POSITIVE PASSION REALLY MADE THE FULL-BLOWN EFFORT TO ACCOMPLISH TO ITS FULLEST, MY LOVE OF LIFE *AND THE LOVING OF MYSELF IN IT*, IN SPITE OF THIS MOSTLY CONTRARY AND NEGATIVE WORLD." And if the answer is no, you haven't to its fullest extent, that simply means you must place INCREASED MEANING ON THE POSITIVE PASSION YOU POSSESS, AND BELIEVE MORE DEEPLY IN IT. Know just how much more you are capable of becoming. That's how you use your love of life to its fullest possible capacity. IT WOULD BE COUNTERPRODUCTIVE AND JUST PLAIN FOOLISH TO DO THE OPPOSITE.

Negative Thoughts From Negative Words

88

We've discussed this in passing, but I want to get more specific. There are certain words more often than not, that can produce long-term results that contribute to a lifestyle more negative than positive. Unfortunately, many people use words more negative than positive several times a day. What can be deceiving is, they certainly seem innocent enough. They're simple words like *can't, won't, don't, wouldn't, couldn't* and *shouldn't.* Now of course there are many instances, that those six words could have positive implications and meanings. But generally speaking, these are the kinds of words that, when used too frequently in a serious discussion, can subconsciously feed self-doubt, cause hesitation, and eventually through repetitious use, cultivate and become breeders of FEAR AND INSECURITY. Those are the two major ingredients that contribute greatly TO PERSONAL LOSS OF CONFIDENCE. As innocent as those six words may sound, it's these exact words that over an extended period of time, can LEAD TO PERSONAL LIMITATIONS, as relates to our overall mentality maintaining a substantially more positive than negative mindset. It seems the older we get, the more these two innocent sounding words – fear and insecurity - creep into our minds, CREATING MORE THAN NORMAL SELF DOUBT. My point: When you use *couldn't, wouldn't, shouldn't, can't, won't,* and *don't* daily, at this stage of your life, as opposed to when you were a twenty to thirty years old, they can contribute to A SHAKIER INSTEAD OF A SOLID FOUNDATION, to your core values and priorities.

So your mission when those words are used too negatively, cut their usage to a minimum. Better yet, as these years of the second half of your life pass, be consciously aware to use those words only when they become your ally, not your enemy, only when their meaning has positive implications.

Simple summary to this subject: *should do* will always produce better results than *shouldn't do*. *Could do* and *can do*, again, positive and productive words as opposed to *couldn't do*, *can't do* and *won't do*. So whatever conversations you are involved in, BE CONSCIOUS OF THESE MORE OFTEN THAN NOT NEGATIVE WORDS. Refuse to let them influence, no less dominate, YOUR THINKING OR YOUR SPOKEN WORD, because they can put a negative slant, on the thoughts you are conveying. USE THEM LESS AND LESS IN YOUR SECOND HALF OF LIFE.

So please, sir, look back on that life of yours, consider all the sacrifices you have made, and are still making. Do that and you will become aware in a positive way, of how to apply the rest of your THOUGHT-PROVOKING, SPOKEN LIFE. You must keep your negative thoughts and the words they represent to a conscious minimum. How many times does The Old Man have to say it to ya: YOU HAVE JUSTIFIABLY EARNED AND RICHLY DESERVE, THAT KIND OF PERMANENT, POSITIVE, POWERFUL, PURPOSE, <u>WHEN SPEAKING YOUR MIND</u>.

Downhill Ride? Not For You!

89

With advancing age, I think we should be careful not to let each passing year, become more of a frustrating preoccupation. I know it was that way for me, and as strong willed as I thought I was, it really tried to take a hold on me all those many decades ago. I finally figured it out, this was just nature at work during my great transition. I learned, the older you get, the more preoccupying this EVER-PRESENT STATE OF MIND CAN BECOME. THAT'S YOUR CHALLENGE. It's your call. Downhill ride for you? Why? What counts where you are concerned, as referred to with repetitious intensity, is to make sure you have an INCREASINGLY POSITIVE STATE OF MIND AS YOU GET OLDER. Only one way to do that. Please, sir, NO FEELING SORRY FOR YOURSELF as these years pile up. Certain natural limitations are a given as we get older. So what! NO BIG DEAL UNLESS YOU MAKE IT ONE. These are natural conditions you can use in an affirmative way. If you think a negative state of mind is creeping in, keep it out by ACCEPTING THE REALITY, what you were CAN NEVER BE LIVED AGAIN. Of greater relevance, YOU SHOULD KNOW YOU ARE NOW A BETTER, MORE COMPLETE MAN THAN WHAT YOU WERE THEN. Why? Because you are now functioning with a highly developed, more emotionally balanced, SUPERIOR STATE OF MIND, which you must encourage to be, MORE POSITIVE AND PRODUCTIVE. That's all it's going to take from you, sir. JUST KEEP YOUR HEAD SCREWED ON STRAIGHT AS THE YEARS PILE UP. You have acquired the experience to make the time you are living in now MORE USABLE and MORE VALUABLE.

Guys, when it comes to vanity and pride, I'm guilty as charged. It's no mystery to me why so many men react in a depressed way to the aging process. It's called EXCESSIVE VANITY AND FALSE PRIDE. How do I know that? Because its effect on me was immense all those years ago. And if expanded upon, we subconsciously, may not know we've started on that LONG-TERM DOWNHILL RIDE, WHERE YOUR MORTALITY IS CONCERNED. You must never let your age have such a strong negative influence where you believe, YOUR LIFE HAS LESS VALUE, LESS MEANING, AND LESS PURPOSE.

Sir, I want your strength of will and sense of self-worth to KICK THAT DAMN DEMON OF FEAR AND INSECURITY, *THE CREATORS OF SELF DOUBT*, COMPLETELY, TOTALLY OUT OF YOUR LIFE. As I state so often, take the realistic experiences of your youth, and always be objective about them. In that way, you will make sure they PROVIDE A PATHWAY TO ELEVATE YOURSELF ABOVE THEM. THERE IS NO REASON TO QUESTION OR HAVE EVEN THE SLIGHTEST DOUBT, ABOUT THE PRICE YOU PAID TO BE WHO YOU ARE NOW. Downhill ride? My ass! You get that sweet ass of yours in gear, sir, and take that uptown, upward bound ride into what SHOULD, COULD, CAN, WILL, AND MUST be you being the maker of this life's second half, the best years of your life. SIR, THAT IS YOUR JUST AND VALID REWARD.

Things We Don't Like

90

Even though as individuals we have singular identities, there are certain things we have in common. Not just physical appearance in general, but even similar likes and dislikes. Do we have prejudices? Of course we do, and not because of another person's color or culture, but there are so many other things in life you may not agree with. And, sir, they could number in the hundreds. Just think about all your daily activities over a lifetime. All the diverse situations you are involved in. CAN'T ALWAYS BE EXACTLY THE WAY YOU WANT IT. Because ninety-nine percent of the time, there's other people involved. If you don't have patience, benevolence, and most important, COMPROMISE, you will not achieve very much success, in any area of human contact. I readily admit, there are lots of things I see and hear that absolutely irritate the hell out of me, and not because they are right or wrong, good or bad, but because they are NOT IN ACCORDANCE WITH MY VALUE SYSTEM. Well that's how I was, that SUBJECTIVE AND SELF SERVING. That's how we can all be! Like most men, most of the time, I feel my opinions, after lengthy evaluation, are accurate and valid, so of course I think I am right because I am being SUBJECTIVE, which comes easier and is more mentally comforting than being OBJECTIVE. Well, in spite of all those things that I don't like or disagree with, I refuse to let them get me down, or emotionally upset me and become unhinged because of them. I have taught myself to love the living of my life in WHATEVER VARIABLE FORMS IT TAKES. And young brother, at that time for this naturally outspoken strong-minded man, it was anything but easy, in fact maybe my toughest single task ever. One of the hardest changes I ever had to make, and took a hell of a long time to achieve. With all my good fortune and my interesting encounters over all these decades, I have made it my mission for SELF PRESERVATION PURPOSES, to love every aspect of life NOW MORE THAN EVER. Excellent reasoning: after living ninety years, how many more do I think I have? I am smart enough to know that even if I live to be a hundred, I have already used up ninety percent of my time. This gray-haired old muscle-man will soon be at the very end of his lifespan. Well rest assured, I'll deal with it, and I'll handle it.

Having used up close to fifty percent of your life, spend as little time as possible out of your next half-century, giving license to any of those conditions, situations, or people that irritate you, and could have a LASTING NEGATIVE EFFECT ON YOU. If you let that happen, you'll find BOTH THE PERPETRATOR AND VICTIM IN THE MIRROR LOOKING RIGHT BACK AT YOU. When you permit things you disagree with to dominate, they will ASSUREDLY DICTATE YOUR ATTITUDE. THE END RESULT COULD EASILY BE CRIPPLING YOUR JOY FOR LIFE, AND DIMINISHING YOUR SPIRIT. So assess accurately the actions and conduct of others. You'll find the majority of the time, they'll be talking about what THEY DON'T LIKE INSTEAD OF WHAT THEY DO LIKE. That's the primary reason so many men past forty half quit on life, JUST BECAUSE OF THINGS THEY DON'T AGREE WITH. Now how silly is that? Every man is entitled to his own opinion, just don't OVERREACT to any opinion, just because you strongly disagree with it. A battle we all fight all of our lives, and thank God, in all honesty, I believe I'm winning it. Why? I HAVE LEARNED NOT TO FIND EXCESSIVE FAULT WITH OTHERS WHEN THEIR OPINIONS DON'T FALL IN LINE WITH MINE, when I am so acutely aware of MY OWN IMPERFECT NATURE. Why in the hell would I do that to myself. Don't let it happen to you, when with just a TOUCH OF TOLERANCE and open mindedness, you can exchange views with people, and still be loving the whole damn hell-bent-for-leather human experience. Never forget, their freedom of choice is just as important as your freedom of choice. So never be intimidated or over agitated by ANYBODY ELSE'S OPINIONS. You must resolve and understand how important that kind of fair and balanced conduct and action is. Just think of the aggravation and annoyance YOU ARE INTELLIGENTLY AND WISELY AVOIDING.

If you are on the low road of life, GET THE HELL OFF IT. The low road is a total waste, a losers lonely and barren road where you could wind up very much alone. Just know and accept there will always be so many things you don't like. Of course they exist. The purpose of this piece: Never let them GIVE REASON FOR YOU TO AGGRAVATE YOURSELF. If you do, they will be a total waste of your valuable time. Know you are much too good, to let THINGS YOU DON'T LIKE take control and DOMINATE, TO YOUR DISPLEASURE AND FRUSTRATION.

297

Longer Stronger

91

You living longer, getting, and staying stronger, also looking better and being that prouder, bolder, more confident man, DOES NOT HAVE AN AGE LIMIT ON IT, unless it is self-imposed.

Let's really look into this longer stronger theme. Activate, but accurately, every month and year of your past memories, and you are going to find that you have invested THOUSANDS OF HOURS OF HARD WORK, that included THOUSANDS OF OBSTACLES AND PROBLEMS, that you worked your way through and successfully resolved, in order to survive and continue on. BE PROUD OF THAT! Being that responsible person, plus a thousand other day-to-day obligations, that went along with those earlier stages of your life. Well after forty or more active years, do you think you deserve the right to get stronger the longer you live? OF COURSE YOU ONE HUNDRED PERCENT DO. After age twenty, for twenty more years, acquiring adequate financial means to support your lifestyle. Should you kick back and smell the roses during this, your great transition? Of course you should, now that you are SMARTER, WISER, AND MORE QUALIFIED. MORE NOW THAN EVER! That's why living longer, justifiably means being stronger in every phase of your CHANGING PERSONA. That's a fact you must accept and believe. So, whatever your needs and wants are from here on out, to achieve your goals for the rest of your life, don't you let anybody suggest or ever tell you anything, that could in any way undermine your ongoing, growing, longer, stronger mindset. Listen, my better than good man, YOU SURE

AS HELL HAVE MORE THAN EARNED AND DESERVE IT. It's like your own insurance policy, PREMIUM PAID IN FULL.

Just because one phase of your life is ending, in no way does that imply your life's journey has less meaning. Your job now: MAKE IT HAVE MORE MEANING. So if you feel it's time to retire from your job, it does not mean YOU RETIRING FROM AN ACTIVE, PRODUCTIVE LIFE. The longer you live, the stronger and more self-assured you will become. Doing nothing will culminate in your producing nothing, which can cultivate a feeling of BEING LESS USEFUL. Now think about this, sir: no matter how rich or intelligent any man has been, if that individual becomes less productive with advancing age, he will semi-consciously if not subconsciously, NATURALLY THINK LESS OF HIMSELF.

So at whatever age it is, that you finally decide to finish doing what you had to do to make a buck, and fulfill your responsibilities, and this is powerfully important, YOU MUST NEVER RETIRE FROM AN ONGOING, ALWAYS GETTING BETTER, ACTIVE, INTERESTING, AND REWARDING LIFESTYLE. This is the perfect time to dream your even bigger dreams, to ensure yourself the just and rightful rewards you so richly deserve. Only one way that is going to be achieved, kind sir, and one word says it all: *Doing.* DOING … DOING AND MORE DOING OF THOSE THINGS THAT FULFILL YOUR FEELINGS, AND SATISFY YOUR NEEDS AND WANTS. Because once you retire from making a living, why would you let yourself believe with advancing age, that you have to live your life with diminished enthusiasm. A whole new world of opportunities are going to open up for you, IF YOU SEARCH THEM OUT WITH CURIOSITY AND PASSION. You *must* seek them out with proven CONFIDENCE AND AUTHORITY, that you have, VALIDLY ACQUIRED. So, you keep STOKING THE FIRE, of your strongest DESIRES, AMBITIONS, HOPES, AND DREAMS. Young brother of mine, for God's and your sake, PLEASE DON'T YOU EVER LET YOUR DREAM FADE, FALTER, OR DIE. Regardless of your age, reach higher and try harder with every hope you have, to make that cherished, heart-felt dream, scheme, or fantasy COME TRUE. However far-fetched you might think a dream is, it will never be BIGGER THAN YOUR LIVING OF LIFE. It is well within your CAPACITIES AND CAPABILITIES to achieve. You know how highly relevant that is? It means YOU OWN IT! IT'S YOURS EXCLUSIVELY a part of every day that you are granted this great gift of life. So keep those positive, confident thoughts always, at the forefront of your thinking. Use your IMAGINATION TO KEEP BUILDING ON THEM. Without question, I found out over my long human journey, the most rewarding and gratifying times of my entire life happened when I WAS PRODUCTIVELY USEFUL. Well chasing my dreams certainly embellished and made more meaningful that positive lifestyle. SO KNOW THIS WITH ABSOLUTE CERTAINTY: If you feed and nourish your self-respect and self-confidence, then it WILL BE ENTIRELY YOURS FOR THE TAKING, FOR YOUR ENTIRE LONGER, STRONGER SECOND HALF OF LIFE.

Valuable Life

92

I've said it a thousand times, and it's a common theme that runs through this book: No matter how well you take care of yourself, every single organ and muscle and ligament and tendon in your forty-plus year-old body, has been working every second of those first forty-plus years. It goes with the territory, so we sure as hell better face up to it and learn to live with this AUTHENTIC, HIGHLY RELEVANT FACT OF LIFE. That being established, let's get to the PLUS FACTOR IN THIS EQUATION. Again I say so it will sink in a little deeper: Don't ever think that just because you are getting older, those years piling up means you are becoming more obsolete, and that your life in the overall picture with the passage of time and natural wear and tear, has less value or meaning. That's another crock of crap YOU MUST NEVER BELIEVE! Please, sir, I implore you, do everything within your positive power to never let that lousy loser of a life take hold, or become any part of your permanent mindset. All around me at this late stage of my life, I witness men ten to forty years younger than me, FEELING MORE REMOTE AND REMOVED from life's vibrant mainstream. Why would any man ever allow life and nature's normal wear and tear, TO LIMIT THE EFFECTIVENESS, OF HIS WHOLE REMAINING LIFE'S PURPOSE.

Boy, I am so vividly aware of how touchy and sensitive a subject this is, having lived through it in full-blown form. But know this about your Old Pops: until my dying day, no matter how many aches and pains or how much wear and tear enters my life, if they

301

were ten-fold, and surrounded me, let me tell you what I have learned and what I've done in my life: I HAVE MADE ABSOLUTELY, POSITIVELY ONE HUNDRED PERCENT DAMN SURE, THAT MY OWN SUPER POSITIVE INFLUENCE ON MYSELF IS EVEN STRONGER, MORE RESILIENT, AND MORE POWERFUL, *AS TIME PASSES.* Of all my hundreds of priorities, number one? Having an active, valuable, and complete life. And until I pull my last breath, THAT IS AND WILL ALWAYS BE MY TRUEST OF TRUTHS.

Now the longest and more than likely most meaningful sentence in the book: If you want to add greater value along with greater purpose, and lend more meaning to every remaining moment, of every day of your life, you must remove, not just from your vocabulary, but ultimately from your mindset, the word *obsolete* <u>WHERE IT CONCERNS YOU PERSONALLY</u>. I sure as hell hope I am getting through to ya. Obsolete, my ass! *Don't you ever think or use that word, in whatever form or fashion it tries to impose itself on your psyche.* OBSOLETE YOU ARE NOT! Come on, kiddo, if I'm still pumping out the positive vibes at my age, you sure as hell certainly can at yours.

So here we go again with our play on words. As you get older, sir, you must find a way in your thinking and in your actions, to go one-hundred-eighty degrees from becoming and feeling obsolete, to a total feeling of being *complete.* Of course I'm talking about you having a COMPLETE AND VALUABLE SECOND HALF OF LIFE. This is an every day, *I know I'm getting older – so f-ing what, isn't everybody* - CONSISTENT

POSITIVE MINDSET. All my life I've tried to make rational, believable sense. I hope you are accepting this observation in that context and perspective. Absolutely nobody, no matter how influential they are, NOBODY BUT YOU CAN FULLY PRODUCE THAT VALUABLE LIFE FOR YOU. Encourage you, of course. But on a day to day basis, your number one responsibility is to yourself and ALL THOSE YOU HOLD NEAR AND DEAR.

Another key to making this a reality, is not depending entirely on ESTABLISHMENT VALUES. No rebel here, this is just common sense. ESTABLISHMENT VALUES CAN IMPLY that as you get older, YOUR LIFE HAS LESS PURPOSE. Talk about established establishment destructive bullshit and negative influence, are you God forbid f-ing kidding me?! WHAT A DOWNRIGHT DAMN INSULT TO YOUR INTELLIGENCE. You being told at this mature stage of your life, things and activities you cannot and must not do or take. NOT A CHANCE IN HELL IN A NEW YORK SECOND DO YOU EVER ENTERTAIN THAT TOTALLY THOUGHTLESS, EMPTY, MEANINGLESS WAY OF THINKING.

So don't you ever let any GENERALLY ESTABLISHED CONCEPT, imply that the QUALITY OF YOUR LIFE IS BEING DIMINISHED, as you climb life's chronological ladder. POINT THE FINGER OF BLAME ELSEWHERE? NEVER! WHEN YOU KNOW IT WAS YOUR CHOICE TO MAKE. You must BE SUPER STRONG OF WILL, AND FULL OF SELF DETERMINATION, and you will be living your life consistently at its HIGHEST VALUE LEVEL. Please, sir, find and make that philosophical mode rock-solid, so that nobody will ever to the slightest degree, be able to alter or even tinker with your thinking. Have the COURAGE AND CHARACTER OF YOUR CONVICTIONS to say *no*. These must always be YOUR SOLIDLY INDEPENDENT INDIVIDUALIZED CONDITIONS.

Don't ever point that finger of yours at anybody else, when you know it's your responsibility, TO ADD THE FULLEST VALUE, TO YOUR LIFE. You must be STRONG OF WILL, and full of COMMITTED DETERMINATION AT ALL TIMES. When those two qualities of *will* and *determination* are strongly activated and exercised effectively, AGE WILL NEVER BE A BARRIER. The results? You being a TREMENDOUSLY STRONG AND RESILIENT LIFE FORCE. It will make other people fully aware of YOUR SELF WORTH! Always display an aura of self-confidence so strong, that no one would think OF ATTEMPTING TO ALTER OR CHALLENGE YOU, NO LESS CHANGE YOUR MIND. What a great way to go through your second half of life, knowing nobody can ever mess with your mind! Why? They will know by your very strong and confident presence, not a chance in hell they can ever make you do anything YOU DON'T WANT TO DO. That's how you demand and get TOTAL RESPECT, and know you are living a highly VALUABLE REST OF YOUR LIFE.

Good, Bad and Ugly

93

You never wear out a paraphrase that sums up so conclusively, so many relevantly essential real-life implications. These three words do exactly that VERY THOROUGHLY AND EFFICIENTLY. Every day of your life you live with the *good*, the *bad* and the *ugly*. I think we can assume almost all people, love that word *good*. We all like to feel good, eat food that tastes good, and of course we want to look good. We all want as much of what's good as we can get in our life. So we'll assume it always means exactly what it says LITERALLY. Then of course just the opposite is true of the word *bad*. And the third word, which is the cousin of bad: *ugly*. So if you've got to live with these three words – where two are negative, causing excessive griping and bitching - and only one is positive, not very good odds if you USE THEM EQUALLY. That could be a problem when you express yourself audibly. One positive, and the other two just the opposite. You and I both know, much of life CONSISTS OF THINGS AND CONDITIONS THAT ARE BAD AND UGLY. It's still a mystery to me, but somehow I knew by mid-life, it was those negative two words – bad and ugly – that could consume a lot of my rhetoric and thought processes, and negatively dominate my mindset and environment, IF I LET THEM. All those years ago I was faced with that task, knowing in the living of my life, how much MORE BAD AND UGLY THERE IS GOING TO BE compared to the good. I just made up my mind I was going to find a way to tolerate, and in positive fashion deal with it all. Naturally the good came easy. But, man, it took a lot of committed learning for an emotional, opinionated guy like me, to develop the tolerance and patience to live productively, with the bad and the ugly ALWAYS BEING THERE, AND STILL LOVING EVERY ASPECT OF MY LIFE. I didn't like what the bad and ugly represented, and it was a tough learning process to reduce their use, but I knew there was no escaping completely THE NEGATIVE CONDITIONS THOSE TWO WORDS CREATED. I for one have learned, as hopefully you have too, THE GOOD, THE BAD, AND THE UGLY ALL GO WITH EVERYTHING IN YOUR LIFE.

So here's my take on the overall picture: When something bad and/or ugly happens, there can be many reactions and alternatives. The circumstances and conditions that fall into bad and ugly can easily create ANGER, FRUSTRATION, DISAPPOINTMENT, DESPAIR, DEPRESSION, EVEN DEEP SADNESS. Now in the course of a long life, we are going to continually have many moments like that. What you must do is recognize them as a part of your living pattern, AND MINIMIZE THEIR IMPACT. I again somehow knew, the more I complained about the bad and the ugly in my life, the more preoccupied I became with them. NOT A SMART THING TO DO. God, man, just think how many things in your life, are going to fall under and be associated with those two nasty words. If you lose your job, have a hard time paying your bills, that sure as hell can be bad and ugly. And with all the people in your life, there can be troubled relationships ASSOCIATED WITH THE BAD, LEADING TO UGLY. How many times in your life, has a good relationship under adverse conditions, TURNED BAD and could easily BECOME UGLY. Example: Even if your point is valid, if

306

it's a heated difference of opinion, that's bad. And if that same disagreement leads to an overheated argument, it sure as hell can get ugly real fast, creating a DEEPER DARKER HOLE, WHERE IT COULD GET VERY, VERY UGLY. Now we both know it's so easy to rationalize in favor of yourself and say: "I know I'm right, why me?" Well, sir, it's not *why me* or *you,* it's everybody who is alive because all of us are going to communicate and relate in different ways. WE ALL BELONG TO THE GOOD, THE BAD, AND THE UGLY *CLUB*. Because all those things - good or bad or ugly - all people experience. Now it's easy to put your SUBJECTIVE BLINDERS ON and FIND FAULT EVERYWHERE YOU LOOK. Or you can make the SMART, SENSIBLE CHOICE where the bad and the ugly are concerned. Apply your positive passion to overpower, neutralize, and take CONTROL OF THE EFFECTS that go with those two JOY-DESTROYING WORDS.

Now let's take it up a notch and thoroughly evaluate its long-term effect. I'm here to tell you that even though I'm inclined to be more emotional than most, the true joy of this long life so far, as much as anything else I've ever done, was to HONESTLY UNDERSTAND OBJECTIVELY, THE PROS AND CONS OF HUMAN NATURE, and learn to live with it all - the giving and taking and all the passions and challenges they created. YOU ARE GOING TO BE FACING, THOUSANDS MORE OF THOSE TOUGH ORDEALS IN LIFE, THAT ARE FULL OF ADVERSITY. What you must do to lighten that load, as I have suggested, if you haven't already, YOU MUST BE TOLERANT IN ORDER TO LESSEN THE LOAD OF THE BAD AND THE UGLY, because, young brother, as implied, there is no escaping

307

it. It is going to keep happening, all around us for the rest of our lives. YOU MUST MINIMIZE ITS IMPORTANCE, REDUCING ITS EFFECT. If you let it over-burden you, it will automatically guarantee PSYCHOLOGICAL AND SPIRITUAL DAMAGE. Over the many years you've lived, and all your future decades yet to be lived, DON'T LET THE WEIGHT OF THE BAD AND THE UGLY DOMINATE. Come on, young brother of mine, for the umpteenth time, being secure and confident means being tolerant and understanding. Lift that head of yours up high, be strong and smart, show that confidence in your facial expressions. THAT'S HOW YOU DEAL WITH *AND DOMINATE* THE BAD AND THE UGLY, and make extra room in your brain, to expand on all the GOOD things in your life. Sir, you do this on an every day basis and that EXPANSION OF GOOD will more strongly influence your POWERFUL, POSITIVE ATTITUDE, which will greatly REDUCE THE IMPACT OF BAD AND UGLY. It is going to take all the mental muscle you can muster up, all the rest of your life, to achieve.

Now, when the bad and the ugly start to do their DESPICABLE DIRTY WORK, that's your cue, sir, to let them know who the hell they are dealing with. You and only you, can bring the f-d up forces of bad and ugly in your life to a SCREECHING F-ING HALT. The results? A FEELING OF LIFE-LONG FULFILLMENT.

Equal To All Others

94

All of us, every last human, is born with insecurities and self-doubts, as I so frequently with cause refer to. We were almost completely dependent on others, so we automatically, naturally, LACKING INDEPENDENCE, FURTHER DEVELOP INSECURITIES AND SELF DOUBTS. I am no exception. Irrefutable fact: Because I was dependent on others, I was a victim of all those similar self-doubts and insecurities, for almost all of life's necessities, during those first fifteen MOST FORMATIVE YEARS OF MY LIFE. But from twenty to forty, I slowly learned to become independent, eventually assuming one hundred percent personal responsibility for my thoughts and actions. So whether you are approaching forty, past sixty, all the way up to eighty-plus in your journey through life, please, sir, DON'T EVER ACCEPT AS YOUR NORM, whatever insecurities and self-doubts you still IMAGINE might exist, from your formative years. Know YOU ARE ANY AND EVERY MAN'S EQUAL.

No matter how self-assured and smart any other man might be, because of his also insecure youth, will he or anyone else ever be COMPLETELY FREE OF THOSE INSECURITIES AND SELF DOUBTS. They may have less effect as we mature, but they linger, if only a little, for life. It is something we all have to live with and deal with. So now let's create a criteria, a standard. No matter how many more brain cells and diplomas another person might have, here's all you have to know to VALIDATE AND AUTHENTICATE YOUR PERSONAL EQUALITY: Of course other people are going to have their own talents and abilities, but don't you ever forget what puts you on an equal footing with ANYBODY ELSE ON THIS PLANET. You, sir, not only have YOUR OWN INDIVIDUALITY, YOUR OWN IDENTITY, YOU HAVE TALENTS AND ABILITIES THAT NO OTHER HUMAN POSSESSES, BECAUSE THEY ARE NOT YOU. If you believe deeply enough in your unique qualities you will realize your capacities and capabilities, of going places mentally, psychologically, physically, and logistically, even spiritually, that no one else in this world can. THAT TRULY MAKES YOU SPECIAL. So don't ever put a thought process in place, that is going to stunt and restrict your own special, ONE-OF-A-KIND growth and development. And as I've mentioned and filtered liberally throughout this book, no matter how much you respect and admire somebody else, you are, by virtue of your HUMAN NATURE, THEIR EQUAL. Now, there are many people I have learned from that I admired. That being said, I never considered them either superior or inferior to me, as human beings. Which meant I never had to sacrifice in any way my independence of thinking or my identity, trying to be anything other than what I authentically was. FROM THAT PERSPECTIVE, I KNEW, I WAS EQUAL TO ALL OTHERS. No better or worse, as nature intended. Well, sir, *SO – ARE - YOU! DON'T YOU EVER ATTEMPT TO BE THE OTHER GUY, BECAUSE YOU BELIEVE OR HAVE DECEIVED YOURSELF INTO THINKING,* HE OR SHE IS SUPERIOR TO YOU. Of course you should admire and respect exceptional achievements of all others, but DON'T EVER TRY TO BE THEM OR FEEL INTIMIDATED BY THEM, when your potential, definitely allows you to know

310

you are equal to AND THEREFORE A MATCH FOR ANY MAN OR WOMAN.

Of course we learn from all others all our life. I learned a long time ago from my father, when I was just a teenager and thought I had all the answers. My father, who was a very savvy, street smart guy, sat me down and these few words have stuck with me for over seventy-five years. He said to me, "*Son, I know you are a sharp kid, but I want you to know this: everybody in this world no matter how LIMITED their education and experience in life is, or how RESTRICTED their travel and their exposure to life has been, TALK A LITTLE LESS, AND LISTEN A LITTLE MORE ATTENTIVELY AND RESPECTFULLY, TO WHAT THAT PERSON HAS TO SAY. Because no matter how much smarter you think you are, son, every human being on this planet, no matter their limitations, KNOWS SOMETHING YOU DON'T KNOW. Remember, for the majority of your life you are going to be conversing, sharing the spoken word with other people EVERY DAY OF YOUR LIFE. That means you are an original, a one of a kind, AND SO IS EVERYONE ELSE! Everybody you meet, is going to say something YOU HAVE NEVER HEARD BEFORE. For God sakes man, keep your ears and your brain open, active, and receptive TO ANYBODY, AND YOU WILL LEARN FROM EVERYBODY.*"

That was the pearl of wisdom my father left me with, all those many years ago. So know, everybody can become your teacher, as you also can become theirs. Of course when other people are successful, there is absolutely nothing wrong with being motivated and inspired by them. That has certainly been a major

311

part of my life's driving force. But there is one thing I want you to sincerely believe, every waking minute for the entirety of your life, sir: Recognize YOU WILL ALWAYS HAVE YOUR OWN ONE-OF-A-KIND QUALITIES TO REMOVE INSECURITIES, TO BUILD AUTHENTIC LASTING CONFIDENCE AND SELF WORTH. That will positively ensure your parity and equality. If you haven't already, hopefully you will develop that kind of mentality to such a high level, that it will by its very nature automatically MINIMIZE YOUR INSECURITIES AND SELF DOUBTS, and MAXIMIZE your incentive to step out with COURAGE, to develop and utilize all that you are meant to be.

Repetitiously repeat and unquestionably believe, under all and any conditions, to never deceive yourself into thinking, YOUR LIFE WOULD BE BETTER IF YOU WERE SOMEBODY ELSE. Fully discover through infinitive pursuit, your AUTHENTIC HIGH HUMAN VALUE. Once your mind accepts that truth, all lingering self-doubts, every last one, will be minimized, DIMINISHED AND ULTIMATELY ELIMINATED. Respecting yourself with increasing validity is how you make advancing age an asset. *It is the key, to unlocking your expanded individuality, during this second half of life.* Sir, JUST KEEP CLIMBING AND REACHING, WITH AN OPEN, CONFIDENT, FREE MIND, AND YOU WILL REALIZE THE FULLEST MEANING POSSIBLE, THAT YOUR LIFE HAS TO OFFER.

Writing Your Book

95

I guess over my long lifetime, I have read more than a few hundred books. And although I may out date you, I'm sure you've done your share of reading. Some people read fantasy or fiction, others like biographies that are hopefully accurate portrayals of real people. There are several great history books. But with all the books you've read, as MEANINGFUL AND INFORMATIVE as they might have been, and as strong an INFLUENCE AS THEY MIGHT HAVE HAD, there is one more book you haven't completed yet, that is personally of much greater importance. The most relevant book that will ever be written, is the one you are currently writing: THE BOOK OF YOUR LIFE, where let's assume EVERY PAGE REPRESENTS A WEEK OF YOUR LIFE. If you live to be ninety to a hundred years old, and play it right, smart, and real, you will have written a very, very long, exciting, and interesting book. And to keep it current, the fact that you are reading my book right now, means you are writing a very small part of your own human journey.

So as you write this book of you, try to make every current page better than the previous one, which essentially means, make every current week AN IMPROVEMENT ON THE PREVIOUS WEEK, with the goal of doing it for a lifetime. No matter how adverse any moment of that week you are living in may be, it will provide the opportunity and incentive TO ADD MORE POSITIVE PAGES TO THE BOOK OF YOUR LIFE. It's not hard to figure and so easy to analogize, compare, and then apply, and watch your book of life get better with each page. You must make this four to five thousand-page history of yours, A PERSONAL BEST SELLER. Please, sir, keep writing this BETTER BOOK ABOUT YOURSELF. I want you to focus on making your life more valuable and meaningful. This is your better way to stay currently and passionately involved, in a fuller, more complete life.

Now, as you write with pride and passion, this purposeful book of your life, let me remind you, no matter how thick that book, and how many positive and interesting pages it has, you and I are only given so much of this *precious, priceless gift called time to write it.* Hopefully that last page of this very thick book of life you are writing, is still several decades down the road. But at all times during these many approaching decades of life that are still to come, know now you will have the opportunity to *successfully complete, to your absolute satisfaction*, your long, productive, rewarding, and *TOTALLY FULFILLING HUMAN JOURNEY*.

Our Bodies, Lest We Forget

96

As so frequently referred to in the previous ninety-five observations, the major meaning of positivity, will only be accomplished by you being the major influence in, CONTROLLING EVERY CONDITION AND ENCOUNTER IN YOUR LIFE. Our main focus as early as our teens, was to get smarter. If achieved, you knew it would put you in a position to not pursue just wealth, but develop and build, a MORE PERSONALLY GRATIFYING, LASTING, HUMAN EXPERIENCE. Again, common knowledge tells us, if we improve the brain by acquiring more education, the net result will be more money in our pockets and the bank. Certainly your top priority from twenty to forty. You and I both know how important having enough money was, to satisfy your lifestyle and all your obligations and responsibilities up to forty-plus.

If these accomplishments are a part of your recent past, PAT YOURSELF ON THE BACK! That's a one hundred percent valid reason, to be PROUD OF AND GRATIFIED WITH WHAT YOU HAVE ACHIEVED. But with all these assets and positive experiences I just related, as good as that sounds, THEY COULD BECOME PROBLEMATIC. Here's why: As we make more money, maturing into our resilient manhood, you will have completed to your satisfaction, almost all your goals. When you were twenty into your late thirties, how fast those fifteen to twenty years went! All of a sudden, you're approaching forty! But because so many things were of such a high priority during that survival mode, it's possible you placed A LOWER

PRIORITY, ON THE CONDITION OF YOUR BODY, not realizing the negative effects it could possibly have. Too many men take youthful resilience for granted.

Now with all those priorities completed between twenty and forty, we've become very conscious past forty of what the so called *normal aging process* is. And it's unmistakable. Of course physical compromise don't happen overnight, but it SURE AS HELL SEEMED THAT WAY with our busy over-loaded schedule. And even though it required months and years as you were going through those personal changes, ON A DAY TO DAY BASIS, PHYSICAL CHANGE IS ALMOST IMPERCEPTIBLE. But we do have eyes, and day in and day out we live with ourselves. And that critical moment will finally arrive WHEN YOU WAKE UP TO THE FACT SOMEWHERE BETWEEN THIRTY AND FORTY, ONE LOOK IN THE MIRROR WILL SURE AS HELL TELL YOU, YOU ARE NOT TWENTY ANY MORE. You don't look like you did when you were twenty, and you don't think like you did when you were twenty. So here you are now, in that first stage of life's second half, your forty to sixty bracket, AWARE OF YOUR MORTALITY, particularly when you see the diminished physical condition of that eighty to eighty-five year old man, THAT YOU JUST THINK YOU MIGHT BECOME, thirty or forty years down the road. All of a sudden you are ACUTELY aware, that is a very real, long-term possibility. Let's face it, when you look at somebody thirty to forty years older than you are, it's obvious that no matter how much money or knowledge they may have, wealth NEVER HAS BEEN A GUARANTEE, OF A STRONG, ACTIVE, HEALTHY, HIGHLY ENERGIZED

BODY. Well, sir, the majority of men past seventy-five are considerably more frail, feeble, or infirmed with limited, even restricted PHYSICAL ACTIVITY. The sad commentary on this deteriorating condition, in most cases is, that seventy-five-plus crowd unknowingly let it happen. Their long and young-man period up to thirty-five to forty influenced them to TAKE THEIR PHYSICAL CONDITION FOR GRANTED. So unknowingly they accelerated their own aging process, because WHEN YOU TAKE YOUR PHYSICAL CONDITION FOR GRANTED, IT IS THE SAME AS PHYSICAL NEGLECT. So let's be very frank and realistic. Not a doubt in my mind, those men thirty to forty years older than you, because the process of aging is so slow, again unknowingly, in fact to be more blunt and specific, NOT KNOWING ANY BETTER, showed disrespect for their body BY NOT CARING FOR IT PROPERLY OVER LONG PERIODS OF TIME. Well be aware and sure of this, kind sir, now that you are past forty, that physical decline can and will accelerate more rapidly with each passing year, let me say it again, IF YOU ALLOW IT.

Make no mistake, and know this as unshakable fact: As that body of yours weakens and loses strength, regardless of how well educated and wealthy you are, the possibility is your reduced physical condition, can and will have a negative effect on your SPIRIT FOR LIVING. Generating accelerated psychological adversity. Believe me, sir, they – the mind and body – are that closely connected and play off each other. But know this as a guaranteed human physical fact, and it has been a constant reminder throughout these pages: THERE IS ONLY ONE PERSON ON THIS GOOD EARTH, WHO HAS THE POWER

TO DO SOMETHING ABOUT THAT CONDITION, AND, SIR, THAT IS YOU! ONLY YOU CAN HELP YOURSELF. Don't leave it to chance, sir. Hopefully you will find, at this age, the respect that body of yours deserves to live at a higher level. YOU ARE ENTIRELY, ONE-HUNDRED PERCENT RESPONSIBLE FOR YOUR PHYSICAL WELL-BEING EVERY SECOND OF YOUR LIFE.

If you have neglected yourself even a little physically during the last decade or two, YOU CAN EASILY TURN IT AROUND IN SHORT ORDER! Do it and do it now if you want to DOUBLE THE QUALITY OF YOUR LIFE FOR THE REST OF YOUR LIFE. Your increase in energy will be so rapid, making you so much more active and productive in every way. And your biggest benefit with your increased strength? YOUR SPIRITS, MAN, I'M TELLING YA, YOUR SPIRITS WILL BE LIFTED TO NEVER BEFORE EXPERIENCED LEVELS. Imagine having those three most important aspects of your life – BODY, MIND, AND SPIRIT - IN PERFECT BALANCE, FUNCTIONING AT THEIR OPTIMUM LEVELS. That wonderful feeling of highly elevated strength, energy, and attitude, will increase your capacity to making it possible for you to absolutely FULFILL TO ITS ULTIMATE, THE REST OF YOUR NOW MORE EXCITING AND STIMULATING, SECOND AND SUPERIOR HALF OF YOUR LONG JOURNEY THROUGH LIFE.

Challenges Of Change

97

As we close in on the end of our observations, and you start down or are well into that second half of life make no mistake in judgment, in no uncertain terms, almost every facet of your life, grows more important with your passage of time. I CAN SAY AFTER ALL THESE YEARS, THE WAY I HAVE LIVED THEM, WERE BASED EXCLUSIVELY ON THINGS I HONESTLY AND OBJECTIVELY THOUGHT, AND OF COURSE THE BIG CHANGES OF THAT CRITICAL, PIVOTAL PERIOD BETWEEN FORTY AND SIXTY. It was absolutely those twenty years, that made the next thirty years of my life, the most self-confident and most self-assured years of my life. And believe me, sir, I must have been in the right place at the right time, because I sure had one hell of a fantastic first forty. But I want you to know, I can say past forty, the last fifty years of my life, have been my most REWARDING, GRATIFYING, AND FULFILLING. Jump on board, pal, I need your company. Don't you NEVER EVER lose heart or hope, in dealing with the challenges of change. STAY DEFIANT, PROUD, STRONG, AND OF COURSE, BOLD over your long-term aging experience. And do it RELENTLESSLY, FEARLESSLY, WITH ENDLESS INTEGRITY, AND GROWING SELF RESPECT. Don't ever allow yourself to be frustrated or anxious about things and people YOU HAVE NO CONTROL OVER AND CANNOT CHANGE. If there's something stressful or distasteful in your life, that needs adjusting or altering, and IT IS IN YOUR POWER TO DO, of course take the necessary, timely action. You must acknowledge, time is always of the essence. Nothing in your life is more important because IT IS LIMITED. That's why, with its passage, you must make it more valuable and meaningful to feel fulfilled. This old boy is telling ya, OVERALL, younger being better, just because it's newer and supposedly more stimulating, is a bucket and a half of exaggerated bullshit! Just use to your potential what is already in you - YOUR MATURE MINDSET, EDUCATED INSIGHT, AND ACQUIRED WISDOM. It would be WASTEFUL, NOT TO IMPROVE THE QUALITY OF YOUR LIFE, *WHEN YOU DEFINITELY KNOW YOU HAVE THAT CHOICE.* Be fearlessly PROUDER, BOLDER, AND MORE FREE SPIRITED with every passing year, taking every essential obstacle head-on that the challenges of change create, and do it from a position of UNBEATABLE STRENGTH, which by your very nature is who you naturally are. DON'T YOU EVER LET ANY CHALLENGES OF CHANGE, CAUSE CONFUSION AND FRUSTRATION, PRODUCING A FEELING OF MISDIRECTION OR HELPLESSNESS. That would be a complete waste of this, THE MOST VALUABLE TIME OF YOUR LIFE.

Psychologically, philosophically, and spiritually, DON'T YOU DARE LOSE HEART OR HOPE AS YOU GET OLDER. Never let that flawed demon of disaster seep into your psyche, weaken your will, and destroy your joy. In fact, better yet, kick that low-life son of a bitch right the hell out of your life. Let "Mr. Lose Hope" know he is not only not welcomed, if he even tried to enter he'll be dead on arrival! I want you to recall as best you can from your memory bank, that CLEARER POSITIVE PICTURE

OF <u>YOUR PAST</u>. Then visualize all those things you've accomplished, up to this point. I know from personal experience we all can create self-imposed problems, with our VANITY and PRIDE. Damp them both down a little bit. It is so important your vanity be minimized, and YOUR REAL PRIDE AND LOVE OF WHO AND WHAT YOU ARE MAXIMIZED. Now when I say *pride*, I don't mean *false-pride*. False pride is for insecure boys and younger men, NOT YOU. Too much vanity and false pride, were certainly a part of my growing up. But, sir, what I'm saying to you right now is, take that real inner strength of yours, that has been developed over these first forty-plus years, and USE IT CONSTRUCTIVELY, TO AFFECT A POSITIVE CHALLENGE OF CHANGE FOR AS LONG AS YOU ARE GIVEN THIS GREAT GIFT OF LIFE'S SECOND HALF.

That's the whole purpose of this thesis. You … Y-O-U, taking this first twenty-year period of your second half of life, and with every damn ounce and gram of enthusiasm, GRAB EVERY BIT OF THIS CHALLENGING PERIOD, RIGHT BY THE BALLS AND SQUEEZE, the results of which will be A NEW HIGHER LEVEL OF PSYCHOLOGICAL AND INSPIRATIONAL FULFILLMENT. Then you will hopefully find, as I did, after this great twenty-year transition, the following thirty years from sixty to ninety, will become one hell of an exciting, interesting, CONTROLLED roller-coaster ride.

The Natural Process

98

As we get down to our last three observations, having come at you from every psychological and philosophical angle, what life really boils down to are YOUR PERSONAL ATTITUDE, INTENTIONS, AND ACTIONS AS YOU AGE. I believe most of us, most of the time, try to have good intentions. But because of our age, if we over activate our impulsive emotions the end result will be, bad personal intentions, that can produce less than accurate judgment. If we allow this mindset of bad intentions to expand, IT WILL DOMINATE ON A DAILY BASIS. That's in real conflict with Mother Nature's plan for the middle age man. But, sir, make no mistake, any time you think you can countermand Mother Nature's rules where age is concerned, you are setting yourself up for a long-term let-down. That good lady is on your side, cooperate. WHY DEFY MOTHER NATURE? SHE HAS A WAY OF WINNING <u>EVERY TIME</u>!

Let's go a little deeper and get a little more definitive in the meaning of those four words, *MOTHER NATURE'S NATURAL PROCESS*. The key that adds strength and support, to those four words, is *honesty*. Certainly it's smart to be as honest as you can, in dealing with all your actions, where other people's feelings and values are concerned. Of course you occasionally may veer off center. But the one person you have to be one-hundred percent honest with, all the time for a lifetime where Mother Nature's natural process is concerned, IS YOURSELF. I'm talking about what this book was totally meant to represent: YOUR, NORMAL, TO BE EXPECTED, AGING PROCESS. Many times we subconsciously or unknowingly, ACCELERATE our own physical and psychological decline as we age. That can happen every time you are not being honest with yourself. It is so easy to bend the truth, to satisfy and soothe insecurities and self-doubts. All of us, including Yours Truly, are inclined to do exactly that, when it's convenient, and makes us MORE COMFORTABLE WITH WHAT WE PERCEIVE AS UNCOMFORTABLE CIRCUMSTANCES. In our minds, bending of the truth has the ability, to offer us TEMPORARY peace of mind. That's a reaction to OUR OWN PLAUSIBLE AND INBORN INSECURITIES. Many decades ago, I remember, as a much younger man, the WELL-HIDDEN INSECURITIES AND SELF DOUBTS I CARRIED AROUND for almost half my life. Talk about a fragile personality, there were certain things I flat refused to hear, because THEY WERE INTIMIDATING REALITIES I SURE AS HELL DID NOT WANT TO FACE. But I knew when I hit my forties, I had to finally GROW THE HELL UP and put that kind of crappy, crippling, deceptive, infantile thinking behind me. Too frequently in our youth, during those years of self-doubt, we can consciously, in a self-serving way, cover them up, by rationalizing their reality, which COMPROMISES AND ALTERS OUR SENSE OF HONESTY, as it did mine, which will DENY YOU TRUE EXPANSION OF YOUR INDIVIDUAL IDENTITY DURING YOUR LIFE'S SECOND HALF.

So now I'm going to tell you, at this late stage of my life, how I became HONEST WITH MYSELF, where the natural and normal, but often UNWELCOME process of aging was

323

concerned. The first thing I discovered, was the importance of what I'd been doing religiously since fifteen: always being in good to excellent physical condition. Building that solid, healthy, strong base. All you gotta do is go back twenty-plus years, and think about your own physical condition through your teens and high school. Of course I knew there were a few fat kids then, but it's very possible you were athletic and in good shape, all the way up and into your early twenties. And that's when a lot of guys, sometimes not even aware of it, START A LIFETIME OF PHYSICAL NEGLECT. Now let me be more brutally honest with you. Up to twenty, during your youthful high hormonal period, you have immense respect for your body. Then somewhere between your mid-twenties and forty, because of self-survival, your priorities dramatically change, and as discussed in several observations, I repeat, too many men go from RESPECT FOR, TO INCREASED NEGLECT OF THEIR BODY.

Let me give you an example: Imagine being in great shape into your early twenties, and then for the next fifty to sixty years of your life, watching your physical condition very slowly falling into a STATE OF CONSTANT DETERIORATION. The key word there is *slowly,* because that physical condition of deterioration is so insidiously slow, that on a month to year time-frame, it's almost imperceptible and unnoticeable. But, sir, make no mistake, THAT IS EXACTLY WHAT IS HAPPENING. Your willpower and discipline will be affected, and the OVERALL QUALITY OF YOUR LIFE, will also decline and suffer at that same slow, imperceptible rate. And if you have any doubts, look at most guys twenty to forty years older than you. But if I can serve as an example, remember, many men ten to

324

thirty years my junior, have reached that time when the negative signs of aging have REALLY SET IN AND START TO CLEARLY SHOW ACCELERATED PHYSICAL DECLINE. So the time has come for you to be brutally self-honest. No matter how long and slow the process is, YOUR BODY WILL GROW WEAKER AND LESS EFFICIENT, BECAUSE OF NEGLECT OR OVER-ABUSE, and your mind and spirit for living, will suffer proportionally. I don't know how much clearer I can make that point. YOUR PHYSICAL BODY IS THE BASE. It dictates every movement and motion you make. Respect it, and make it a top priority. IT IS THE SOLID FOUNDATION OF EVERY MINUTE OF EVERY DAY THAT THE WHOLE OF YOUR LIFE IS BUILT ON. So make no mistake, as your body loses strength, your mind and spirit can also be reduced. YOU MUST RECOGNIZE AND ACKNOWLEDGE, THE STRONG POSSIBILITY OF THIS CONDITION EXISTING, *AND TURN IT AROUND*. If you don't, you limit and restrict the prospects, of what can be the most rewarding time of your life - THE SECOND HALF. Why would any self-respecting man deprive himself the opportunity, of living the balance of his life TO ITS *FULL* POTENTIAL.

Now, if you are permanently infirmed, be it genetic or by accident, that's understandable. But in any and all other natural conditions, IF YOU PERMIT SELF NEGLECT AND ABUSE TO TAKE PLACE, there will be nobody to blame – one more time - except to point your finger at the guy in the mirror. So whatever your state of mind is right now, you have to recognize, what you'll find in many different descriptive narratives in most observations, are all the POSITIVES OF A PERFECT,

325

ASCENDING, NATURAL AGING PROCESS. And your body is by far the biggest part of you. It is just aching to be activated, whatever age you are. Age is no barrier to MORE MUSCLE AND STRENGTH. Your body is DESIGNED to react to your POSITIVE INPUT. I'm here to tell ya, DON'T EVER TELL YOURSELF IT'S TOO LATE IN LIFE. God, man, don't ever become a victim of that kind of thinking. That's a cop-out for the clueless! The one person you should never ever bullshit is yourself. As long as you are pulling a breath, IT WILL NEVER BE TOO LATE for your body, mind, and spirit, to be at their absolute best. YOU CAN ALTER YOUR PHYSICAL AGING TO YOUR ADVANTAGE. What in the hell or in God's good name (whichever you prefer) could be holding you back? So what's that you just said? Of course, if you haven't already, you should start now! Why wouldn't any forty to sixty- or seventy-year-old man NOT? YOU ABSOLUTELY STILL CAN. IT'S NEVER TOO LATE TO CREATE, A ROCK-SOLID PHYSICAL FOUNDATION. Then, as this older man knows all too well, MOTHER NATURE WILL NOW BE YOUR GREATEST ALLY AND LEND YOU A HELPING HAND. Again, one more time: don't screw with Mother Nature. THAT OLD GIRL? WILL RETURN THE FAVOR EVERY DAMN TIME!

Possibilities

99

Let me recap, and give you something to think about as we come to the end of these observations. Because our values and technology are changing so rapidly, being just one generation removed can create major differences, which can, if allowed, produce continuing problems. Just look around. We are possibly more than two, even three generations removed from each other. But you reading this book means we are still connecting, because we still have SO MANY THINGS IN COMMON. So whether it's my generation of eighty to a hundred, or yours from forty to eighty, you must never let getting older year by year, negatively define you in any way. You must not allow NATURE'S NATURAL PROCESS, to impose exaggerated unreal and unnecessary restrictions or limitations, to creep into your subconscious and stifle, or worse yet distort, YOUR MOST AMBITIOUS POSITIVE, AND VERY REAL AND ACHIEVABLE POSSIBILITIES. Whether it's me at my age, or you thirty to fifty years younger, REGARDLESS OF CURRENT TECHNOLOGY, we must always pursue our strategically important priorities in life. And that's exactly what I do every day, REGARDLESS OF MY AGE, and I do it with gusto, guts, and CONSISTENT PERSISTENT DETERMINATION, *AND SO SHOULD YOU*!

As said and read throughout this book, in order for dreams to come true, you not only have to have them, YOU MUST NEVER COMPROMISE YOUR WILLPOWER AND DESIRE TO PURSUE THEM ENDLESSLY. The more mental muscle you

COMMIT TO BEING OPEN-MINDED, the MORE YOUR IMAGINATION WILL BE STIMULATED AND EXPANDED. Your dreams can only come true, if you make the long-term, timeless, tireless commitment to the ones you believe in passionately. I want you to chase with endless pursuit those dreams that IGNITE AND INSPIRE your most MEANINGFUL reasons for being alive. I want you to do it FEARLESSLY AND FEROCIOUSLY, with an OPEN AND FREE-SPIRITED, UNFILTERED MIND. And as you are relentlessly chasing them, they will create even more exciting hopes and dreams for you to ENHANCE THE CHASE. I don't want you to rationalize or self-impose limits, when it comes to your dreams. You find the wildest, most way-out fantasies imaginable, and infuse them not just with passion, BUT BELIEVABILITY. Make those dreams of yours bigger than life, because without them, you will have less of a life. Part of every single day, CHASE THEM. Ten dreams or a hundred dreams, chase every one every day! Now, are they going to be evasive, even elusive? Of course they are! BUT YOUR MAIN JOB IN LIFE, YOU WILL *NEVER LOSE SIGHT OF THEM,* AS LONG AS YOU KEEP UP THE CHASE. One of the major responsibilities of your positivity, is to keep them in CONSTANT, CRYSTAL CLEAR FOCUS. Don't ever allow any barriers to get in the way. And, young brother, I do mean any obstacle, no matter how imposing it may seem, that you think has the potential to diminish or kill your dreams, DISPEL THEM, OVERCOME THEM, AND CRUSH THEM IMMEDIATELY. When it comes to your dreams, that are of such a high value to your lifestyle, you must bust your balls to bust through ANY PSYCHOLOGICAL DETOURS OR

328

MENTAL ROAD BLOCKS. Go after every single one with unstoppable determination, as strong as your mind can muster. Even at this late stage of life, IF I QUIT ON MY DREAMS, IT WOULD ALMOST BE LIKE BRINGING MOST OF MY LIFE'S FORCE TO A STANDSTILL. Not for one precious priceless minute, should you ever stop pursuing your dreams. I'll personalize it for ya: I would never compromise or abandon my never-ending quest in pursuit of my dreams. That, more than any other single aspect, has kept me vitally alive and highly energized all these years. Well, sir, why not you, WHO HAS SO MUCH LONGER TO LIVE, AND SO MANY MORE EXCITING DREAMS FOR YOUR MIND TO IMAGINE.

Now if by some fortunate long-shot chance of fate I make it over the next ten years to a hundred, you can bet your ass I WILL NEVER STOP MAKING THE SUPREME EFFORT IN PURSUIT OF MY DREAMS. Why not you, with fifty to sixty more years to live. You must stay DETERMINED. Sir, those dreams you are chasing? THEY ARE EXCLUSIVELY YOURS. Right now, millions of men are in that critical, transitional mid-life age category. Well may I suggest this little piece of advice: As convoluted as life can get, or may actually be, you will hopefully never forget, all those people you know, having so many different opinions, you must make this commitment to yourself, and do it with laser focus: CHASE ANY DAMN DREAM YOU WANT TO CHASE, as long as it harms no one else in the process. That is the only thing that counts, and (be like The Old Man!) don't throw an unnecessary guilt trip on yourself, if it flies in the face of SO-CALLED ESTABLISHMENT VALUES.

Most important, never to be forgotten, remember always, that long, exciting dream you are endlessly chasing? TO CHASE IT, IS JUST AS IMPORTANT, AS CATCHING IT! The main excitement of living, is always in the chase. If you catch that dream, terrific! BUT IT'S THE CHASE that will always take you to that UNKNOWN, EXCITING, BIGGER-THAN-LIFE PLACE. Therein lies the essence of living your life one day at a time. PLEASE, KIND SIR, DON'T WASTE ONE DAMN MINUTE OF IT. Why wouldn't you use the highest level of positive energy for your entire human journey, when you know unequivocally, YOU WILL ALWAYS BE THE BENEFICIARY. So chase, chase, and keep chasing relentlessly, with sharp focus, every hope and dream you have ever had, every day of your life. And if they are old dreams you still believe in, BREATHE NEW LIFE INTO THEM. Remember who you are now, YOU ARE UNIQUE AND YOU ARE THAT ONE-OF-A-KIND. God, man, please believe that's as true as the blood that runs through your veins and keeps you alive. IT WILL NEVER BE TOO LATE, to make the living of your life more super and exceptional, THE OLDER YOU GET.

DON'T YOU NEVER, EVER, *EVER,* QUIT ON YOURSELF. MAY ALL THE POSITIVE BLESSINGS OF GOD AND NATURE, AND ALL THE OTHER ASSETS THEY PROVIDE, BE YOUR CONSTANT AND GROWING COMPANIONS UNTIL YOU ARE AT LEAST ONE HUNDRED YEARS OLD. *Then, sir, you're on your own!*

More Confident

100

During the second half of your life, you must make every extra concerted effort, to make yourself feel more confident, and elevate to its highest possible level *your self-worth* about who you are, and what you say and do, and that's a must, for every day for the rest of your life. It will never happen by chance, it's always up to you, to make your best choice. And most relevant, keep it that way, all the way, day after day, in a never ending, ever growing, positive way. Get out there and grab life by the low-hangers like the man you know you are. MAKE AND LIVE EVERY TOMORROW EVEN BETTER THAN THE DAY YOU ARE LIVING IN. It absolutely can be done, AND YOU ABSOLUTELY CAN PUT YOUR MIND TO IT AND DO IT.

Ken's Cornerstones

It All Starts With Honesty

Fear

Slavery

Hope

Now that you've learned from these many observations, here are some final thoughts in the form of Ken 's Cornerstones that will tie it all together and help you put it all in play. Four simple cornerstones to help you become the best man you can be and make the second half of your life, the best half.

"It all starts with honesty" deals with how you conduct yourself.

The cornerstone on fear is an honest look into what contributes to the decisions you make which will affect each day of your great transition and beyond.

The slavery cornerstone will no doubt *not* be what you are expecting to hear, but will open your mind to new thoughts and ideas.

And finally, there is "Hope", the most appropriate cornerstone to finish off these many thoughts and observations.

Read them, refer back to them often, and keep moving forward in your great transition.

It All Starts With Honesty

There are over one hundred thousand words in the English-speaking dictionary. Let me tell you what I think just may be the most important five words, in the successful living of your life. HONESTY, TRUST, LOYALTY, COMMITMENT and FRIENDSHIP. And they follow in that exact order. There is no doubt in my mind, that they are the five most important, closely connected words in this world, in any language. They will definitely determine irrevocably how your entire life plays out. They will strongly influence and affect permanently, whether you are a success or failure, in every function and facet of your life.

The first of those words, and more likely than not the most important one of all, the foundation all other words in this dissertation will be based on: HONESTY. You must understand how fundamentally critical it is, for you to make the fully concerted effort to be as near as you can, totally and completely honest. Nobody knows better than me how near impossible a task that is. BUT IT IS AN ABSOLUTE MUST, where the most important, meaningful, and most closely connected people in your life are concerned. It's a tempting human tendency to bend the truth. But this I know as irrefutable: When it comes to those very special people who are committed to you unconditionally, if you are not honest to the core, not only will the consequences be heavy, they can be irreparable. I want you to think long and hard about it. With family and friends, the people that are really important in your life, no matter how strong and tight that bond is, if those people so dear to you are given any reason, even the smallest little suspicion to question your honesty, THEY WILL

NEVER BE ABLE TO TRUST YOU COMPLETELY EVER AGAIN. If there is any lack of honesty, to any degree, there will be no TRUST. Think about the adverse consequences and scope of that statement. Not almost, this is an absolute must for your successful survival. To have the people in your life, that over a long period of time have trusted and confided in you, to have those same people, because of a lack of total honestly lose trust, could create an incalculable, tragic loss.

Now it's time to get to our third word, and understand succinctly how closely and completely these words relate. We have just strongly established that if you are not honest there is no way for mutual trust to exist. And they follow in that order. No honesty - no trust. When trust is lacking, there will be no LOYALTY. I want you to think, all the years you've already lived, and you will know as you think and remember, just how powerful that word *loyalty* is. The words *loyalty* and *absolute* are connected. People are either one hundred percent loyal or not. Loyalty, my friend, is very, very hard to find. And when we do find this very rare human quality, those people that are one hundred percent iron-clad to the bone loyal to us, how foolish it would be if you were not equally, one-hundred percent loyal to them. When loyalty is lacking, life will lose much of its meaning. Because then and only then, under those exact conditions, total loyalty, will they to you or you to them, make a COMMITMENT. Another super powerful word.

I want you to imagine living a long life, and no matter how successful you have been, or how intelligent you are, having you committed to nobody, and having nobody committed to you.

What a catastrophic disaster that would be. That's why you will cherish those people that are loyal to you: because they have taken their honesty and trust in you, and created loyalty to you. There is no other way for you or them to become committed unconditionally.

So now we've connected these four valuable words that are very important: HONESTY, TRUST, LOYALTY and COMMITMENT. And I repeat, they will always, in every aspect of your life, follow in that exact order. But the reason they do, the reason trust follows honesty and loyalty follows trust is, they create commitment. And once a person makes their commitment to honesty, trust, and loyalty, it will culminate with only one purpose that can never be replaced or duplicated: REAL, LASTING FRIENDSHIP - without question, the most important element of all. No speculation here, this is a rock-solid fact. If you have no real friends in life, and I'm talking about those trusted, loyal, committed friends, then you have no real mutual human rewards. Talk about a lousy, rotten, unrewarding fate. You could be rich in dollars, have an IQ of one hundred sixty, and you will know that all the money and intelligence in the world, CAN NOT AND WILL NOT BUY YOU ONE SINGLE REAL FRIEND.

Look how simple and sensible that was. And all you gotta remember, is where it all starts. It all starts with not being a liar. It starts with being honest. And that takes principled character. Know that honesty will gain the trust and the loyalty needed for commitment. And don't you ever forget, trust, loyalty, and commitment cannot exist without HONESTY. So check that

337

conscience of yours when you wake up to the gift of life for one more day. I know it's not easy in this reckless, contrary, compromised world we live in, but you must always make your most concerted effort, to operate from a position of honesty. There is no other way that you will ever earn the trust and loyalty from any human being, that will allow you to develop a true, committed friendship. And don't you ever forget, in this world there is nothing more important. Not a ton of gold or a pound of diamonds, Make sure you say that to yourself every day: "There is nothing more important." And that's why you should make these the five most important and valuable words in your life. Always giving them as high a priority AS YOU HONESTLY CAN. If you attempt to do that every day of your life, the end result will be A LIFE TOTALLY AND COMPLETELY WORTH LIVING.

Fear

It's not only strange, it's unique how one simple little word can have such a monstrous meaning and impact on your life past forty, and create such frightening results. I know this may sound like a stretch, but I honestly believe that this one word we're talking about can be more influential, than a four-hundred-page book with a hundred thousand words. This little one-syllable word not only can, but will frequently affect nearly every aspect of every part of the second half of your life. Now of course it's there all your life, but I think its meaning peaks after forty. And that little four-letter word, which I'm sure you have already surmised by the title, is FEAR.

From a perspective of true reality, total authenticity, it becomes our true mortal, second half of life, enemy. All through our lives we are always fighting the influence of fear. Of course, growing older and developing greater insights and wisdom, is certainly a big advantage in fighting fear. That is the hard fought for positive perspective needed, but know there is a downside that we have to deal with. As we age we become, in certain areas, a little more frail. We are a little less mobile and not quite as well coordinated. All those little losses, if you let them, can result in being less self-assured. And even though the effects of the aging process at your stage can be that subtle, especially as we start to lose our physical prowess, it can make us question our confidence. And when that happens it will lead to us being A LITTLE MORE FEARFUL. Now what I am about to say is absolutely critical to improving the quality of our lives. With fear we only have two choices, because it's always going to be there on a daily basis, no matter

339

how fearless you think you are. But those two simple choices? They will lead to one of two conclusions: EITHER WE CONTROL FEAR OR LET FEAR CONTROL US. We can permit fear to have the upper hand and eventually exercise complete control over us. Well, to be realistic, the older we get, as I have just mentioned, because of our ongoing limitations, the more doubts we can develop, and the more control fear can impose. That is exactly what will happen if we allow fear to dominate, that's how that bastard of a bad-boy works. Imposing its will on our thinking, hoping to influence our every thought. The results of that kind of situation are going to be very obvious. Indecision, lack of confidence, immobilization, will ultimately result in a failure to function in a positive, effective way. If we let that happen it can and will restrict, confine, and limit out of frustration, every potentially positive aspect of our life. Therefore we must make this commitment, if we are going to have a successful experience in the living of our life's second half. WE CANNOT AND WE MUST NOT LET THAT KIND OF MINDSET TAKE HOLD *AND DESTROY OUR POSITIVE DESTINY.*

So let's establish some rules and conditions to live by, knowing that whether we like it or not, we're going to live with this very worst of all negative influences called fear, because it's all around us. And I do mean every single day for the rest of our lives. Let's examine in detail how this mental monster of misery called fear operates. Any time we allow fear to play a major influence or take command, it won't just occasionally, to a greater or lesser degree, be one thing or another. That tricky bastard – fear - will intrude into every aspect of your life. Here's how fear functions:

When any person finds that very rare moment where they can muster up the self-confidence and courage needed to make a bold decision, IN A FEARLESS WAY, sitting right there on their shoulder? You got it. That bad-intentioned Boogie Man - fear. Whispering into their ear, creating doubt and indecision, with the sole purpose of trying to hold them back. In spite of that, every one of us are going to have those super confident moments in life, that are so rare. We all know the feeling: finally building up the courage to step forward with boldness and real determination. And there is no feeling in the world exactly like that. It is capable of producing the ultimate in satisfaction and gratification. Resulting in a real feeling of inspired personal pride. But guess who is sitting right there ready to do his dirty work, tugging at your mental sleeve, trying to create doubt and hold you back. Why of course, who else? It's that clever, cunning, conniving, deceiving, low-life bastard called *fear*. And there is a reason I use the words CUNNING and CLEVER. You see, fear is a master at disguise. Fear has the ability to take those easy to hear words, words you and I are so comfortable with, words we use to connect thoughts dozens of times daily. The word *doubt*. It's one of our most basic human natures to have doubts. Then there's indecision. That happens so frequently, sometimes on a minute to minute basis. Of course there is alarm, anxiety, hesitation. And these are words that are not just a part of our vocabulary. These are not throw-away words, they are truly a part of the majority of our thought processes. But, when they have their fundamental meaning stripped away by fear, those seemingly harmless sounding, exact same words translate and become SHOCK, IMMOBILITY, SELF DOUBT, LACK OF CONFIDENCE

341

AND ULTIMATELY SELF DEFEAT. That is fear at work at its worst. That's how deceptive and morally destructive this low-life bastard called fear can be. And you must be ready to confront it, deal with it, and take it head-on to fight it off. That is the only way you can reduce its influence, impact, and after effects. Now know this and know it as a life changer: If you don't make that fully focused effort, then you are conceding to fear ALMOST COMPLETE POWER TO VICTIMIZE YOU. So you be astutely conscious, cautious, and on guard always of this low-life bum called *fear*. You must be strong minded. Show real strength of your resolve to serve as a barrier. And again, always, and I do mean every waking moment, be alert and aware of this wicked, evil doer. Because every day, acting like your friend, this debilitating, down and dirty no good demon called *fear*, is going to come knocking at your mental door. And what a high pressure, super sophisticated salesman this dealer of doom is. *Fear* is going to claim to be PRUDENCE, CAUTION, CARE, EVEN DILIGENCE, AND DISCRETION. Every single one of those most positive words are associated with actions we all take on a daily basis. Well with *fear* it's not prudence, caution, or care, or diligence and discretion. When *fear* is done with you, it's debilitating self-doubt, hesitation, stagnation, and restriction. So in assessing fear, know exactly what it is. FEAR IS A ROBBER, A THIEF AND A BANDIT. And once you let it in it starts doing its dirty work. *Sapping your energy, weakening your body, and negatively altering your mind!* Fear has but one motive: TO RESTRICT AND LIMIT ALL YOUR NATURAL ABILITIES AND ASSETS.

So we've got to fight with all our eternal might to battle, beat, and defeat fear. And I want you to know how effectively that can be done by every last one of us. We possess a powerful weapon that we don't always activate and use. It's in all of us, and it's also a single word, and it is the only word in the world that when you have it in abundance and use it to its optimum potential, can it and will it defeat fear. And that word, my friend, IS FAITH.

Oh boy, what a life-rewarding joy is the power of FAITH! When you properly apply it, it is one of the strongest, most meaningful words ever conceived, right up there with the word *hope*. No matter whatever your religious, personal, or universal faith may be, there is only one main power behind that faith: YOU! Only one powerful mental motor: YOU! First, sir, you must have, or acquire if you don't have, unshakable, unmovable, rock-solid FAITH IN YOURSELF. *THAT MEANS BELIEVING IN YOURSELF*. Every time you look in the mirror, you must have complete faith in what you see. Let me show you how powerful a word this can be. You know as an absolute, that all your hopes and dreams would be meaningless, if you didn't have the deepest faith in those beliefs. Make no mistake, FAITH GOT YOU THIS FAR! Faith allowed you to accomplish and achieve what you have over your long, hard fought first forty years of your life.

Now there's another word closely associated with fear, and that word is *guilt*. Guilt and fear are not only related, they are almost exact twins. They are partners in crime, working together in your mind to restrict you, but only if YOU ALLOW THEM ENTRY AND THE POWER TO ASSUME CONTROL. They nourish and feed off each other, always at your expense. But when you take that potent force called faith, and encourage it to take a powerfully immovable meaning in your mind, FEAR DON'T STAND A CHANCE IN HELL, because when those qualities of unbreakable resolve are built into your faith, only then can you outgun this felon called fear.

If we could go back several thousand years, essentially to the first beginnings of humankind, as in men and women, when they had their first awakenings on this planet, what do you think brought them this far? All these many millenniums later, just think of all the hard elements that our ancestors had to face, and what it took to survive and stay alive on a day-to-day basis. If you can possibly conceive, think about a human life before modernization and technology. How they had to acquire food, shelter, rest, and repair. And how generation followed generation and how century followed century. I honestly believe from the core of my being, the most powerful mental ingredient WAS THEIR FAITH. I am completely convinced that without the power of faith on an every day basis, THEY WOULD HAVE NEVER SEEN THEIR NEXT TOMORROW. It was faith more than anything else that created the courage to keep reaching out and pushing forward, millennium after millennium. That's why you must persevere. You must maintain at its highest level your rock-solid, absolutely indestructible faith, to achieve your highest goals and ideals. THAT'S WHAT OUR ANCESTORS HAD TO DO. So make no mistake, it was faith and faith alone, that created the confidence and the willpower and the discipline and all their other positive beliefs necessary to survive. So right now, today, only with your faith strongly in place as a top priority, knowing that it is constantly present and well established in your belief system, CAN YOU BEAT FEAR.

And faith, like fear, has a twin too, and that twin is *confidence*. They also support and nourish each other. And you need them both, and they are both in your possession in endless abundance. BUT YOU CAN'T LET THEM LIE DORMANT. Your faith and confidence must be activated to their highest levels, and guaranteed, every remaining moment of your life's second half, you will feel the true joy, the deep appreciation of your faith. You can be that human powerhouse, who has the strong unbreakable barrier of belief in his faith. You know that's in you, but you gotta use it.

So when that diminisher of life – *fear* - comes knocking, that's your signal to show the unshakable strength of your DEEPLY ROOTED FAITH. And do it powerfully and forcefully. IT WILL ABSOLUTELY OVERPOWER AND DISSOLVE, THE UGLY, DESTRUCTIVE SHADOW OF FEAR, AND KILL IT DEAD ON THE SPOT. FAITH IS YOUR GREATEST BLESSING AND YOUR BIGGEST ASSET. THERE IS ABSOLUTELY NO LIMIT TO THE AMOUNT OF FAITH AND CONFIDENCE YOU ARE ALLOWED. Sir, make no mistake or misjudgment, waiting right there in every cell of your body is your faith. Tap into it every single day. Get your fill of it right up to your spiritual and mental capacities, always keeping faith at the forefront of your consciousness, and do that for the rest of your natural life. It is the most effective way to MAKE EVERY DAY OF YOUR SECOND HALF AS FEAR-FREE AS POSSIBLE, producing full peace of mind.

Slavery

Slavery, *slavery*, **SLAVERY**. I don't think there's any doubt in anybody's mind, one of the most disgusting, abusive, ugly, and despicable words in any language is *slavery*. My God, man, just think of it, the concept of slavery and its degrading inhuman history throughout the centuries. It's always had that one singular meaning, and that's why we all know the story. It almost always involves two human beings, and one of those human beings, like a true dictator, dictates with total and absolute authority, what another human being can and cannot do or say. Which literally means one person has total power, to impose as much sub-human treatment on another human being as he so chooses. Now think what that does to the enslaved person. It's a process that cripples and destroys for even the slightest infraction of the so-called masters' word. That's the true, literal definition and history of slavery. Creating total extremes in self-respect and self-worth. And I think you'll agree, in this day and age, I believe that would be OUR NORMAL AND ACCURATE INTERPRETATION OF THE CONCEPT OF SLAVERY. Let me be more graphic in how brutally destructive this is to human dignity and self-worth. We're talking about being held in bondage here. Becoming a total and complete victim of that seemingly inescapable grip, that one person could have the power to hold another in COMPLETE SUBSERVIENCE. You bet, that word *slavery* is one of the ugliest, most vulgar words in the world. There is nothing I know of, and I mean absolutely nothing, not any other word in your Webster's dictionary that could be more degrading and despicably subhuman.

Now, I think you'll agree that's a fair and just, accurate description of slavery. Thank god we live in this later time. Thank god you and I don't have to go through that in this world of our current values. You know that what I just described would and could never happen in your life. Out of self-pride and self-respect, not for one single second would you, let any other human TREAT YOU THAT WAY. So let me ask you this: If you wouldn't tolerate that kind of treatment from another human being, WHY WOULD YOU DO EXACTLY WHAT I JUST DESCRIBED, *TO YOURSELF*?

And this is not a contradiction in terms. Let me tell ya where I'm going with this. That is precisely what can happen in our pursuit of all those things in life, that can offer us the greatest rewards. Question: If you wouldn't be a slave to another human, why would any man in his right mind, with an ounce of common sense, BECOME A SLAVE TO HIS OWN DESIRES AND OBSESSIONS. Let's run the gamut: be it food, booze, tobacco, sex, drugs, gambling, even hate and anger, or any other potentially overwhelming base instinct. When we surrender our will to any one of these, THEY BECOME OUR MASTERS. What I'm saying very specifically is any uncontrolled habit, any out of control indulgence, can put you in a SELF-IMPOSED STATE OF SLAVERY. And it doesn't matter one way or the other, where any one or all of your desires are concerned, how exciting they may be or how euphoric they make you feel, creating your insatiable desire to have it. IF YOU DON'T CONTROL IT, SURE AS HELL, IT WILL CONTROL YOU. All that will ever produce, every time, is you becoming the slave to it. And I couldn't be more accurate because that's an actual fact. If or when you let that happen, you will have enslaved yourself. Simply put, you have placed yourself in self-imposed bondage. So out of self-respect, self-esteem, and personal pride, if you wouldn't let any other human make a slave out of you, why in the hell would you let any habit, no matter how strong your urges and desires for it, PUT YOU AND KEEP YOU IN A STATE OF BONDAGE? No matter how gratifying you think any moment could or would be, there is no reward, there is no winning under those conditions. In the long run, that person will lose.

Know that going in, but also know when to get the hell out. Nothing wrong with a great meal or having a drink now and then. Gambling, sex? You bet. They are two of the most satisfying things in life. But iron-clad in your mind, you must understand completely, they are only rewarding AS LONG AS WE CONTROL THEM. So if you've lost control to any degree, now may be the time to take your head out of your ass, breathe some fresh air, oxygenate your brain, and take that control back. And don't tell me you can't. No bullshit excuses. You absolutely can. Then and only then do some of life's greatest rewards, remain the relevant pleasures they were designed to be. So if you feel enslaved by any one of many human desires, starting right now, don't overeat foods you love. Have a drink or two - not a drink or ten! Sex and gambling? You always win when you know when to TAKE A BREAK. That's how you control all the rewarding activities in life. Because no mature, self-respecting man would ever BECOME A SLAVE TO THEM EVER AGAIN.

Hope

It's a simple little word that's been alluded to in many of my observations. It's a one syllable, four letter word. Think of all the powerful words that we use repetitiously. I am sure there are hundreds in your vocabulary, that are words that reassure you and support your wants and needs. And that's why you use them again and again, in the course of living your life. Well I personally believe, the most powerful word in the world is HOPE. The implications of that word are immensely powerful. And when you get right down to the precise fundamentals, it's really very easy to examine and evaluate. All you have to do is go back to the time you were a child of five or ten, and evaluate realistically and practically the major influence of that word *hope*. There is not a fantasy, a desire or an ambition you have ever had in your entire life, and I do mean not one, that was not driven and kept alive by your belief in that word, HOPE. To be specific and accurate, you, without exercising your highest hopes, not even one single fantasy, desire, ambition, or goal would have come to fruition. In fact, they would have died and never happened, IF NOT FOR THAT LIFE-SAVING AND LIVE-GIVING WORD, HOPE.

I guess it starts off when you're a boy of about twelve or fourteen with those raging hormones, as mentioned in so many previous observations. And by exercising those thoughts, think of all the discoveries made during those first formative years. All, every last one, driven by hope. Back then hope came easy because there were so many things during that time to hope for. Oh boy those first twenty years. HOPE AFTER HOPE AFTER HOPE. And you chased every damn one. Good for you. Now of course, one of your first big strategic hopes, was to get yourself educated and get a good job. Then with continuing and intensified hope, backed by the DISCIPLINE AND WILL to achieve that hope, you did everything you had to do to advance yourself. Once those hopes were satisfied, you could support a family. So you hopefully fell in love and had a family. And once you made that commitment, it created a myriad of more hopes. And if you think of it on a day to day basis, that could and would not ever have happened, not one single day of it, without you having the HIGHEST HOPES THROUGHOUT THAT ENTIRE PERIOD.

Now here we are at forty-plus, and I don't think there should be a doubt in your mind, during those first forty years, all those hundreds, even thousands of expectations were fueled and driven by that one single word, *hope*. All those day-to-day hopes are what got you this far. And now, during your second half, it's of even greater importance.

In one way or another, we all start to see and feel the effects of aging. Sound dismal? It's not! It's a natural process that each and every man forty to sixty years of age and beyond, is going to experience. All these changes are normal, and that does not mean they should necessarily impose a negative aspect on you. With age, they can make us start to question our confidence and doubt our manhood. When all those things are accumulated, that not only could, but it will if you allow it to, INITIATE A MENTAL PROCESS OF YOU STARTING TO LOSE HOPE.

That is such an easy psychological trap for you to fall into. Going from those younger years when you had the highest of hopes, to going through those transitional years. If you lose your confidence and start developing those self-doubts past forty, you could convince yourself to become hopeless. Well you can bet your ass you and I are going to do everything possible to keep that from ever happening. Because if you have one ounce of authentic self-respect and self-pride, you are not going to, I repeat emphatically, YOU ARE NOT GOING TO LET THAT HAPPEN. But the reality is, the battle is on, and that battle for you to maintain your highest hopes, is going to get even bigger. We are in this uphill fight, and it is going to get harder with every passing year. So I'll say it again, BRACE YOURSELF, STIFFEN THAT BACK, AND GET READY FOR THIS BIGGEST BATTLE OF YOUR LIFE. You must strengthen and reinforce your power of will, discipline, and long-term commitment. Say to yourself honestly, realistically, with the highest hopes you can possibly muster: "This is my challenge. It is a never-ending battle worth undertaking." Am I serious? Are you f-ing kidding me? The only words I can think of are *totally*, *absolutely* and *positively*! I don't know if there are words strong enough to express that core-value feeling, knowing your natural aging process could potentially cause increasing self-doubts and insecurities, culminating in a state of hopelessness. The one key weapon you possess that has the potential to win this battle, that we all have in endless abundance, so you can fight all of your life against self-doubt, insecurity, and a lack of confidence, and it's always going to be there, is that simple little four-letter word, *hope*. So not for one single hour or minute of the rest of your life, should you ever surrender your will, and lose hope. All your hopes should be kept alive, and expanded, every last one.

Without question, I reemphasize, IT'S MUCH, MUCH MORE IMPORTANT PAST FORTY TO KEEP YOUR HOPES ALIVE, THAN WHEN YOU WERE YOUNG. You must hold on to all the hopes you have. Cherish them, nourish them, I can't say it enough, ALWAYS KEEP THEM ALIVE AND PROTECTED. Now another Dab-Row fundamental, hear me good, please: Don't you never ever allow anybody, anything, any condition, any situation, to diminish their importance and meaning to you, because there is nothing of greater value. HOPE IS YOUR GREATEST ASSET. And when you exercise it from your most positive perspective, only then will you be aware of how fortunate you are, to have been given the privilege of the aging experience, and know and believe fully, instead of age becoming a liability, with the power of hope in your possession, your aging process becomes your biggest ally and your most valuable asset.

It's important that you know, at this late stage of my life, I have never for one single second, lost hope. I still have the highest hopes for every aspect of my remaining life. Now let me tell you how I keep those hopes alive. I know that waking up to every day is not a fairy tale. I know it's a harsh, cruel world out there, and most of it is not going to be good. But this I do know:
Ken Dab-Row, by virtue of the strength of his hopeful nature, will muster up every damn ounce of physical and mental energy he has to HOPEFULLY take complete charge of the day he is living in. And HOPEFULLY I will practice that every day of the rest of my life, no matter how little is left.

So here's what you have got to say to yourself every day of your entire life: "I will not, never, ever, let the negative circumstances or conditions that could happen to me on this or any day, no matter how adverse they may be, diminish or damage MY HIGHEST HOPES. And there is not a single word that will represent any single subject that I will ever take more serious. It's only through my highest hopes that I can discover and know who I am and where I am at in my long, interesting, human journey."

Well, as of this writing, after all these years, I realize I'm very blessed. Still got a lot of muscle and energy left, still exercising my love for life. And believe me, I would have had a hell of a lot less meaning in my life, without the constant spirit lifting power of that most important of all words, HOPE. Please, kind sir, for your own self-preservation, never, ever, for one second of your life, let the destructive and deceiving seed of HOPELESSNESS take root in even one cell of your brain. I want you to know for sure, that your long, interesting life, and all the long years you still have to live in front of you, can and will become more interesting and meaningful when supported and driven by the power INFUSED IN ALL YOUR HOPES. Only then will your life never become hopeless. DO THAT WITH EVERY LIFE-GIVING BREATH YOU SUCK IN, AND YOU WILL NEVER LOSE THE MEANING OF THAT PRICELESS, PRECIOUS WORD. Once that is accomplished and deeply believed, HOPE WILL NEVER DESERT YOU.

Some Final Thoughts

Well, that's it guys! I hope I've shed a little more light on your life, and have given you valid reason to watch and feel and know, that you are getting stronger in every aspect, phase, and focus of your life.

As long as it took your Old Pops to write this book, what is of even greater importance, is to know you have spent your valuable time reading it. I am thankful and so are my spiritual mother and father – MOTHER NATURE AND FATHER TIME. They never fail to show their appreciation for your cooperation!

Now let me tell you about this poem you are about to read, and why I chose it to end this book. Over sixty years ago, my philosophical mentor, a gentleman named Edgar Brewer, and I would meet in front of Millie 'n Ken's restaurant in Arizona at five in the morning and watch the sun rise over barren desert as far as the eye could see. A setting that made a man feel as free as he could possibly feel. And after discussing almost every aspect of life over a period of months and years with this wonderful man, Edgar said to me: "Ken, now that we've covered almost all things tangible and intangible that men could talk about, the one thing we haven't talked about is your soul. So let me ask ya" … and Edgar said to me: "Ken, what would you do if YOUR SOUL WERE FREE?" I thought about it long and hard, and that was over sixty years ago. Now I'm going to pass that thought on to you, and I want you to take it a step further now and allow me to ask you how far could and would you stretch and expand your imagination WERE YOUR SOUL FREE. That's what I hope this poem will convey to you.

Were My Soul Free,
To Pursue *Infinite Liberty*

Would I …

       pause beneath a rainbow sky, surrounded by

       soft green earth for timeless hours,

       and in silence taste through breath,

       the fragrant flowers

Or would I …

       in focused thought contemplate how,

       to live forever in the priceless now

Were My Soul Free

Would I …

       lie peaceful by a quiet river, with thoughts of me,

       or travel to wondrous places on an endless sea

Or would I …

       idly rest, fond memories to recall,

       beneath calm eddies by a flowing waterfall

Were My Soul Free

Would I …

        linger under a shady pine,

        breathtaking mountains to visually define

Or would I …

        on earth's lush surfaces softly tread,

        floating clouds whispering breezes

        all around me, and overhead

Were My Soul Free

Would I …

        perch on a vista-bound ledge,

        while to myself I'd solemnly pledge,

        no more of a yester-world would I endure,

        but in this new-found moment forever assure,

        no longer confined by fear,

        of a limit-lived tomorrow day,

        but in my newfound eternity-bound soul,

        perpetually stay

Were My Soul Free

Would I …

        dwell in the bosom of a raging sea,

        of rugged wave scared rocks and cliffs,

        and in that same moment,

        be on a calm fringed isle, with coral rifts

Or would I …

        with thoughts calmed, on earth's most golden sands,

        listen with intent to wise voices

        from far and distant lands

Were My Soul Free

Would I …

        upon some fleecy cloud lie,

        drifting blissfully in a sun warmed sky,

        far above turbulent strife,

        of futile frustrations of earth-bound life

Or would I …

        have barren deserts beckon me,

to reflect in quiet solitude of what should be

Or would I ...

gaze upon the infinite cosmos,

where billions of stars light up the night,

millions of light-years far

but within my sight,

to remind me that short lived fame

of man's made man,

seems meaningless and small

to God's universal man

Were My Soul Free

Would I ...

travel back through time and clearly see,

to measure accurately all eternity

and in moments rare, with time's

exceptional and elect few,

share a thought or two

I would then ...

sit like a child with learning intent,

at the feet of great ageless souls who have been sent,

like a beacon in a black night,

to light the way for lost souls

who endlessly stray,

and with vision not yet known they will reveal,

God and nature's master plan,

for me to know and feel

So, If My Spirited Soul Were Totally Free

I would …

from gravity bound earth travel light years far,

to a peaceful perfect distant star,

with soul and spirit now body-free,

would I be confined to this speck of cosmic dust?

NO NOT ME

with my now wizened soul I'd go beyond infinity,

and LIVE THROUGHOUT ETERNITY

Made in the USA
Las Vegas, NV
11 April 2023